LAST POST

Gerald Weland

HERITAGE BOOKS
2025

HERITAGE BOOKS
AN IMPRINT OF HERITAGE BOOKS, INC.

Books, CDs, and more—Worldwide

For our listing of thousands of titles see our website
at
www.HeritageBooks.com

A Facsimile Reprint
Published 2025 by
HERITAGE BOOKS, INC.
Publishing Division
5810 Ruatan Street
Berwyn Heights, MD 20740

Copyright © 1990 Gerald Weland

— Publisher's Notice —
In reprints such as this, it is often not possible to remove blemishes from the original. We feel the contents of this book warrant its reissue despite these blemishes and hope you will agree and read it with pleasure.

International Standard Book Number
Paperbound: 978-1-55613-286-5

*To care for him who shall have borne the battle,
and for his widow, and his orphan*

Abraham Lincoln

TABLE OF CONTENTS

Spawn of an Ideal:
Arlington becomes a government burial ground ... 1

The Last Posts ... 7

Historic Sites in the National Cemetery System:

Alabama

    Mobile National Cemetery ... 9

Alaska

    Sitka National Cemetery ... 11

Arizona

    Prescott National Cemetery ... 13

Arkansas

    Fayetteville National Cemetery ... 15
    Fort Smith National Cemetery ... 17
    Little Rock National Cemetery ... 19

California

    Fort Rosecrans National Cemetery ... 21
    Golden Gate National Cemetery ... 23
    Los Angeles National Cemetery ... 25
    San Francisco National Cemetery ... 27

Colorado

    Fort Logan National Cemetery ... 29
    Fort Lyon National Cemetery ... 31

Washington, D.C.

    Battleground National Cemetery ... 33
    U.S. Soldiers' and Airmen's Home National Cemetery ... 35

Florida

    Barrancas National Cemetery   37
    Bay Pines National Cemetery   39
    St. Augustine National Cemetery   41

Georgia

    Andersonville National Historic Site   43
    Marietta National Cemetery   47

Hawaii

    National Memorial Cemetery of the Pacific   51

Illinois

    Alton National Cemetery   53
    Camp Butler National Cemetery   55
    Danville National Cemetery   57
    Mound City National Cemetery   59
    Quincy National Cemetery   61
    Rock Island National Cemetery   63

Indiana

    Crown Hill National Cemetery   65
    Marion National Cemetery   67
    New Albany National Cemetery   69

Iowa

    Keokuk National Cemetery   71

Kansas

    Fort Leavenworth National Cemetery   73
    Fort Scott National Cemetery   75
    Leavenworth National Cemetery   77

Kentucky

    Camp Nelson National Cemetery   79
    Cave Hill National Cemetery   81
    Danville National Cemetery   83
    Lebanon National Cemetery   85
    Lexington National Cemetery   87
    Mill Springs National Cemetery   89
    Perryville National Cemetery   91
    Zachary Taylor National Cemetery   93

Louisiana

Alexandria National Cemetery	95
Baton Rouge National Cemetery	97
Chalmette National Historic Park	99
Port Hudson National Cemetery	101

Maine

Togus National Cemetery	103

Maryland

Annapolis National Cemetery	105
Antietam National Battlefield	107
Baltimore and Loudon Park National Cemeteries	109

Minnesota

Fort Snelling National Cemetery	111

Mississippi

Biloxi National Cemetery	113
Corinth National Cemetery	115
Natchez National Cemetery	117
Vicksburg National Military Park	119

Missouri

Jefferson Barracks National Cemetery	123
Jefferson City National Cemetery	125
Springfield National Cemetery	127

Montana

Custer Battlefield National Monument	129

Nebraska

Fort McPherson National Cemetery	133

New Jersey

Beverly National Cemetery	135
Finn's Point National Cemetery	137

New Mexico

Fort Bayard National Cemetery	139
Santa Fe National Cemetery	141

New York

Bath National Cemetery	143
Cypress Hills National Cemetery	145
Long Island National Cemetery	147
Woodlawn National Cemetery	149

North Carolina

New Bern National Cemetery	151
Raleigh National Cemetery	153
Salisbury National Cemetery	155
Wilmington National Cemetery	157

Ohio

Dayton National Cemetery	159

Oklahoma

Fort Gibson National Cemetery	161

Oregon

Roseburg National Cemetery	163
White City National Cemetery	165
Willamette National Cemetery	167

Pennsylvania

Gettysburg, National Battlefield Park	169
Philadelphia National Cemetery	173

Puerto Rico

Puerto Rico National Cemetery	177

South Carolina

Beaufort National Cemetery	179
Florence National Cemetery	181

South Dakota

Black Hills National Cemetery	183
Fort Meade National Cemetery	185
Hot Springs National Cemetery	189

Tennessee

Chattanooga National Cemetery	191
Fort Donelson National Cemetery	193

Tennessee (continued)

    Andrew Johnson National Historic Site — 195
    Knoxville National Cemetery — 197
    Memphis National Cemetery — 201
    Mountain Home National Cemetery — 203
    Nashville National Cemetery — 205
    Shiloh National Military Park — 207
    Stones River National Battlefield — 209

Texas

    Fort Bliss National Cemetery — 211
    Fort Sam Houston National Cemetery — 213
    Houston National Cemetery — 215
    Kerrville National Cemetery — 217
    San Antonio National Cemetery — 219

Virginia

    Alexandria National Cemetery — 221
    Balls Bluff National Cemetery — 223
    City Point National Cemetery — 225
    Cold Harbor National Cemetery — 227
    Culpeper National Cemetery — 229
    Danville National Cemetery — 231
    Fort Harrison National Cemetery — 233
    Fredericksburg and Spotsylvania National Military Park — 235
    Glendale National Cemetery — 237
    Hampton and Hampton V.A. National Cemeteries — 239
    Poplar Grove National Cemetery — 243
    Richmond National Cemetery — 245
    Seven Pines National Cemetery — 247
    Staunton National Cemetery — 249
    Winchester National Cemetery — 251
    Yorktown National Cemetery — 253

West Virginia

    Grafton National Cemetery — 255

Wisconsin

    Wood National Cemetery — 257

The Future — 259

Appendix A — 265

Appendix B — 267

Appendix C	269
Appendix D	271
Appendix E	277
Appendix F	281
Index	283

SPAWN OF AN IDEAL

The thundering volleys at Fort Sumter had barely ceased when Winfield S. Scott, national hero, conqueror of Mexico and commander in chief of the United States Army, summoned a distinguished but relatively unknown brevet colonel in the U.S. Corps of Engineers to his office. To Commander Scott's considerable surprise, Robert Edward Lee, scion of one of Virginia's wealthiest and best-known dynasties and youngest son of "Lighthorse" Harry Lee (who had served so well as Washington's cavalry leader), was not immediately receptive to his offer. The offer was to assume overall command of the United States Army and end the secessionist revolt brewing in the South.

As a native Virginian, Lee did not feel he could answer without reflection. Thus, he temporarily declined the offer to await events. He would be neither the first nor the last Southerner in the U.S. Army to decline the command. But his decision would prove to be the most momentous.

Over the following weekend, he brooded in the palatial family estate across the Potomac River at Arlington, Virginia; he spent some of his time in the famous rose garden, and some time in prayer in the upstairs library. On 19 April 1861 Lee made his fateful decision, one which would fundamentally alter the course of American history. Except in defense of his native state, he would never again take up the sword.

On Sunday night, 21 April, his written resignation from the U.S. Army was dispatched to Scott at the War Department. Shortly before dawn the following morning, Lee and several companion officers rode away from Arlington and headed south to Richmond to offer their services to the fledgling Confederacy.

Behind him he left an estate that was one of the most notable in the Western hemisphere. Its construction was begun in 1802 by George Parke Custis, adopted son of George Washington, and by 1861 it was one of the pre-eminent showplaces and architectural triumphs in the vicinity of the nation's capital.

Nobody will ever know for certain what went through Lee's mind that chilly morning as he rode toward Richmond. As both a military strategist and a realist, he must have suspected that his beloved abode would be denied him and his family in the future, especially should the South face ultimate military disaster. No, of his thoughts we can never be certain. But there is one thing we do know. Robert E. Lee never again set foot on the estate at Arlington.

For the first year of conflict, neither Lee nor Arlington had any special significance in or influence on the Civil War. True, soon after his Southern hegira, Union cavalry clattered across the bridge, seizing the edifice and its strategic heights, and within weeks, numerous military encampments had sprung up in the area. However, Lee himself remained an obscure commander of fortifications on the Carolina coasts and an aide to Confederate President Jefferson C. Davis. Arlington was just another base camp, Lee just another rebel.

Then, on 1 June 1862, Confederate commander Joseph E. Johnston was seriously wounded at the Battle of Seven Pines during McClellan's Peninsula Campaign. He had to be relieved of duty. Another commander was urgently sought.

Some authorities believe that Lee superseded the stricken Johnston because he was the only one available in Richmond to take command. Whatever the reasons, Lee began a meteoric rise to fame. Not only did he repulse repeated Union efforts to capture Richmond, but twice he led invasions of the North in an effort to encircle Washington and inflict shattering defeats on Union forces; he wanted to earn for the South a negotiated peace which would insure its independence.

Even after the decisive defeat at Gettysburg, which ended forever Southern hopes of victory and independence, Lee's star remained in the ascendancy. Thereafter, it was often only his unflagging spirit, military genius, personal charisma and, some say, monumental ego which sustained the flagging Confederate spark.

If Lee had suspected that the estate at Arlington would be outlawed to him, his own continuing success in the remaining months of bitter struggle assured that fact. Battles in the Wilderness Campaign were proceeding as well, moving Arlington inexorably toward its rendezvous with history.

The entire United States had gone to war in a cavalier and unsophisticated manner; it was many months before the combatants on both sides learned that valor combined with ignorance of the demands of war rarely gained one anything but an unmarked grave. Almost no logistical support was initially available to sustain what would prove to be a lengthy, grinding struggle.

Nowhere was this lack of support more evident than in the handling of battle casualties. Throughout 1862 and into 1863 the windrows of blue and gray dead were fortunate to receive interment even in the most rudimentary of mass graves. Especially was this true after larger battles where the numbers of fallen reached unmanageable proportions. All too often they were left as carrion. For many months the only winners of the American Civil War were the vultures. There simply was not manpower or equipment available to handle the situation in an expeditious and humanitarian way.

It became common for Union troops to band together to see that fallen friends were turned over to those private embalming and mortuary firms which infested each battlefield. Collections were taken to defray the expenses of transporting fallen soldiers home.

Before long, rumors arose that morticians were collecting their pay, then simply heaving the fallen man into the nearest unmarked grave--sometimes with Confederate dead!

It is an undeniable, if unpalatable fact, that Northern war profiteers ran rampant during the Civil War. Union troops soon came to loathe this particular brand of civilian "supporter" more than they ever did the average Southern soldier. Beyond question, most of these private morticians did their best under all but impossible conditions, exercising their responsibilities with good conscience. But the stories persisted and it is difficult to believe that all were spurious or without documentation.

At any rate, gossip about this spread from one end of the Army of the Potomac to the other. Eventually it even reached the usually obtuse ears of the Union high command in Washington.

Among the most active, dedicated and ruthless members of this group was Secretary of War Edwin McMasters Stanton. An Ohio lawyer who had held several minor political offices in that state prior to serving as attorney general in the Buchanan administration, Stanton was beyond doubt the most flamboyant and selfless man in Washington when it came to pursuing Northern war aims; he was imbued with the sanctity of the cause of Union and emancipation. Regrettably, he was not above ignoring the advice and directives of others, even his commander in chief, when he felt the situation called for it. He had little respect for the opinions, motives or intelligence of others. It was said, even by Union commanders such as Ulysses Grant, that Edwin M. Stanton believed he had a divine ukase to prosecute the war single-handedly.

To Stanton, the scandalous situation concerning burial of Union war dead was intolerable. (There were few men who fell wearing Union blue that Stanton did not regard as strong candidates for sainthood.) Indignation about this among the military and the concomitant public outrage incited President Lincoln to "order" Stanton in 1864 to acquire a secure area somewhere in the vicinity of the capital as a final resting place for Union war dead. It was the type of task and sacred charge Stanton could take to heart.

Two years earlier, the government had obtained ownership of Lee's estate at Arlington. This was pro forma for all property belonging to those in active rebellion against the Union. The government acquired the property through a rather shady, if effective, tax condemnation. When Lee's invalid wife could not make the trek through Southern lines to personally pay the $92.00 assessment as required, the government put the eleven-hundred-acre tract on the auction block and purchased it for the appraised value of $26,810. Even government apologists of the period admit this was at best a boondoggle. Whether or not this was standard procedure against proscribed rebels is unknown. However, it would appear likely.

At any rate, the government now had Arlington and showed no inclination to let go of it. This was the situation two years later when Secretary Stanton turned over the search for a "government burial ground" to his quartermaster general, Montgomery Cunningham Meigs.

Meigs was a character even by the standards of that time. There were few more enigmatic, unyielding and bitter personalities to come out of the great American trauma of civil strife. An 1836 graduate of West Point, he was fifth in a class of forty-nine and had enjoyed a long, prosperous, peacetime career in the Artillery Corps. In 1861 he was promoted to the colonelcy of the U.S. Eleventh Infantry. Within days he was promoted to brevet brigadier general, a promotion subsequently confirmed by Congress, and assigned the position of quartermaster general. Even for a man of greater talent, this would have been a rise of alarming rapidity. The reasons for Meigs' promotion are now shrouded in the mists of history, perhaps for the best.

Be this as it may, Meigs filled this position throughout the war and finished the conflict in the rank of major general. Like many soldiers in noncombat roles, he developed an unreasoning revulsion for the enemy. His hatred knew no bounds when it came to things Confederate. The death of his son John (also a West Point graduate) in October 1864 near Dayton, Virginia, merely heightened this virulence. Not that it required much stimulation. Meigs had already mastered the art of petty vindictiveness quite well--his behavior regarding Arlington is a perfect example.

There was never any doubt about what site Meigs would choose for the government burial ground. The family home of the Republic's greatest traitor lay vulnerable before his eyes. Meigs set out with the zeal of an avenging angel to make certain this abode would be denied the traitor forevermore.

Only twenty-four hours after Stanton had instructed him to search for a suitable location for the burial ground, Meigs reply was on the secretary's desk. There was, of course, only one selection--Arlington.

Though Arlington has since been expanded several times to reach its present size of over eight hundred acres, the initial authorization by Stanton was for only two hundred acres immediately adjacent to the mansion itself. It is unknown whether Meigs was aware of the official directive dated 15 June 1864--or even would have cared. Under Meigs' direction, burials commenced as early as 13 May 1864 with the burial of Pvt. William Christman, Company G, Sixth-seventh Pennsylvania Infantry at Arlington. Two days later Pvt. William B. Blatt, the first battle casualty, joined him.

Meanwhile, an entirely new lexicon was needed to describe the violence and bloodshed that was becoming part of American history. Grant plunged south with a massive army in the spring of 1864, attached himself to Lee and held on with the tenacity of a bulldog. The Wilderness ... Spotsylvania ... Cold Harbor ... The battles came fast, the casualties faster. Perhaps it is understandable why Meigs jumped the gun, but within weeks thousands of Christman's comrades had joined him at Arlington, brought north in wagon trains from the sanguinary hell of the Wilderness Campaign.

Meigs seemed to take fiendish delight in supervising the destruction of Arlington's habitability. He ordered Mary Lee's rose garden to be surrounded with Union graves to render it unsightly and unapproachable--this despite the government directive that the location was to be used for "charitable and educational" functions. Amazingly enough, over the years this actually has transpired--one of the few instances where governmental aims and results correlated. However, none of this was the fault of Montgomery C. Meigs. He understood little of the government view. He only knew what he wanted.

In August 1864 Meigs visited Arlington to see the progress of his work. To his horror, he discovered not a single grave near the edifice itself. The rose garden was unchanged. Many Union officers were in residence at the mansion, and living in the middle of a cemetery had generated less than an ideal level of enthusiasm. Therefore, Union officers had redirected all burial details to a distant segment of the estate. A lovely cemetery filled with white markers could be seen in the distance, several hundred yards to the southeast of the house. But not a single marker stood anywhere near the house.

Lee, with son to his right, and an aide named Taylor
--*National Archives photo*

Purportedly almost hysterical with rage, Meigs ordered all available Union bodies to be brought from various hospitals in the capital. Some twenty-seven arrived shortly thereafter. Then, throughout that hot August afternoon, the quartermaster general of the United States Army personally oversaw the interment of these Union dead placed in a large "L" surrounding two sides of the manse.

Meigs supplied what he no doubt considered the final indignity to Robert E. Lee when he himself died in 1892. Meigs ordered that his own body be interred in Arlington. There he still resides, not far from the main house itself. Standing at Meigs' grave one can see the Union markers still encircling the now reconstituted rose garden.

Thus did the obscure quartermaster general of the Union army accomplish what only Ulysses S. Grant had also been able to do: He had won an irrevocable victory over the great Lee that would endure to the end of time. Somehow, Grant's effort seems more memorable.

Not that all ran on greased wheels for the government after the cessation of hostilities. In 1882, Lee's son successfully sued and gained a judgment in the Supreme Court which stated, in effect, that the estate had been stolen and the government was trespassing. However, young Lee had to be content with a moral victory. He did settle title to the estate on the government for $150,000, but even by the standards of the times, it was a shockingly low price. Of course, by 1882 some forty thousand war dead and other soldiers resided below the verdant acreage of Arlington. Young Lee obviously realized that evicting these "trespassers" was not feasible. Apparently, like his father, he was realist enough to take what he could get.

In September 1866 Arlington changed from a bucolic, pastoral cemetery into a national shrine. At that time some 2,111 unknown Union dead, lately collected from the battlefields of Virginia, were buried in a mass grave there. They joined between 17,000 and 19,000 of their comrades already on the estate.

On 30 May 1868 General John A. Logan, commander in chief of the U.S. Army, declared that day as a Memorial Day to all those who fell in defense of the Union. Even the graves of several hundred Confederate dead, whose markers were pointed so no "damnyankees" could sit down on them, were decorated with flowers for the first time. In 1873 Ulysses S. Grant, now President Grant, made the first executive trek to the cemetery on Memorial Day. It became a presidential duty that has rarely been violated. Memorial Day soon evolved into a major American tradition.

By 1873 the pastoral abode of the Lees was gone forever. So in fact was Robert E. Lee. He had died in 1870. His last words were "Strike the tent!" Perhaps delirium. Or perhaps an epitaph for the palatial estate he loved so well.

However, a national concept and an American tradition had been born!

THE LAST POSTS

The following pages present a treatment on each historic locale of the National Cemetery System. The emphasis is on the general history of the area where the installation is located and the reasons it was established there. In some cases, the past and present contributions of the surrounding environs are more significant than the cemetery itself, and thus are given more treatment. At other sites, the people and monuments within the confines of the facility, and how they came to rest there, are the most important aspects of that entry.

However, a format giving general background and whatever specific data are available on the installation has been followed.

For those hoping to find a "Pollyanna" patriotism herein, the body of this work may prove most distressing. The U.S. National Cemetery System owes its very existence to the American Civil War, which casualty ratios indicate was one of the most savage and ruthless in recorded human history. Much of America's past contains events of which modern man finds it difficult to be proud. Some of the information offered here will give the sober individual much cause for thought.

On the other hand, the reader seeking another example of the current American literary obsession with chronic despair and self-castigation, is best advised to search elsewhere. He will be greatly disappointed here. The following dissertation diagrams the broad stream of American history, a course of events which America need not apologize for. Throughout their development, the American people have traditionally shown restrained and progressive behavior which compares favorably with that of any other nation.

I have attempted to set forth in an objective, occasionally analytical style the first two centuries of this nation's life, centuries in which, for the first time, a true democracy exercised prominence in the affairs of mankind. No doubt the text contains errors and misinterpretations. I can only hope for a modicum of absolution for undertaking what I feel was a necessary historical task. To quote Woodrow Wilson as he sought to halt America's drift into World War I, "Hear [and forgive] me for that cause."

This, then, is a tome dedicated to the men and women and who have served the cause of democracy, knowingly or unknowingly, volunteer or conscript. Here in all its triumph and tragedy, humor and pathos, is the U.S. National Cemetery System and the two centuries of American history it represents.

And here too are two centuries of America's citizen soldiers--and their last, most honored posts.

Admiral Farragut at Mobile

MOBILE NATIONAL CEMETERY

Mobile, Alabama

Mobile, Alabama today is one of the crown cities of the American South. It remains, as it always has been, a major trade port. Cotton, textiles and other software are its most significant commodities.

Since its founding, Mobile has controlled the Alabama River Valley to the north. The possibility of gaining this rich prize led to strident Western demands for war with Britain and its Spanish ally, which occupied the city. Inevitably the War of 1812 erupted and Alabama played a crucial part.

During the early days of the nineteenth century, the local Creek Indians had lived in peace with the arriving American settlers. But British machinations soon stirred them to violence under the driving leadership of a young half-breed chief named William Weatherford.

In August 1813 Weatherford led his warriors against a flimsy stockade built around the home of a farmer named Samuel Mims, thirty miles above Mobile on the Alabama River. Major John Beasley, commander of the garrison of the grandiosely styled Fort Mims, unwisely left the front gate open on that fateful morning of 30 August. Around noon the Creeks leaped from the tall grass and stormed the site. For hours the savage battle ensued. But eventually the "fort" was reduced to smoldering ruins and all but a handful of men, women and children there were massacred.

The incident aroused horror and wrath throughout the nation, and brought to prominence a brawling ramrod of a man called Andrew Jackson. He subdued the Creeks in a long, costly campaign, went on to repel the British invasion of New Orleans and culminated his operations by throwing the Spanish out of Florida even before that European monarchy had concluded the sale of Florida to the United States.

With the outbreak of Civil War, both sides recognized the strategic location of Mobile Bay. A terminus of two major railroads, the Alabama and Florida and the Mobile and Ohio, the bay was a natural point of export for Southern products and a most effective base for Confederate blockade runners. All that ended on 5 August 1864 when Admiral David G. Farragut strapped himself into the rigging of his flagship, U.S.S. *Hartford*, and led a force of Union blockaders into the bay in one of this nation's most memorable and thrilling naval actions. Smashing past Forts Gaines and Morgan, he defeated a mosquito fleet of Confederate vessels, including the ram *Tennessee*, and efficiently closed the port. When the Union monitor *Tecumseh* struck a mine (torpedo) and went down with all hands, he deigned to notice with the words, "Damn the torpedoes, full steam ahead!" Mobile remained in Southern hands for many more months, but by the end of this critical day, its use to the Confederacy had ended.

A Torpedo

In March 1865 two Union columns marched on Mobile, one from the coast and another overland from Pensacola. On 12 April 1865 General E.R.S. Canby accepted the surrender of Generals Richard Taylor and the colorful, much-quoted Nathan B. Forrest to end the war along the Gulf Coast.

Mobile National Cemetery was opened in 1865 as a final resting place for those Union soldiers who fell in this final campaign or during the days of Union blockade. Among the others known to be interred here are four Confederate war dead (though the number may be much higher) and Chappo Geronimo, son of the famed Apache war chief.

However, due to lack of space, the 5.24-acre facility was closed in 1963. No further expansion is planned, despite the large number of veterans and retired personnel to be found along the Gulf Coast.

SITKA NATIONAL CEMETERY

Sitka, Alaska

On Baranof Island, along Alaska's beautiful "Marine Highway," Sitka is located 151 miles southwest of present-day capital, Juneau. Baranof Island (named for the driving genius of colonial expansion in the area) and Sitka in particular, were once the headquarters of Russian America. In many ways Sitka retains its Old World heritage, right down to the crumbling headstones in the ancient Russian cemetery. Among these is the marker of Princess Polina Maksoutoff, wife of the last Russian governor. Madame Maksoutoff was a cousin of the ruling Romanov rulers of Russia. In 1855, while on an outing with her maid and a soldier escort, she was caught in an uprising of the Tlingit Indians, and slain. She thus became the only member of European royalty ever killed in the American Indian wars. Every year on 18 October a full-dress ceremony reenacts the transfer of the region from Russia to the United States. Secretary of State Seward obtained the area for the bargain price of seven million dollars. His acumen has outlived the appellation given to the transaction at the time, "Seward's Folly."

Sitka today still contains St. Michael's Orthodox Cathedral, displaying some of the last authentic relics and icons of the once monolithic Russian orthodox church. Nearby Sheldon Jackson College, the state's oldest educational institution, maintains one of the finest collections of early books on the Pacific Northwest as well as a number of priceless Russian and Indian artifacts.

Sitka National Historic Park marks the site of the old fort where the Tlingit Indians made their last stand. This so-called Battle of Alaska occurred in 1804 and ended native resistance to Russian encroachments.

Sitka National Cemetery is part of the fifty-four-acre historic park. Little information is available on the cemetery, which was created as a result of the 1973 National Cemetery Act and the concomitant expansion of the Veterans Administration. Thus it is among the newest installations in the entire system. Due to the relatively low population in the area, the cemetery, though small, should be able to serve those area veterans for the foreseeable future. Space for gravesites is expected to be available well into the twenty-first century.

PRESCOTT NATIONAL CEMETERY

Prescott, Arizona

> "The recent discovery of gold near the San Francisco Mountains within the district of Northern Arizona and the flocking thither of many citizens of the United States ... renders it necessary that a small military force be sent to these gold fields to preserve order and give security to life ..."

With those words, General James R. Carleton, commander of the Department of Arizona, ordered the establishment of Fort Whipple on 23 October 1863. It commemorated General A. W. Whipple, who as a first lieutenant of engineers, had explored the territory in 1853 and had been killed in action at Chancellorsville a few months before Carleton's edict.

In the wake of the gold rush, the town that would become Prescott bloomed overnight. And, aside from Apache raids, there were compelling reasons for establishing a military post. Most of the Arizonans of the time, striving for survival in the harsh pioneer life, had no particular adherence to the Union cause. The Confederacy was hungry for hard cash to use in foreign purchases. By planting a Union fort in the heart of the area, Carleton neutralized any potential Southern inroads among the populace.

Fort Whipple had less than an auspicious beginning. The night the initial detachment arrived, Apache war parties made off with forty-three of the forty-four mules available for transportation of supplies. But commanding officer Major Edward Willis overcame this and a myriad of other difficulties. By May 1864 a permanent location had been established along the banks of Granite Creek.

Campaigns against the Apaches from 1864 to 1871 have been described as "frequent but not outstanding." However, the headquarters of the Department of Arizona remained at Fort Whipple until 1886. By then, Geronimo, the last of the feared local raiders, had been brought to heel. With the end of the fighting in the Southwest, Fort Whipple had little value. Though carried as an ungarrisoned post until 1918, it became U.S. General Hospital # 20 in that year.

With the establishment of the Veterans Administration on 21 July 1930, the facility was taken in hand by that organization. In 1946 a domiciliary was opened for disabled and/or homeless veterans whose injuries required proximity to a medical center. Today it is but one of 171 such hospitals operated by the Department of Veterans Affairs throughout the nation.

Indian Raiders

Prescott National Cemetery was developed to provide a final resting place for veterans who had succumbed in government hospitals. But all such restrictions were eliminated in 1973 and this raised the number of interments considerably. The cemetery now averages sixteen committals per month. The 15.6-acre site has six acres developed for burials. As of this writing, the small location is expected to provide burial space only through 1990, with a final total of about ten thousand interments.

FAYETTEVILLE NATIONAL CEMETERY

Fayetteville, Arkansas

Located in the northwestern part of the state, Fayetteville today is the home of the University of Arkansas. The area was first explored by French trappers in the seventeenth century. Ranging out from New Orleans in search of furs and other valuables, these *couriers de bois* noticed the prowess of the local Indians with bow and arrow and bestowed the name "Aux Arcs" on the state. The appellation somehow became corrupted to "Arkansas" and stuck.

To the north and east of the city lie the legendary Ozarks. Though long the brunt of tiresome Depression jokes, the Ozarks today provide a thriving business and retirement area. Thousands of midwesterners have been drawn as permanent residents due to the incredible amount of recreational areas in the vicinity. Cost of living indexes traditionally remain lower than elsewhere in the nation. Table Rock Reservoir alone, a massive project finished by the U.S. Army Corps of Engineers in 1958, provides forty-three thousand square acres of vacation sites for boating and fishing. To the south of Fayetteville, Ozark National Forest remains one of the most rugged and attractive in the country.

History abounds around Fayetteville. At the turn of the century William "Coin" Harvey constructed his famous pyramid near Mount Ne to hold all those objects he believed to be doomed by the advance of civilization. Its exact location is now known by few--it is deep under the water of one of the innumerable new reservoirs of the Ozarks. At Eureka Springs, fabled prohibitionist Carrie Nation spent her declining years running a boardinghouse she purchased in 1908. Cave Creek, a tributary of the Buffalo River, has long yielded some of the better prehistoric animal finds in the United States. In the days following the Civil War "Bald Knobbers" patrolled the countryside, acting as informal vigilantes to end the depredations of bushwhackers and renegades from both North and South.

Not far to the north of Fayetteville lies the battlefield of Pea Ridge. Though now largely overlooked in the greater tragedy of the Civil War, a key battle was fought on this site. Confederate attempts to occupy Missouri had been repelled in late 1861 by Union forces under Nathaniel Lyon. Union General Samuel Curtis replaced the slain Lyon and pursued the withdrawing Southerners under Generals Sterling Price and Earl Van Dorn. Here on 7-8 March 1862 he met and defeated them again, ending for all time serious Confederate attempts to bring Missouri into their new nation. Their later efforts were only harassing raids.

Over two thousand men fell on this location and the Union found thirty of its dead scalped by Confederate troops recruited from Indian Territory. Infuriated, they began to retaliate in kind, and this further fueled the war of atrocities that reigned in that area for the duration of the war. Today most of this is forgotten. To most of the area's citizens, Pea Ridge is merely the site of a large iron-mining complex.

Fayetteville National Cemetery, like most of those dating from the Civil War period, was primarily used as a reinterment center for Union war dead from battlefields in the area. Few Confederates found a final resting place here. Since then, the location has provided burial space to Americans from both sides of the Mason-Dixon Line who have fallen in the service of a united land. It remains open at the present time, and for the foreseeable future.

FORT SMITH NATIONAL CEMETERY

Fort Smith, Arkansas

Historically, this small military outpost at the junction of the Poteau and Arkansas rivers in western Arkansas was a manifestation of the worry in Washington about the constant warfare between the local Osage and Cherokee Indians and the damage it might do to eventual westward migration. In the summer of 1817, area military commander General Thomas A. Smith, for whom the encampment would be named, received orders from Andrew Jackson to garrison the area. A detachment of eighty-two men from the Rifle Regiment of Philadelphia was sent via the Ohio and Mississippi rivers to undertake the task. On 1 October 1817, Major William Bradford met his new command at the juncture of the two rivers and they arrived at Arkansas Post at the eastern terminus of the Arkansas River by the middle of that month.

There the force was detained by illness and logistical problems. However, Major Stephen Long, a topographical engineer, proceeded by skiff up the river to survey the area and selected Belle Point as the site of the fort. Beautiful the area may have been, but its name proved a misnomer.

Though buffalo and other game were abundant, and food could be grown on the fertile land, yellow fever and other virulent illnesses also abounded. The first death occurred within months of establishing the post and records indicate that twenty-five percent of the command died during 1823 alone. These provided the first graves in what would become a national cemetery.

In 1824 the fort was abandoned and five companies of troops moved to build a fort at the mouth of the Verdigris River in Indian Territory. This became Fort Gibson, Oklahoma, also the site of a national cemetery.

From 1824 to 1833 the post stood abandoned. Then, in 1833, troops again returned to be strategically positioned to intercept whiskey and other illegal goods headed for Indian Territory. But illness once again forced an abandonment until 1838.

On 23 April 1861, even before Arkansas officially seceded from the Union, a Confederate detachment under Colonel (Senator) Borland arrived at Van Buren, Arkansas and occupied the fort as its small garrison abandoned it. Though no major battles occurred in the area, there was considerable guerrilla activity. To the north two significant actions took place in 1862 at Pea Ridge and Prairie Grove. Fort Smith changed hands several times during the fighting.

Two Confederate generals lie buried at Fort Smith, James McIntosh, who died at Pea Ridge, and Alexander Steen, who fell at Prairie Grove. They are among 437 known Confederates interred there.

In 1867 an act of Congress specifically directed that a national cemetery be established at Fort Smith. On 23 March 1871 the post was officially closed. However, ubiquitous Quartermaster General M.C. Meigs obtained exclusion of the sale of the property for the cemetery and it remained inviolate.

The city of Fort Smith soon became administrative center for the federal territory that would become Oklahoma. The Dalton and Doolin gangs were but two of the desperado bands that terrorized the area. There may not have been any law west of the Pecos but there certainly was no God west of Fort Smith.

One of those later buried at the cemetery was Judge Isaac C. Parker. Though he had served in the Sixty-first Missouri Infantry, as well as two terms in Congress after the war, his greatest fame arose when he took the bench at Fort Smith's federal court. Vilified in song, legend, and Hollywood scripts as "The Hanging Judge," he has become the epitome of blind and merciless justice. For twenty-one years he held sway over Indian Territory. He tried over thirteen thousand cases, carrying such a load on his docket that the court had to convene six days a week. However, legend notwithstanding, only eighty-eight men went to the gallows in the courtyard behind his fortress court, an average of but four men per year.

Parker died on 17 November 1896, only weeks after the jurisdiction of his court was reassigned to areas in Indian Territory. In addition, some of his more famous marshals (Randolph Creekmore, Calvin Whitson and Jacob Yoes) are also buried at Fort Smith.

The cemetery contains over 4,000 gravesites, 1,464 of which are marked "unknown." Veterans of every American conflict since the War of 1812 rest there. Though one of the smaller national cemeteries, the Fort Smith location is one of the most interesting in south-central United States.

LITTLE ROCK NATIONAL CEMETERY

Little Rock, Arkansas

Little Rock, capital of the state of Arkansas, took its name from French explorer Bernard de la Harpe who explored the Arkansas River Valley in 1722. He wrote on the map "Le Petit Roche" at the spot where the city grew, and somehow the odd handle stuck.

Not far to the southeast lies Pine Bluff and its well-known arsenal, today one of the nation's most controversial military facilities due to its experiments and manufacturing of agents for chemical and biological warfare. To the southwest on Lake Catherine is the resort community of Hot Springs, during the wild 1930s a temporary hideout for many a gangster. Ouachita National Forest to the west is one of America's largest and most rugged. Also in the area one will find the Crater of Diamonds, the only diamond mine in the United States where private citizens are allowed, even encouraged, to dig.

At the start of the Civil War, Little Rock was the site of a large U.S. arsenal. It surrendered to Confederate militia on 8 February 1861. The city became a major Confederate base after Union withdrawal from Missouri, though enough local citizens held Union sentiments to comprise at least two known cavalry regiments for the Northern cause.

At any rate, Little Rock held off Union forces for two years. Not until September 1863 did Union General Frederick Steele occupy the area and force Confederate forces under General Kirby Smith to fall back on Arkadelphia further south. From here in the spring of 1864

Army Huts

Steele launched his Arkansas Campaign to support Union operations on the Red River in Louisiana. However, both Union offensives met disaster; Steele's command was smashed at Jenkin's Ferry on the Sabine River near Pine Bluff. He returned to Little Rock minus five hundred Union casualties and most of his military prestige.

However, overwhelming Union strength held Confederate Trans-Mississippi Department troops under Kirby Smith at bay until the end of the war. Little Rock National Cemetery was thus established on 9 April 1868 due to the large number of Union war dead from all causes in the Arkansas Campaign and occupation of Little Rock. In fact, the cemetery today sits on the very ground used as the Union encampment during hostilities.

From Devall's Bluff, Jenkins Ferry, Pine Bluff and many other locations came the Union dead to be reinterred here. At first, Confederate war dead were denied burial in the cemetery. But within twenty years, attitudes changed. In 1884 some 640 fallen Southerners were removed from Little Rock's Mount Holly Cemetery and transferred to the Confederate Section of Little Rock National Cemetery. Simultaneously, the trustees of Mount Holly raised a monument to all Confederate dead there. A later monument was erected by the state of Minnesota in 1916 to the Union men who fell in and around Little Rock.

The twenty-five-acre cemetery remains open at the present time, and indefinitely to future interments. Only half of its space is now utilized.

FORT ROSECRANS NATIONAL CEMETERY

San Diego, California

High above San Diego, on the slopes of rolling Point Loma, the seventy-two acres of Fort Rosecrans present one of the most unique settings for a national cemetery, and, along with Arlington, has one of the most panoramic views. Lying below and stretching to the horizon is the beautiful, graceful San Diego Bay and its surrounding metropolis.

First trodden by Europeans in 1542, it was the point of land upon which Juan R. Cabrillo landed in that year. Like all conquistadors of the sixteenth century, he was strictly interested in locating the cities of gold which the Spaniards believed existed, despite all evidence to the contrary. However, he did take note of the natural harbor at his feet, and the lighthouse at the tip of Point Loma today bears his name.

However, after his passing, there was little colonization in the area except for an occasional mission as Jesuit priests sought to spread the gospel among the Indians whom Cabrillo and his ilk had found merely encumbering. Not until some years after California was conquered by the United States, did the area receive more than cursory examination. Then, Executive Order Twenty-six of February 1852 designated one thousand acres of land on the peninsula for a military reservation. This was eventually named in honor of Major General William Starke Rosecrans, Union army, in 1899. One of the crustiest commanders of the Civil War, he was also one of the most controversial. His campaigns in Tennessee achieved both mixed results and decidedly mixed reviews. When they culminated in the 1863 defeat at Chickamauga, he was relieved of command of the Army of the Cumberland and was eventually appointed head of the Department of Missouri on 30 January 1864. This Ohio graduate of West Point eventually served as minister to Mexico, made a fortune acting as advisor to local railroad construction there, and finally retired to California. Upon his death in 1898, he was buried at Arlington with full military honors.

The fortification evolved into a highly sophisticated and supposedly impregnable series of coast defense gun emplacements designed to guard San Diego Bay and its approaches. Fortunately, the guns never had to be fired in anger. The German fleet of World War I proved something less than a threat to area residents and no Japanese battle fleet came closer than Hawaii during World War II--and that was only for a few short hours one Sunday morning in December 1941.

Prior to that however, pursuant to War Department Order Number Seven of October 1934, eight acres were designated a national cemetery. This land primarily included the old post cemetery and officers' section. Additional land was placed under proscription for expansion until its final size was reached. It was formally closed on 15 September 1966 when all available gravesites were either claimed or committed. As of 30 June 1976, a total of 47,147 interments had been made.

Fort Rosecrans has a pronounced uniqueness as well, in that some of those interred there predate the admission of California to statehood. Among these are the U.S. Dragoons of Brigadier General Stephen W. Kearny, who fell at the Battle of San Pascual some forty miles northeast of the city in 1846. It was the first conflict between American and native Mexican forces in the area during the Mexican War. These eighteen dead were reinterred in 1874 at Fort Rosecrans. Today their burial site is commemorated by a large granite boulder removed from the battlefield in 1922 by the Native Sons and Daughters of the Golden West. A plaque bearing the names of the fallen is attached to it.

But the most outstanding monument in the cemetery, and one of the more memorable to be found through the National Cemetery System, is that of the Bennington Spire, located in the older section of the cemetery. Towering seventy-five feet in the air, it is dedicated to the sixty-six officers and men killed when the gunboat U.S.S. *Bennington* was destroyed by a boiler explosion in the San Diego Bay on 21 July 1905. Made of flecked, grayish granite, the obelisk is among the more attractive structures of its type to be found in America.

Listed among those interred at this location are a number of men awarded the Medal of Honor. These include Boatswain William S. Cronan of the *Bennington* disaster and Ensign Herbert C. Jones, who fell on the U.S.S. *California* at Pearl Harbor while leading ammunition parties during the fateful attack. Several Medal of Honor winners from Vietnam are also found interred here. In addition, 158 memorial plaques commemorate local men whose remains were never recovered after making the supreme sacrifice during various American conflicts.

GOLDEN GATE NATIONAL CEMETERY

San Bruno, California

Golden Gate National Cemetery is one of many which reflects the current urban needs of the United States; it is not associated with a particular event or historic site. National cemetery legislation after World War I was designed to provide burial space for the huge number of eligibles brought about by that conflict, and Golden Gate was created as a result of this legislation. San Francisco National Cemetery, at the old Presidio in the heart of the city, was suffering from rapidly diminishing grave space by the 1930s. So, in 1937, another cemetery was authorized in the area for the large number of veterans, especially retired personnel, who made their homes there.

In 1938 a 162-acre tract of land was made in San Bruno from the old Rancho Buriburi land grant. The next year the name "Golden Gate" was bestowed on the cemetery, commemorating the name first applied to the San Francisco area by General John C. Fremont during the Mexican War of 1846 to 1848. At dedication, it was felt the large site would prove adequate for a century. But the huge number of veterans created by World War II and subsequent conflicts has disproven that assumption.

Among the more illustrious military men to rest here is Fleet Admiral Chester Nimitz. As U.S. commander in chief in the Pacific, he won the greatest naval war in history and is generally regarded as one of the great naval captains of the century. The American naval campaign against Japan from 1941 to 1945 was both a concept of daring and brilliance as well as a masterpiece of resolution and firepower. Much of its success must be credited to this former Texas farm boy.

Nimitz rests in section C-1, within yards of the graves of three of his finest subordinates who themselves shared tremendous responsibility for the war effort. They are Richmond K. Turner, commander of amphibious forces; Charles A. Lockwood, commander of submarines; and Raymond A. Spruance, victor of Midway in 1942.

There are seven Medal of Honor winners interred at Golden Gate. These include four army veterans, two navy and one marine veteran. Most were decorated for action in World War II and three of them received the medal posthumously. Also, one hundred commemorative markers reside here, erected in memory of American servicemen whose final disposition of remains is unknown.

Some forty-four members of the German armed forces, all of whom died in captivity, are also located here. Most were captured in North Africa in 1943, veterans of Erwin von Rommel's legendary Afrika Korps.

In 1977 an avenue of flags was commenced here at Golden Gate, a popular phenomenon that is rapidly becoming a tradition at national burial grounds throughout the nation. Lining the central drive from the entrance to the flag staff are 536 American banners, each received from the next of kin of an American veteran interred here and originally used as the covering of his or her bier. By 1980, local veterans' groups had added the fifty state flags to the display.

Despite the size of the location, Golden Gate National Cemetery was closed due to lack of space in June 1967. As of 1980, all 107,000 available gravesites had been filled.

LOS ANGELES NATIONAL CEMETERY

Los Angeles, California

Los Angeles National Cemetery, like most of those near large metropolitan areas, has primarily evolved as a facility to provide burial services to the large numbers of veterans to be found in those locales around the country which have become traditional retirement havens. Such a mecca is southern California. The cemetery lies in the heavily populated section of West Los Angeles about twelve miles from the civic center. An equal distance to the northwest is scenic Malibu, while the skyscrapers of Santa Monica and Westwood tower above it on either side. Lands belonging to the monstrous educational installation, UCLA, lie adjacent to the cemetery, just across Veterans Avenue. Running parallel to the northern border is fabled Sunset Boulevard. Follow it for a fifteen minute drive to the east and one encounters the tinseled, if cold, heart of Hollywood.

Los Angeles National Cemetery was initially established as a part of the National Home for Disabled Volunteer Soldiers which lies next door, now separated from the burial grounds by the San Diego Freeway. The home was one of ten located across the country by act of Congress in 1866 to aid former Union war veterans who remained permanently injured as a result of the Civil War. In 1933 the Veterans Administration assumed jurisdiction over the home and continues to operate it at present. The location became a national cemetery site with the establishment of that enlarged system in 1973.

The first interment here was of Abner Prather, Fourth Indiana Infantry, on 11 May 1889. By 31 October 1978 there had been 68,163 interments. Also, a columbarium contains niches for the committal of cremated remains and approximately 5,600 will be made with available space. Otherwise, the 114-acre site is closed to below ground burials after about 77,000 interments.

The cemetery possesses no less than ten different memorials. However, the most visible is at the corner of Veterans Avenue and Wilshire Boulevard. It is a gigantic figure of a woman carrying the light of peace and surrounded by sculptures of American soldiers. Its inscription reads, "To those who volunteered and extended the hand of liberty to alien peoples." Donated by the United Spanish War Veterans, the monument was erected in 1950.

This national cemetery is the final resting place for six recipients of the Medal of Honor. Three of these were former cavalrymen, all of whom were exemplars of heroism in the 1870s during the Texas Indian Wars. Another, Coxswain Timothy Sullivan of the Union navy, was decorated for coolness and bravery in several of his ship's engagements during the Civil War.

Among the other notable men here is Nicholas Earp, father of the gunfighting marshal of Tombstone and other locales. The younger Earp died in nearby Colton, California in 1929 following a long California sojourn. Also found here is a former mountain man and army scout named "Liver-eating" Johnson. His twenty-year personal feud with the Crow Indians in the wilds of Colorado became the basis of a popular 1971 movie entitled *Jeremiah Johnson*. Six memorial markers have also been raised to veterans of Vietnam whose final resting place was never determined.

With the exception of the columbarium mentioned above, the first active edifice of its type in the National Cemetery System, the location was closed due to space limitations in 1976.

Monument to All American War Dead
by the Spanish-American Veterans at the
Los Angeles National Cemetery
--*photo courtesy of the author*

SAN FRANCISCO NATIONAL CEMETERY

The Presidio, California

San Francisco National Cemetery is located within the confines of the Presidio of San Francisco. Pine and eucalyptus trees dot the landscape, and the beauty of the scene is completed by the long span of the Golden Gate Bridge towering in the background.

The same year Americans stood on the steps of a meeting hall in Philadelphia and declared their independence, the Spanish Empire in the New World began to stir. It established numerous missions and military posts along the west coast of what would become the United States. The most northern of these was placed at San Francisco and given the name "Presidio," a derivation of the Latin term for "garrison" or "fortified encampment." In 1821, following Mexican independence, Spanish troops were supplanted by Californio militia. They occupied the site until conquered by American troops in 1846 during the Mexican War. Today the location is the headquarters of the U.S. Sixth Army area.

The reservation comprises fifteen hundred acres of land set in the northernmost end of the San Francisco Peninsula. A major landscaping effort undertaken in the 1880s has made a lush facility of an area originally scant in vegetation. It remains the oldest continuously active military post on American soil.

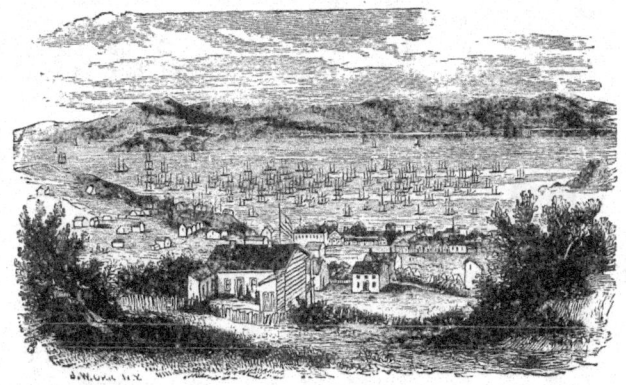

General Order 133 of December 1884, designated 9.5 acres here to establish the first American national cemetery on the West Coast. Incorporated into this parcel of land was the old post cemetery, containing remains of men buried there dating back to its original founding. Interments made immediately after 1884 included veterans from post cemeteries at abandoned forts and other locations throughout the American West. Later transfers of land from the local army command increased the installation to its current size of 28.3 acres.

No less than eleven recipients of the Medal of Honor are interred here and a twelfth, a U.S. Navy man whose final resting place is unknown, is also commemorated by a memorial marker. Four of these men received their awards for service in the Indian Wars. One of them, Sgt. William Wilson, U.S. Fourth Cavalry, was decorated twice for gallantry in Indian campaigns in Texas. Among the others to receive the nation's highest medal for valor are General William Shafter, whose name remains alive in the Hawaiian fortification which is currently headquarters of the U.S. Army, Pacific. Still another is General Frederick Funston, originally from Kansas. He planned and executed the coup which captured Filipino guerrilla leader Emilio Aguinaldo to help end the Philippine Revolt in the days after the Spanish-American War. Others at rest here were honored for heroism in such diverse campaigns as the Civil War, the Boxer Rebellion and World War I.

Among many famous Americans resting here is Pauline Cushman, commonly referred to as the Mata Hari of the Civil War. Though how much valuable intelligence she gathered and how many Confederate officers she fooled is problematical, she was arrested and sentenced to be hanged as a spy. Only advancing Union troops, who liberated her from jail in Shelbyville, Tennessee, saved her life. Originally an actress, she returned to the stage to tremendous crowds. She died in Arizona in 1893 while married to a local sheriff named Fryer. The Grand Army of the Republic association arranged for her reinterment here in 1907.

Also found here is Union General Irwin McDowell, commander of Northern forces at the first major battle of Civil War, Bull Run. At rest in the Presidio is General Robert Van Horn, who won great acclaim during World War I, and Colonel Edward D. Baker, the consummate politician whose military acumen failed him dismally at Balls Bluff, Virginia. The circumstances of his defeat and death are discussed elsewhere.

Four monuments have been raised at the facility. A tall, granite shaft erected in 1893 by the Grand Army of the Republic commemorates all Civil War dead. A similar edifice dating from 1897 was placed by the Army-Navy Union of the Pacific Coast. It is surmounted by a figure with a battle flag. A rough-hewn monument in a small plot near the main entrance is dedicated to the unknown dead of all our nation's conflicts. Some 517 such men lie in the nearby grounds. A final memorial was raised in 1934 to the American War Mothers, all those women who have sacrificed sons and daughters to their country's call.

Due to its small size, the Presidio was closed to future committals in 1962. Through 31 December 1976, interments numbered 25,363.

FORT LOGAN NATIONAL CEMETERY

Denver, Colorado

Fort Logan represents one of the few major expansions of the National Cemetery System since World War II. It is located on the site of a former army post established in 1887. The old post cemetery is incorporated into the present national facility. On 1 November 1950 the U.S. Army officially accepted jurisdiction over the location as a national burial ground. As with all other army installations, with the exception of Soldiers Home and Arlington, its administration was transferred to the Veterans Administration in 1973.

The post commemorates Union General John A. Logan of Illinois. A lawyer by trade, he had served in the Mexican War of 1846 to 1848 and had subsequently been elected to Congress. A Democrat, he was briefly suspected of Southern sympathies. However, after assuming the colonelcy of the Thirty-first Illinois, he served with distinction throughout the war and was wounded at Fort Donelson, Tennessee in 1862. He took an active part in Grant's capture of Vicksburg, and was appointed to succeed General James B. McPherson as commander of the Army of the Tennessee. He was replaced when he found logistics a science beyond his ken, but there was no longer any doubt about his loyalty and he served well during Sherman's Atlanta Campaign. In August 1865 he resigned his commission to reenter politics as a Republican and was the unsuccessful vice-presidential candidate under Harrison in 1884. One of the founders of the Grand Army of the Republic, he served as its president on three separate occasions.

On 17 February 1887, less than two months after Logan's death, the army opened a new facility on the outskirts of Denver, occupying a site chosen by General Philip Sheridan. The state of Colorado donated six hundred forty acres of land for its construction without cost to the government.

The post was in keeping with the new army policy of eliminating small western garrisons and consolidating troops at large railheads where they could be rapidly deployed to necessary locales. The post was occupied by the U.S. Infantry in October, 1887. Its first uninspiring appellation was "Camp near the city of Denver." For some time it was informally referred to as Fort Sheridan. But on 5 April 1889 it was officially designated "Fort Logan." It remains active, but since 1939 has been merely an adjunct of Lowry Air Force Base.

Fort Logan National Cemetery contains one notable monument to

American veterans, a large sundial donated in 1939 by the Women's National Defense Association. Two former Medal of Honor winners and one known prisoner of war from World War II are at rest here. The large installation should allow for available grave space well past the year 2000, but, due to the fact that much of its terrain has not been developed, the final size of the cemetery cannot as yet be determined.

FORT LYON NATIONAL CEMETERY

Fort Lyon, Colorado

Actually there were two Fort Lyons. The first was established at Bent's New Fort on 29 August 1860 on the left bank of the Arkansas River in southeastern Colorado near present day La Junta. The locale was leased as a supply base, and intensive fortification was undertaken by the U.S. First Cavalry commanded by Major John Sedgwick. It was originally given the appellation "Fort Wise" after the governor of Virginia. But, on 25 June 1862, it was redesignated "Fort Lyon" in honor of Union General Nathaniel Lyon, killed at Wilson's Creek, Missouri while expelling Confederate forces from that state.

Lyon, an 1841 graduate of the U.S. Military Academy at West Point, was one of the bright young lights of the Union army. He served in the Seminole and Mexican Wars, as well as in occupation duty during the period known as "Bleeding Kansas." As a captain of the Second U.S. Infantry, he protected the St. Louis Arsenal early in the Civil War as secessionist sentiment swept the state. Promoted to general of volunteers due to his writing advocating the cause of the Republican Party and Abraham Lincoln, he launched operations which culminated in his demise at Wilson's Creek on 10 August 1861; however, his efforts kept Missouri from the Confederacy. Lyon was the first true military hero of the Northern cause.

The original fort was abandoned in June 1867 due to constant flooding from the Arkansas River. The land was given to the Department of the Interior in July 1884. The fortification was relocated to a spot two and a half miles below the Purgatoire River. It remained active until transferred to the Department of the Interior in 1890.

But it is the earlier site which has become a part of American history, for here one of the nation's most despicable events transpired.

In the spring of 1864, Cheyenne Indians under Black Kettle, generally regarded as a wise and gentle chieftain, began to seek an accommodation with the government. In September of that year he met with U.S. officers at Camp Weld near Denver, and left the conference believing his people were now at peace. He was even granted permission to camp on Sand Creek, a tributary of the Arkansas, about forty miles from Fort Lyon.

Enter one John M. Chivington, Colonel of the Third Colorado Cavalry. An over-zealous ex-clergyman and unscrupulous politician, the so-called Fighting Parson apparently intended to ride an Indian war into the U.S. Congress. Regrettably, the only Indians available to fight with were those of Black Kettle's peaceful band. This slowed up the good Colonel Chivington not even a little.

Despite vociferous demurrers from the U.S. regulars at Fort Lyon, Chivington deployed his troops around the Cheyenne village on the morning of 29 November 1864. In the frigid air, one could see the U.S. banner and a white flag hoisted high above Black Kettle's lodge. But it bought no immunity this day.

The ensuing "Sand Creek Massacre" saw the lives of two- to three hundred Indians, mostly women and children, snuffed out. Though Black Kettle escaped, nine other chiefs perished. Chivington and his "Bloody Thirdsters" paraded in triumph through Denver and even exhibited hundreds of scalps from the stage of a local theater.

However, the substantial political career the former preacher so desperately sought eluded him. He died in obscurity a few years later. While he never paid for his machinations, thousands of other settlers did. Following Sand Creek, the Cheyennes reached a fever pitch of destruction. Within two years they had severed lines of communication across Kansas and Nebraska. Estimates range between seven hundred and one thousand for the number of settlers who died. An untold number of others fled to the sanctuary of the nearest army fort, abandoning their farms and homes and the years of labor invested in them. Not until the army launched a major three-pronged offensive in 1868 was the Cheyenne War concluded. Among those who pursued the hostilities was a column of troopers from Fort Lyon, many of them the same men who had been unable to deflect Chivington from his path four years previously.

In 1934 Fort Lyon became a regional medical center under Veterans Administration auspices and continues to serve in that capacity. Though not large by the standards of the system, Fort Lyon National Cemetery remains open to veteran interments. It serves southern Colorado, western Kansas, northern New Mexico and the Oklahoma and Texas panhandles.

BATTLEGROUND NATIONAL CEMETERY

Washington, D.C.

Battleground National Cemetery commemorates the only battle ever waged within the confines of the nation's capital. The Battle of Bladensburg during the War of 1812 occurred several miles to the north in Maryland.

In June 1864, in order to relieve some of the pressure put on Lee by the Army of the Potomac during the last year of the Civil War, Confederate General Jubal A. Early undertook an offensive through the Shenandoah Valley to threaten Washington. With but ten thousand men he managed to inflict a series of defeats on Union forces opposing him. Though his cavalry destroyed the bridges of the B & O Railroad across the Potomac, it was not until Early crossed that river on 5 July that Grant believed he was launching a serious offensive.

Four days later Early defeated a Union force under General Lew Wallace at the Monocacy River in Maryland, driving them into retreat to Baltimore. His military career never prospering, Wallace turned his talents to literature, where many years later he turned out the Roman epic *Ben Hur*.

Ulysses S. Grant

Once he realized the capital was threatened, Grant quickly dispatched the VI Corps under General Wright to protect it. By the time Early reached the outskirts of Washington at Silver Spring, Maryland on 11 July, the area had already been reinforced. The following morning, with Lincoln watching from Union parapets, Early launched a dispirited attack on Fort Stevens in what was little more than heavy skirmishing. However, this position, part of the great ring of fortifications surrounding Washington, was given credit for having repulsed the Confederates' advance.

Early withdrew, his cavalry pausing to hold for ransom the town of Chambersburg, Pennsylvania. When the money could not or would not be raised, Early ordered it evacuated and burned in reprisal for Union destruction of much civilian property in the Shenandoah Valley by Union troops in 1862 and 1863. Two-thirds of the town was destroyed in the conflagration.

Grant concluded that steps would have to be taken to remove Confederate bases from the Shenandoah. This led to the successful campaign of General Philip H. Sheridan a few months later; but by the time the campaign ended the following March, campaigns against the South no longer really mattered because Lee's Army of Northern Virginia was tottering toward the brink of oblivion.

Battleground National Cemetery was established in June 1864, as were Arlington and the cemetery at Alexandria, Virginia. Today Battleground National Cemetery lies in the northwestern section of the capital on Georgia Avenue between Whittier and Van Buren Streets. From the day Battleground opened, it was clear that this small facility could not compete with the much larger Arlington as a national shrine. Many of those interred here were Union soldiers who died while serving in the area fortifications, and others were those who fell on battlefields during Early's abortive raid. At present all grave sites have been committed and no expansion seems possible due to surrounding land usage. The cemetery is administered by the Department of the Interior.

U. S. SOLDIERS' AND AIRMEN'S HOME NATIONAL CEMETERY

Washington, D.C.

Located at 21 Harewood Road in the northwestern section of the nation's capital, Soldiers' and Airmen's Home is one of the oldest medical center/national cemetery complexes in the United States. Originally known as Soldiers Home, it existed to provide accommodations for disabled or otherwise homeless men who formerly served in the ranks of the U.S. Army. Since the day it was founded, the installation has given sanctuary to thousands of veterans who did not prosper in later life, generally due to factors beyond their control. In 1972, Air Force personnel were extended accommodation as well, and that year the facility officially became Soldiers' and Airmen's Home. However, for whatever reason, the name of the cemetery was not changed from Soldiers Home National Cemetery to Soldiers' and Airmen's Home National Cemetery until 19 July 1983.

The facility today lies in the heart of Washington. Surrounded on three sides by Howard University, Catholic University and Gallaudet College, Soldiers' and Airmen's Home is almost next door to Washington's Union Station. The grounds of the Capitol Building and the White House, two miles distant, can be seen from the windows of its structures.

Today open to the public, the home is at the hub of everyday Washington life. But when opened in 1851, it was situated in a rather isolated and pastoral locale.

At the instigation of two famous American warriors, General Winfield Scott and Major Robert Anderson (later commander of Fort Sumter), the facility came into being. Though now of prodigious proportions, the original Soldiers Home was merely the summer residence of banking magnate George W. Riggs. The purchase was made for $100,000, using tribute money from Mexico City following the Mexican War of 1846 to 1848. For some obscure reason, the check for war reparations from the Mexican to the U.S. government was erroneously made out to Scott himself, probably because he was U.S. commander in Mexico. He simply endorsed it over to create what he termed the "military asylum."

During the Civil War, Fort Stevens sprang up next to the home. This installation defended the capital from Confederate General Jubal Early's raid in the fall of 1864. And it was here in Anderson Cottage, (the residence of Major Anderson when he was administrator of the home) which then commanded an unimpeded vista of central Washington, that Abraham Lincoln wrote his final draft of the Emancipation Proclamation.

For over a century, Congress has never appropriated a cent for the upkeep of the home. All expenses are met by a large trust fund composed of court-martial fines, unclaimed estates left by decedent American soldiers, and voluntary contributions by army enlisted men. Yet, for over a century, it has not varied in its function or in its quality of service to U.S. service personnel.

Soldiers' and Airmen's Home National Cemetery, adjacent to the large Veterans Hospital, is at present open only to interments of home residents who die there. Its acreage has been filled over the years almost entirely by army enlisted personnel. Some burials even predate the Civil War. Aside from Arlington National Cemetery, Soldiers' and Airmen's Home is the only other burial installation presently maintained by the U.S. Army. The number of interments in the 15.8-acre cemetery will not much exceed the present number of about twelve thousand.

BARRANCAS NATIONAL CEMETERY

Pensacola, Florida

Barrancas National Cemetery is located within the U.S. Naval Air Station, Pensacola, and officially became a national cemetery in 1866 in the wake of the Civil War. British, French, Spanish and American forces all fought over Pensacola in the eighteenth century before Pensacola emerged as part of the state of Florida in 1819.

Pensacola came to prominence during the Civil War. On 10 January 1861 Florida became the third state to leave the Union. At the time, Pensacola was the finest harbor along the Gulf of Mexico. It was guarded by three American forts, the most significant being Fort Pickens on the western tip of Santa Rosa Island. On the very day of secession, Lt. A.J. Slemmer and the men of Company G, U.S. First Artillery, destroyed the two other forts and occupied Fort Pickens. Eventually obtaining a garrison of five hundred men, the fort was never lost to the Union. Because of this, though the Pensacola Navy Yard surrendered to the Confederates, their ability to use Pensacola Bay was nullified by Fort Pickens.

Numerous actions occurred in the area before the Confederates evacuated Pensacola. Even then, not until General Braxton Bragg attempted to storm the fort in an amphibious assault on 8-9 October 1861 did the Confederates finally admit defeat.

Many U.S. Navy and Army personnel originally buried at the post cemetery at Fort Pickens now are at rest in Barrancas National Cemetery, as are seventy-two fallen Confederates. Veterans of all subsequent struggles also reside there.

One of the more unique interments was Ga-ah, wife of Geronimo, the Apache chieftain who proved to be one of the most cunning Indians the U.S. Army ever had to chase. With amazing skill and determination, the wily Apache led detachments a merry chase until General Nelson A. Miles ran him to earth for the final time in the Guadalupe Mountains of Arizona in 1886.

Following the surrender, Geronimo and his more recalcitrant followers were removed to Fort Pickins. In 1887 his wife died there and was buried at the national cemetery. Eventually returned to Fort Sill, Oklahoma, the old warrior became an Indian scout for the U.S. Seventh Cavalry. He died there in 1909 at the age of eighty.

A number of other distinguished servicemen rest at Barrancas National Cemetery. Among these is Admiral J.W. Reeves, awarded many citations for service against the Japanese in World War II and as commander of N.A.S. Pensacola afterwards. Two Medal of Honor recipients of the Vietnam conflict lie here--Major S.W. Pless, USMC, and Sgt. C.C. Sims, U.S.A. There are also thirty-seven memorial markers to those whose final resting place is known but to God.

Barrancas National Cemetery reveals a variety of headstone markers. Rounded tops indicate Union casualties, while those with points signify fallen Confederates. Larger granite markers have been used for more modern interments. A large monument in Section 22 was erected in 1884 by the Marine Corps in memory of the many servicemen who perished in a yellow fever epidemic the year before.

Barrancas National Cemetery covers approximately thirty acres. It is the only one of the three national cemeteries in Florida still open to receive interments, and will be indefinitely. Of over twelve thousand committals here, nearly one thousand are of unknowns.

Headstone of Ga-ah, Wife of Geronimo
Barrancas National Cemetery
--*photo courtesy of the author*

BAY PINES NATIONAL CEMETERY

Bay Pines, Florida

The national cemetery at Bay Pines and its adjacent V.A. Medical Center are located in a suburb of St. Petersburg on the western side of Tampa Bay. The increasing numbers of retired veterans seeking homes in the Florida area, especially St. Petersburg, made this a logical choice for such an establishment. However, the area is rich in history as well.

Across the bay on the southern shore stands the De Soto National Monument, commemorating famed explorer Ferdinand De Soto. Originally serving with the conquistador Cordoba in Nicaragua in 1524 and with Pizarro in Peru in 1532, he arranged an expedition to pursue the great wealth thought to be contained in Florida. Receiving financial assistance from Spanish monarch Charles V, he was granted the title "Governor of Cuba and Florida," and began his sojourn in 1538. Landing at Tampa Bay the following year, he engaged in numerous brouhahas with the Indians, but found not an ounce of the precious yellow metal. Finally, accompanied by surly and near-mutinous troops, he decided to travel overland to New Spain (Mexico). In doing so, he became the first European to set eyes on the great watershed known as the Mississippi River. Contracting a fever of undetermined cause, he died in 1542 at the age of forty-six. His followers wasted little time mourning him. They struggled on to Mexico, having received such unflattering reports of Florida's conditions that the area was virtually ignored thereafter by the Spanish crown.

In 1819 Spain ceded Florida to the United States and settlers poured into the area. Taking over the territory, they soon restricted the Seminole Indians to a reservation in central Florida. When the promised supplies and annuities were not forthcoming, many of the natives took to the warpath. In 1835, General Wiley Thompson, a Georgia militiaman the government had made Indian Agent, called the recalcitrant Indian leaders to Tampa Bay for what became known as the Treaty of Payne's Landing. However, when one rebellious warrior named Osceola rendered his opinion by burying his knife in the paperwork, he was clapped in irons and the treaty was short-lived. Osceola agreed to "touch the paper" in order to gain his release, and promptly launched the worst Indian war east of the Mississippi.

One confident American general after another saw his reputation evaporate in the insect-infested swamps. Not until Colonel Zachary

Taylor (a rigid, inflexible commander like Andrew Jackson) arrived on the scene did the army inflict enough damage on the enemy to restore order. Even then, some of the Seminoles' descendants refused to register for the draft in World War II, claiming to be citizens of a sovereign Seminole nation which had never been conquered. It was a doubtful assertion in view of Taylor's successes, but it posed an interesting legal wrangle still not settled today.

The 21.2-acre Bay Pines National Cemetery was opened in 1933. It is one of the most perfectly uniform sites in the system. Near the entrance is a large monument to all American war veterans. The burial areas are divided into forty-two symmetrical plots of one-half acre each. Among those interred here is former Bay Pines Veterans Administration Director Mizell Bryson.

Due to lack of space, the cemetery was closed in 1969 with some fourteen thousand interments.

ST. AUGUSTINE NATIONAL CEMETERY

ST. Augustine, Florida

Though it did not officially become a national cemetery until the latter half of the nineteenth century, this small location has played a colorful part in American history, just as the city in whose heart it lies. The first Spanish colony here included a Franciscan monastery, and the land on which the national cemetery now sits was a part of that religious property. In fact, the boundary of the location is bordered by the walls of the original town.

With the British occupation from 1763 to 1783, the monastery became an army barracks, and with the resurgence of Spanish suzerainty, it remained as such. With American conquest in 1821, a small part of the reservation was set aside as a post cemetery. Burial records indicate the first interment occurred in 1828.

Most of the early interments were of soldiers who fell in various Indian wars or who succumbed to subtropical illnesses, always rife in the area. Among these are Major Francis L. Dade and the 108 men of

A Swamp in Florida

his command wiped out by Seminoles in the Wahoo Swamp of the Withlacoochie River in 1835. Marching from Tampa to Fort King (now Ocala), Dade failed to take precautions against surprise and blundered into an ambush from which only one soldier escaped. He and his men were originally buried on the spot, but with the cessation of hostilities in 1842, they and the other fallen troops from areas scattered about Florida were reinterred at St. Augustine. Three squat pyramids of native coquina stone were erected as a monument to these war dead.

When Florida seceded from the Union in January 1861, Confederate soldiers seized Fort Marion and St. Francis Barracks. Soon the fourth flag to fly over St. Augustine was hoisted. However, as all coastal towns, St. Augustine was hard hit by the Union blockade and the interruption of trade. Therefore, when a Union gunboat entered the harbor in March 1862, the city surrendered to avoid a potentially devastating confrontation. St. Augustine reverted to U.S. control and never again was controlled by Southern forces.

By 1881 the port city was once again flourishing. In that year the quartermaster general's office suggested that the post burial grounds be declared a national cemetery. Funds were appropriated for its upkeep and a wall of coquina was constructed to enclose the site. Also, a white obelisk was raised as a monument to those Americans who fell during the Florida Wars. The cost of this spire was met by the donation of one day's pay by each soldier stationed in the area. Presumably this contribution was voluntary but no documentation concerning that fact exists.

In 1913 additional land was set apart to double the size of the cemetery. Today nearly a thousand American veterans rest in the St. Augustine National Cemetery. But due to its small size, it is now closed to future interments.

ANDERSONVILLE NATIONAL HISTORIC SITE

Andersonville, Georgia

"About midnight the train stopped and we were ordered off. Five hundred weary men shuffled along between double lines of guards. Five hundred weary men moved towards the gates that would shut out life and hope for most of them forever."

Thus did John McElroy, Sixteenth Illinois Cavalry, recall his arrival at one of the most infamous prisons in all of human history.

Andersonville Prison, or Fort Sumter as the Confederates called it, was the largest prison camp during the American Civil War. It was

Drawing of Andersonville Prison Camp (Fort Sumter)
--National Archives photo

established in early 1864 when the Confederate high command realized that the area around Richmond was no longer secure enough for holding captives due to constantly encroaching Union forces. Over a fourteen-month period, some forty-two thousand Union troops were confined in Andersonville, and of these, over twelve thousand perished of various causes.

Lying southwest of Atlanta and just north of Americus and Plains, Georgia, Andersonville was nothing but an open stockade surrounded by fifteen-foot-high pine logs. The prisoners were herded into the rectangular camp some twenty-seven acres in area where they lived either in the open or in small, tattered tents. Only two gates at the northwest and southwest corners provided entrance to the stockade. About twenty feet inside the logs was a "deadline" over which prisoners wandered at the risk of being shot. How often they actually were shot is unknown, but reputedly it was not uncommon.

Originally, the only source of water to the compound was a branch of Sweetwater Creek which flowed through the grounds. Unfortunately, it was also the only sewage system available, and disease soon spread. Prisoners dug many wells to the north of the creek and some of these are still visible today.

The stockade was surrounded by "star forts," earthworks containing rifle pits and artillery. Designed to quell disturbances inside the prison, they were also bastions to fight off Union cavalry raiders. To the south was a small hospital compound, but it too provided only tents for the sick prisoners. The Union blockade made obtaining medical supplies impossible and there was little Southern doctors could do to alleviate suffering. To the west of the encampment sat the so-called Dead House, a structure of logs in which dead prisoners were held until graves could be dug in what became the national cemetery half a mile to the northwest. The number of grave diggers employed must have been awesome, as deaths averaged nearly one thousand a month.

Admittedly the situation was abhorrent, but it is doubtful the Confederacy could have done better. Richmond was finding it difficult to feed and supply its armies, much less enemy prisoners. The Union refusal to continue the prisoner exchange system exacerbated the problem, and evidence indicates that Confederate guards at Andersonville ate little better than their captives.

All this not withstanding, the cessation of hostilities saw camp commandant Henry Wirz arrested and charged with "murder, in violation of the laws of war." A handsome, bearded man originally from Switzerland, Wirz had practiced medicine in Louisiana and been a clerk in Libby Prison. Wounded in 1862, he later served as a Confederate agent and propagandist in Europe. He returned to Georgia in January 1864 to take over administration of the prison. This sealed his fate.

Just what he was guilty of, except being the camp commandant, has not been pointed out. At worst, he appears guilty of errors of omission over which he had little control. However, he was hanged in November 1865 in Washington, D.C. for his war crimes. His hanging was the sole post-war reprisal emerging from the American Civil

War.

After the war, Andersonville deteriorated almost completely. In 1891, Union veterans living in Georgia purchased the land and it was eventually turned over to the government in 1910. Until 1970 the U.S. Army administered it as a national cemetery only. At that time it was turned over to the Department of the Interior and designated a National Historic Site.

Today no less than nine major monuments are found within the stockade itself, and numerous others are located in the national cemetery to the north. Of some twenty-seven acres in extent, Andersonville National Cemetery continues to be an active facility. Of the 15,700 men buried there, some 13,669 are Civil War decedents.

Badger Monument at Marietta, Georgia
Dedicated by the State of Wisconsin
--*photo courtesy of the author*

MARIETTA NATIONAL CEMETERY

Marietta, Georgia

Located just ten miles north of Atlanta, Marietta National Cemetery is yet another facility made necessary by the dreadful, fratricidal conflict of 1861 to 1865. During the Union drive on Atlanta under General William Tecumseh Sherman, some of the most vicious battles of that conflict occurred--Resaca, Dallas, Peachtree Creek, Kenesaw Mountain, Jonesboro and the fighting in and around Atlanta itself. Finally, on 1 September 1864, the city fell and the Confederates under General John B. Hood withdrew to the north to threaten Sherman's lines of communication to Tennessee.

But the Union commander refused to be so handicapped. Instead, he simply abandoned his supply lines and hurled his massive army towards the sea in what became the most famous march an American army ever made. When he reached Savannah three weeks later, he left in his wake a swathe of destruction sixty miles wide and two hundred long. Many military authorities, including his original biographer,

General Sherman

Theodore Lyman, and the *Encyclopedia of Military History* as well, state that no section of terrain has ever been as thoroughly devastated in human history. Possibly one hundred thousand non-combatants died from direct or indirect causes of this campaign. It took Georgia a generation to recover.

The land where the national cemetery at Marietta is located was originally donated by Henry G. Cole, a local citizen who had remained loyal to the Union. His idea was to offer a burial ground which would receive the fallen of both sides and thus stimulate future peace and understanding. But the bitter dregs of reconstruction made this a chimera for many years.

The Department of the Army administered the twenty-four acres acquired as a national cemetery from its inception in 1870 until 1973. Most of those interred were Union war dead from battlefields around Atlanta. However, by the early twentieth century, numerous Confederate veterans had also been accepted.

Since then, the cemetery has become final resting place for many veterans of struggles both before and after the Civil War. One of these is General John Clark, who served heroically in the American Revolution and later went on to serve Georgia as governor, congressman and senator. Late in life he was appointed Indian Agent for Florida by President Andrew Jackson. However, his last assignment ended tragically when both he and his wife died of disease there. In 1923 the Daughters of the American Revolution reinterred both of them in the national cemetery at Marietta.

Cpl. L.H. Phillips, USMC, who won the Medal of Honor on the battlefields of Korea, is also interred here. Though he survived the action for which he was decorated, he fell in combat just twenty-three days later.

Monuments abound at Marietta. One of the more impressive is the Wisconsin Monument, twelve feet of granite dedicated on Memorial Day, 1926 to the 405 Union men from that state who fell in and around Atlanta during 1864. Perched atop it is the image of a badger, Wisconsin's symbol of heroic tenacity. A fifty-bell carillon has also been donated by the AMVETS of Georgia as a tribute to those who have fallen in subsequent American conflicts. In 1960 the Gold Star Mothers of Atlanta funded the purchase of a marble monument to all Americans who remain missing in action.

Marietta National Cemetery was closed to interments in October 1970 due to lack of space. As of 31 October 1976, a total of 16,383 burials had been made there. It has since been replaced by the Fort Gillam National Cemetery south of Atlanta, which was completed and opened in mid- 1984. It is believed the new facility will last at least half a century.

Speaker's Rostrum at Marietta National Cemetery
—*photo courtesy of the author*

Central Rostrum and Memorial Area
The Punchbowl, Hawaii
--photo courtesy of the author

NATIONAL MEMORIAL CEMETERY OF THE PACIFIC

Honolulu, Hawaii

Almost a century separated the establishment of the National Memorial Cemetery of the Pacific and those of the earliest cemeteries on the North American continent. On 2 September 1949 in a location half a world away from the cockpit of the great civil strife of 1861 to 1865, the U.S. flag was raised in a dedication ceremony over the hallowed resting place for American veterans who fell in a mighty conflict whose battlefields spanned the world.

Commonly referred to as "The Punchbowl," the cemetery dominates the view of Honolulu from its position in the crater of Oahu's long-extinct volcano. It is particularly appropriate that this locale was chosen. To the ancient Hawaiians the crater was known as Puowaina, "Hill of Sacrifice."

During the time of the Hawaiian monarchy, heavy cannon were mounted on its slopes to aid in the defense of Honolulu harbor. It was later used as a training ground for the Hawaiian National Guard, and from 1940 to the end of World War II it served as an observation and fire control point in the defense of Oahu proper. From its verdant slopes one can see Pearl Harbor sparkling in the distance. In the opposite direction looms the purple majesty of Diamond Head. Behind Pearl City to the west stretch the masses of Oahu's pineapple fields. These extend the length of the central rift valley to Schofield Barracks. Behind the crater loom the Koolau Mountains, and the highway which passes the Punchbowl leads directly to the fabled Pali. Not far away on the "Big Island" to the south, lies the City of Refuge, long a sanctuary for those Hawaiians guilty of crimes or breaking taboos.

In 1943 the territorial governor offered the nation the crater as a site for a national cemetery. In 1948 the Eightieth Congress appropriated over one million dollars for construction and development. On 4 January 1949 the first interment was made, an unknown American killed in the Japanese assault on Pearl Harbor. Ernest T. Pyle, perhaps America's foremost war correspondent, beloved and admired by servicemen for his accurate and sympathetic portrayals of their lives in combat, also lies in Section D of the cemetery. After a distinguished career in Europe, he had been killed in April 1945 on Ie Shima Island near Okinawa.

Since then, over thirteen thousand American servicemen from

World War II have been buried at the Punchbowl. Perhaps the most poignant dedicatory service was the burial on 23 October 1953 of 44 Marines, 3 sailors and 131 civilians who perished in the defense of Wake Island in 1941. It was also here on 15 May 1958 that the selection of the Unknown Soldier from the Korean War was made by M. Sgt. Ned Lyle of the Twenty-fifth Infantry Division.

However, the Punchbowl is best known for its magnificent statue at the head of the cemetery as well as its "Courts of the Missing." Engraved on marble walls about the cemetery are the names of 18,093 American servicemen from World War II and 8,187 more from Korea whose final resting place is known but to God. In no other national cemetery will one find the Emblem of the Wheel, the authorized Buddhist religious symbol, inscribed on so many markers due to the high percentage of Americans of Asian background buried here.

As of 30 June 1973 a total of 23,335 interments had been made in the National Memorial Cemetery of the Pacific. This includes 2,920 men whose graves are marked "unknown." Twenty-two winners of the Medal of Honor lie here. No other national cemetery contains a higher percentage of war dead or more genuine heroes than does the Punchbowl, Hawaii.

ALTON NATIONAL CEMETERY

Alton, Illinois

Alton sits on a great loop of the Mississippi River, approximately fifty miles due north of East St. Louis, Illinois. At the outbreak of the American Civil War, Alton was the location of a large state prison. It was immediately incorporated into the Union prison system for the detention of captured Confederates.

One of the few such facilities used by the U.S. government during that struggle, the penitentiary at Alton was actually constructed as a prison and fulfilled that function in as humane a way as possible. Consequently, the death rate was generally low. Most of those who did perish were apparently removed to the Jefferson Barracks location in St. Louis.

Information on Alton National Cemetery is scanty. It was established as a Soldiers Plot in the Alton City Cemetery for local casualties returned home for interment. The earliest known burial occurred in 1862. Presumably, only Union dead are at rest here. Its small acreage (one-half acre) would indicate that no more than a few hundred men were committed here. Maintenance is done via contract with the Alton City Cemetery Complex.

The site was officially closed in 1949, but became inactive even before then. It is administered by the cemetery director of the Jefferson Barracks National Cemetery, St. Louis, Missouri.

French Fort

CAMP BUTLER NATIONAL CEMETERY

Springfield, Illinois

Throughout the latter part of the seventeenth century, French traders swarmed over the plains south of the Great Lakes, seeking to establish good relations with the Indians and maintain economic ascendancy in the area. But French leadership in Quebec realized that cheaper English goods would inevitably erode their economic control and, therefore, colonization attempts were entrusted to missionaries. The first permanent settlement in Illinois was created in 1699 at the Indian village of modern-day Cahokia.

The final result of French colonization was a foregone conclusion. Via the Seven Years War, the British occupied the area. By 1763 few vestiges of French control remained visible. But England herself had to surrender the region less than a generation later following the successful seizure of it by George Rogers Clark's expedition during the American Revolution.

Though the local Indians "ceded" the land to the infant United States, not until 5 October 1813 was conquest assured. On that day, American militia defeated Tecumseh and his British allies at the Battle of the Thames in Canada, and the last significant foreign opposition evaporated.

Following Indiana by two years, Illinois entered the Union in 1818. The first capital was at Vandalia, but in 1837 a coalition of younger legislators led the movement which transferred the capital to Springfield, where it remains. One of those legislators was a twenty-eight-year-old representative from nearby New Salem in Sangamon County. His name: Abraham Lincoln.

He became and remains today Springfield's most celebrated citizen. First elected to the state legislature in 1834, he served four terms before running unsuccessfully for national office, a campaign in which gave the world the Lincoln-Douglas Debates, perhaps the most fabled series of verbal badinage in American history. The issue of slavery is no longer relevant, and thus the debates are basically forgotten outside of Illinois. But those towns which hosted the oratorical struggles still consider themselves honored.

Eventually elected President in 1860, Lincoln became the savior of the Union in those terrible and tenebrous days which began with shells falling on Fort Sumter. Not until May 1865 did "Long Abe" return home to Springfield. For two weeks after John Wilkes Booth had

Abraham Lincoln

ended Lincoln's political career, the President's funeral train had crept across the nation. By the time it reached the Illinois capital for the last rites on 4 May 1865, an estimated one and a half million Americans had seen their fallen leader lying in state. His final resting place is a giant tomb in a Springfield park. A magnificent obelisk towers to the midwestern sky; surrounding its base are bronzed figures emblematic of the great civil struggle.

Thus it is that Camp Butler National Cemetery, one of those spawned by the Civil War, is so appropriately situated within a few miles of the final resting place of the man who led the Union cause. Located on Rural Route 1 just north of town, Camp Butler is the only cemetery available to veterans in the heavily populated farming and industrial communities of central Illinois.

Originally opened in 1862, the post was a prison for captured Confederates. Numerous men on both sides of the Civil War found their final home here. A Confederate section contains the remains of 848 Southerners who perished in detention. Nearby lie the Union soldiers who died here as guards or in training accidents at Camp Butler's training facilities.

The total area of the site is thirty-nine acres, but only twenty-six and one-half acres have been developed for use. Thus, it appears Camp Butler National Cemetery will serve area veterans until at least the year 2000, according to government projection. As of April 1980 approximately eighty-two hundred committals had been made. These include Americans who have served in every national conflict since the Civil War.

DANVILLE NATIONAL CEMETERY

Danville, Illinois

Danville, Illinois lies on U.S. Route 74, just across the border from Indiana and just east of Champaign-Urbana, home of the University of Illinois. As most communities in the wooded stretches of Indiana and Illinois, Danville was settled in the days following the War of 1812. Immigrants, largely from the southern uplands, poured into the area in what became known as the Lake Plains Settlement. Many of them were seasoned pioneers from Kentucky and Tennessee. One was a gangly, overgrown rail-splitter named Lincoln.

With the government selling land as low as $1.25 per acre, it is little wonder that hordes of settlers stampeded west along the National Road between Indianapolis and St. Louis. A few stopped along the way, some here, others there. By 1830 the lands between the Wabash and the Mississippi teemed with new people and towns.

Danville was fortunate enough to escape the ravages of the early Indian uprisings and those of the great civil strife of 1861 to 1865. A major stop on the Great Western of Illinois Railroad, the city prospered in handling supplies on their way to such points as St. Louis and Cairo, Illinois.

However, with the cessation of hostilities, Danville and its surrounding communities began to feel the first shocks of conflict. Illinois had contributed thousands of men to the Union cause and the number of local men consequently disabled was high.

Shortly after the war, the Danville National Home for Disabled Volunteer Soldiers was established. In 1898 a small plot of ground northwest of the current national cemetery was set aside as a burial ground. Information is sparse, but apparently this small plot was closed shortly thereafter, and a larger piece of terrain taken for development as a national cemetery. Today the site comprises some thirty-four acres.

With the mushrooming of the newly established Veterans Administration in 1930, the Danville National Home was taken over as a veterans hospital complex. It serves both eastern Illinois and western Indiana.

In 1909 the remains of the first governor of the Danville National Home, Colonel Isaac Clements, were reinterred from the old cemetery to a position of honor in Cemetery Center Circle in the national cemetery. A monument in honor of the war dead of all American struggles was erected over his grave.

Danville National Cemetery is presently open to future committals, though now expected to be filled by the year 2000.

MOUND CITY NATIONAL CEMETERY

Mound City, Illinois

Mound City National Cemetery was established in 1864 due to a pressing need for interment space for the myriad Union soldiers who had become fatalities of the Civil War through one cause or another. Though never a combat theater, Mound City and its neighbor, Cairo, Illinois, became two of the most important Union staging bases of the war, located as they were at the crucial confluence of the Ohio and Mississippi rivers. At Cairo, Ulysses S. Grant was appointed commander of U.S. forces in the area on 28 April 1861. After repulsing a Confederate drive into southeastern Missouri at Belmont, he leap-

Federal Gunboats

frogged to Paducah, Kentucky to begin his famed Mississippi Valley Campaign that would cut the Confederacy in two. Most troops and supplies he received were funneled to him via Mound City and Cairo.

Many of the famous Eads ironclad gunboats, which offered such exemplary service in the Mississippi Campaign, were built at the marine works at Mound City. Two of the vessels which became most famous in the river war in the West bore the names *Mound City* and *Cairo*.

All this notwithstanding, the primary reason for the location of a national cemetery here was the large Union hospital complex maintained in the area. As early as 1861, a large brick building was taken in hand in Mound City. At maximum capacity it could handle fifteen hundred patients. Nursing service was provided by Catholic nuns of the Order of the Holy Cross from South Bend, Indiana.

The first patients here came from the Battle of Belmont. Afterwards, such titanic struggles as Fort Donelson and Shiloh added their numbers. Disease, as always, exacted its grim scroll. Thus, by 1865, no less than 1,644 Union soldiers had been buried at the nearby burial grounds. Additional reinterments from locales up and down the Ohio and Mississippi rivers brought the total to over 4,800 by 1869. Of these, 2,441 were of decedents known but to God.

Mound City National Cemetery is today located one mile northwest of the city along U.S. Highway 51. Its current area is ten and one-half acres, acquired in two separate parcels at different times from local citizens. Its most notable monument is a towering obelisk dedicated to the memory of all Union servicemen from the state of Illinois. Costing $25,000 at the time of erection, it has dominated the site since 1874.

Since that time, Mound City has provided interment space for American veterans of all later American wars. There are presently about sixty-four hundred such individuals or their dependents at rest here. Though still open, statistics indicate that available space will reach saturation in the early 1990s.

QUINCY NATIONAL CEMETERY

Quincy, Illinois

Quincy lies about one hundred miles north of St. Louis on the Mississippi River, and an equal distance west of the capital at Springfield. Quincy was once a true American boom town. As the terminus of the Chicago, Burlington and Quincy Railroad, it was a major transshipment point for river traffic to New Orleans and all points south. Though occasionally closed with ice, the "port" of Quincy enjoyed a prosperity unknown to most midwestern towns throughout most of the nineteenth century.

All that has changed of course. Gone are the huffing paddle-wheelers and their armies of steerage passengers and roustabouts. Gone also are the revenues from the C. B. & Q., now just a spur line, left behind by the westward shifts of industrial and population centers. The hustle and bustle is gone but much of the wealth remains. Quincy is a thriving, if modest-sized, community whose citizens have an attitude of contented prosperity.

The prosperity exists primarily because the Illinois waterway passing to the west (a virtual extension of the St. Lawrence Seaway) acts as liaison between Chicago and the Mississippi River. While Quincy profits little from the waterway directly, the farms around the city are some of the most productive on earth.

Some fifty miles north lies Nauvoo, Illinois. Here, in 1839, Brigham Young and his followers briefly sought respite from the persecutions that had followed them from the East. However, they were soon driven to flight again and began their epic anabasis to found the Mormon homeland of Utah.

Just to the northeast lies Lewistown, Illinois, boyhood home of Edgar Lee Masters. His *Spoon River Anthology* and other writings made him one of the foremost voices of Americana.

Quincy boasts one of the more unique city centers in the Midwest. The heart of Quincy, called Washington Square, is based on a New England town square. It was here in 1858 that the sixth of the Lincoln-Douglas Debates transpired.

However, the establishment of a national cemetery here is due to the Civil War and the patriotic ardor of the Illinois population in their service to the Union cause. The Thirty-sixth Illinois Regiment, one of the Union army's finest elements, was mainly recruited in the western part of the state, including Quincy. It saw action at Pea Ridge, Corinth, Chickamauga, Stones River (Murfressboro), Missionary Ridge and the Atlanta Campaign of William T. Sherman. It delivered the key counterattack at the Battle of Franklin in 1864, where the remnant of John B. Hood's Confederate army was destroyed in Tennessee. It was mustered out on 10 October 1865. Few regiments suffered more casualties and one of its commanders, Colonel Silas Miller, was killed at Kenesaw Mountain shortly before the fall of Atlanta.

Most of the graves in Quincy National Cemetery are filled with Union soldiers who were returned home after falling in the battles named above. In 1861 a one-half-acre plot in Woodland Cemetery was assigned as a Soldier's Lot for use by the government. Interments occurred there as early as 1861. In 1870 the city of Quincy donated the land to the government in perpetuity.

The site became a national cemetery in 1882. A superintendent was placed in charge briefly, but in January 1883 the secretary of war canceled the appointment. Subsequent care was arranged under contract with the Woodland Cemetery Association. This continued for a number of years. But in 1899, the government purchased a small plot in nearby Graceland Cemetery and transferred the remains of the three hundred Union soldiers to that site. It retained the name "Quincy National Cemetery."

It remains one of the smallest national cemeteries anywhere. All those interred there are Union army veterans, most of them Civil War casualties. The cemetery is not open to further burials. It is currently administered by the cemetery director of the Keokuk National Cemetery, Iowa.

ROCK ISLAND NATIONAL CEMETERY

Rock Island, Illinois

Rock Island, located in the Mississippi River, is the site of a major United States arsenal and lies almost equidistant between the towns of Davenport, Iowa and Moline, Illinois. In addition to supplying ammunition and armaments to the U.S. government during the Civil War, it also saw duty as a principal prison camp for Confederate troops.

From 1863 to 1865, numerous enemy prisoners were held here. The first contingents were taken in late 1863 during the battles of Lookout Mountain and Missionary Ridge near Chattanooga, Tennessee. By the cessation of hostilities, twelve thousand Southerners had been held here at one time or another. Of these, almost two thousand died, victims of northern winters, poor rations and diseases such as smallpox, which struck numbers of their guards as well.

Consequently, a small site known as the Confederate Cemetery was developed about one and one-half miles northwest of the arsenal post cemetery. It has since been included in the overall structure of Rock Island National Cemetery, and thus makes the location one of the few with burial areas not contiguous to each other.

In August 1868, General Lorenzo Thomas, Inspector of National Cemeteries, visited Rock Island to establish a burial ground on the arsenal reservation. He concurred with the then commandant of the arsenal, General Thomas C. Rodman, that Union dead from Davenport, Iowa and the Rock Island post cemetery be reinterred to a more suitable site on the island. By 1874, some 295 Union soldiers had been buried in what would become the national cemetery grounds.

Among those at rest here is Rodman himself. A distinguished Union officer, he became commandant of the arsenal until his own demise in 1871. His gravesite is marked by a large obelisk and surrounded by cannon produced here. This is appropriate since Rodman invented the new fabrication-casting process that had increased reliability and longevity of American cannon. He also pioneered in bettering the propellant qualities of various gunpowders.

More than a century has elapsed since Thomas authorized Rock Island National Cemetery. Since then, it has supplied burial space for veterans of all subsequent American conflicts. As of 31 December 1985, about eleven thousand interments had been made. Among these are 154 men buried in mass graves because of identification problems. The largest group is of 19 Americans who perished on 10 January 1945 on the armed transport U.S.S. *Warhawk* at Lingayen Gulf, Philippine Islands during World War II. They were brought here in 1950. Also, ten memorial markers are found here to those whose last resting place was never determined.

Rock Island is one of the few cemeteries which hosts ceremonies in memory of the Confederate dead. Each Memorial Day an impressive military ceremony is held, and each grave is decorated with the U.S. flag and the Stars and Bars.

At present, the regular and Confederate sections comprise 31.5 acres of usable land. It is open to continuing interments, but space may be exhausted by year 2000.

Confederate Section at Rock Island National Cemetery
--photo courtesy of the author

CROWN HILL NATIONAL CEMETERY

Indianapolis, Indiana

The rush of settlement into Ohio beginning in 1805 was so great that many of the newcomers simply forged on to what was known as Indiana Territory. By 1821, Indianapolis had become the premier city of the area and remains so today; it is the state capital and has the largest population of any city in the state.

Much American history transpired within a brief drive of the city. To the southwest lies the town of Vincennes, the old British post captured during the American Revolution by George Rogers Clark in what is often regarded as the spark that heralded American expansion into the Midwest. Only one hundred miles north lies the Battlefield of Tippecanoe where, in 1811, General Benjamin Harrison broke the power of the Tecumseh Revolt. He later succeeded in riding this triumph to the White House.

During the Civil War, southern Indiana was occasionally a battleground due to the depredations of Southern raiders. And few states displayed more patriotic ardor in defense of the Union cause. One of the best-known units the state supplied to the Union army was the Nineteenth Indiana Infantry, sometimes called the "Iron Brigade." Organized in Indianapolis on 29 July 1861, it fought in almost every major battle from the Peninsula Campaign to Appomattox. At Gettysburg, in one sanguinary afternoon, it lost 210 of its 288 men. Other units which helped uphold the state's pride in the struggle were the Twentieth and Twenty-seventh Indiana Regiments.

Many of those local men who fell during the Civil War were returned home to Indianapolis and buried in old Greenlawn Cemetery.

By 1863, this site was near capacity due to the sudden influx of decedents. Therefore, on 25 September 1863, a commission was chosen to select a new location. The massive Crown Hill Cemetery complex soon arose in what was known as the Strawberry Hills.

Part of this area was designated a national cemetery and it lies on a gentle slope to the northwest of the central chapel. Buried here are hundreds of Union casualties of the war and over sixteen hundred Confederate war dead, most of whom succumbed to wounds or perished while in captivity. Also at rest here is a former drummer boy of the Revolution.

Down through the years, the location has provided interment space for veterans of all later wars. The cemetery is now closed due to lack of space, but the huge five-hundred-acre complex of which it is a part continues to offer service, and it is known for the vast spectrum of civilian and military personalities who lie there. They are as diverse as President Benjamin Harrison and notorious bank bandit John H. Dillinger.

A complete list of those distinguished Americans buried here would be too exhaustive for this small study. However, below are some of the more notable:

Charles Warren Fairbanks, vice president under Theodore Roosevelt

Thomas A. Hendricks, vice president under Grover Cleveland

Jacob Cox, famed Indianapolis portrait and landscape artist

Richard J. Gatling, inventor of agricultural implements and the precursor of the modern machine-gun

Caroline S. Harrison, wife of President Benjamin Harrison and first president--general of the D.A.R.

Colonel Eli Lilly, a distinguished Union soldier and founder of Eli Lilly Pharmaceutical Company

Booth Tarkington and James Whitcomb Riley, both famed writers of Americana

Robert H. Tyndal, commander of the Forty-second (Rainbow) Division during World War I and a long-time mayor of Indianapolis

A number of monuments will be found here. In the national cemetery section is a memorial to the Confederate dead who lie there. Also raised have been monuments to the men who served in the Rainbow Division in World War II and another erected by the D.A.R. to all Americans who have served in the armed forces.

Crown Hill Cemetery Complex will continue to provide burial space for American veterans into the next century. The location is also one of the few facilities of its type to be listed on the register of National Historic Places.

MARION NATIONAL CEMETERY

Marion, Indiana

Situated on the banks of the Mississenewa River, which runs through the rolling plains of east-central Indiana, the town of Marion possesses one of the newest national cemeteries in the entire system. Its location also places it at the hub of some of America's most noteworthy culture and history.

To the west one will find the town of Kokomo, its unusual name surfacing in more anecdotes and popular songs than perhaps any other community in the nation. One hundred miles beyond, along the banks of the Wabash River, lies the battlefield of Tippecanoe. It was here, in November 1811, that General Benjamin Harrison repulsed the dawn assault of the Indian warriors in Tecumseh's federation and won a decisive victory over them. Though not on the field that day and thus escaping the fate of so many of his men, the Indian leader was to fall two years later while aiding the British in the defense of Canada during the War of 1812. Harrison, for his part, rode his military triumph to the White House, although he died before his term expired.

To the north of Marion, around Elkhart, lies the heartland of the state's huge Amish and Mennonite sects. The largest concentrations are to be found around Berne and Goshen. But just to the south along U.S. Route 6 is located Amish Acres, the only such farmstead in the country where guided tours are available year-round.

South from Elkhart is Fort Wayne. Beginning as a crude military outpost, it became one of the most cosmopolitan cities in middle America. However, for more than a century and a half it was the center of innumerable battles between French, British, American and Indians. Thousands of men on all sides fell on dozens of bloody fields before ownership of what was known as the Northwest Territory was resolved in favor of the burgeoning American republic.

Not far to the south of Marion, near present-day Richmond, Indiana, is Wilbur Wright Historic Park, dedicated to the famed aerial inventor and pioneer, and his brother Orville. And at Fountain City just a few miles away, is the former home of one Levi Coffin. For a generation, from 1827 to 1847, it was the Grand Central Station of the Underground Railroad for fugitive slaves fleeing north to freedom.

Slave Chain

Marion National Cemetery is an adjunct of the large V. A. Medical Center located in the town. It officially became part of the National Cemetery System with the expansion of the concept in 1973. Located to serve the heavily populated areas of southern Michigan and western Ohio, Marion remains a highly active installation. The national cemetery is currently the only facility of its type open to veteran interments in the Indiana-Ohio-Michigan region. The situation was alleviated in 1984 with the opening of the huge national cemetery at Fort Custer, Michigan, halfway between Detroit and Chicago. However, so much land is in demand that the 680-acre Fort Custer facility is expected to be as much as twenty-five percent exhausted by the year 2000. Most of those buried in the 39-acre Marion National Cemetery are veterans of twentieth-century conflicts and died in the Veterans Administration hospital there. Burial at Marion is now confined almost exclusively to such disabled veterans.

NEW ALBANY NATIONAL CEMETERY

New Albany, Indiana

Located just across the Ohio River from Louisville, Kentucky, New Albany and its environs abound in nineteenth-century nostalgia. From 1816 to 1830 a young man named Abraham Lincoln grew up about fifty miles west of New Albany. His mother, Nancy Hanks Lincoln, worn out and killed by hard, pioneering work at the age of thirty-five, is buried at the old Lincoln cabin, now maintained as a historic site.

Southern Indiana, including New Albany, was a major recruiting area for the Union army during the Civil War. Among those units which comprised levies from the town was the Twenty-seventh Indiana Infantry. Its war record was so splendid that its commander, Silas Cosgrove, was eventually brevetted to brigadier general.

Leaving the state in September 1861, the Twenty-seventh served first under General Nathaniel Banks during Jackson's famous Valley Campaign of 1862. Later, it suffered heavy losses at Cedar Mountain, Antietam, Chancellorsville and Gettysburg. Moving back West in 1864, it played a great part at Resaca during Sherman's Atlanta Campaign, and was credited with inflicting five times as many casualties as it lost.

The five-acre New Albany National Cemetery was initially established as a final resting place for Union war dead returned home, and its earliest interments date from well before the cessation of hostilities. Other American veterans were interred there for a short time thereafter, but the facility has been closed since 1900 due to limited space and the committal of all available gravesites.

The Mississippi River

KEOKUK NATIONAL CEMETERY

Keokuk, Iowa

Situated on the Mississippi River in the extreme southeastern corner of the state, Keokuk was long the center of area farming and possesses the only national cemetery in the state. Keokuk was founded in 1833 as a result of the Black Hawk Purchase, which was a manifestation of the failure of the Black Hawk Revolt the year before. Settlers from states to the east poured into the area. The winter of 1833 to 1834 drove many of them out, but the heartiest stayed and scratched a living from the rich soil.

By 1840, forty-three thousand people resided in eastern Iowa. The name of the state was chosen from the Indian word for "Home of the people." Keokuk himself, "Watchful Fox" in the Indian dialect, was the foremost "statesman" of his tribe and the city was named to commemorate his sagacity. In addition to keeping many of his tribe from joining Black Hawk's debacle, he was an astute politician and forceful orator who served his people well. Reasoning that dying in defense of a land they could not protect was foolish, he counseled his people to submit to the white settlers and sell the land prior to moving to a new homeland in Kansas.

With the finesse of an Arab trader, he chivied the greatest price from the greatest number in the interests of his people. Supposedly he once sold the same land to no less than three different groups. The legal wrangle was further complicated upon learning that he did not even own that piece of property. At any rate, he eventually lived peacefully in Kansas until his demise in April 1848 from the consequences of what was delicately described as a "drunken frolic."

Keokuk National Cemetery, like most of those in the Midwest, was created as a result of the Civil War. A legion of Iowans flocked to the Union banner. The Sixth Iowa (XVI Corps) fought in such epic contests as Shiloh, Vicksburg, Missionary Ridge, the Atlanta Campaign and Sherman's march to the sea.

During this time, several Union hospitals were established in and around Keokuk. Keokuk's location on the Mississippi gave ease of transport and was far enough removed from the guerrilla battleground of central Missouri to be secure.

The national cemetery was established by Congress on 17 July 1862 and was originally a part of Oakland Cemetery, apparently operated as part of it for some years. It was officially recognized as a national cemetery in 1870 when a superintendent was assigned and improvements began. Most of those interred there are Union soldiers who died in the general hospitals of the area. The first interment was one Thomas Lurch, Union army, on 23 September 1861, and burials have continued since.

The most visible aspect of the location is a granite obelisk dating from 1912. It was erected by members of the Women's Relief Corps and sits over the Tomb of the Unknown Soldier of the Civil War. Inscribed on it is a life-sized figure of a soldier at parade rest. In addition, the cemetery contains a cornerstone of the old Estes House, a local mansion which served as a hospital during the struggle and which was razed in 1929.

One Medal of Honor recipient is interred here. He is Pfc. John Thorson, U.S.A., who fell in the liberation of the Philippines in 1944.

Six new acres were added to the original plot in 1978. This should allow for continued interment space until after the year 2000 with some ten thousand interments when filled. The director here is charged with overseeing the inactive facility at Quincy, Illinois, just a short distance away.

FORT LEAVENWORTH NATIONAL CEMETERY

Fort Leavenworth, Kansas

Though basically associated with the Civil War, Fort Leavenworth and its accompanying national cemetery encompass much of American history prior to that struggle. One of the most important early day posts in the West, it honors Colonel Henry Leavenworth, the man who selected the site on the banks of the Missouri River as a suitable location for a permanent cantonment in 1827.

Leavenworth himself enjoyed an illustrious military career. Entering the army during the War of 1812, continuing service brought him west in 1819. He began construction of Fort Snelling, Minnesota and then spent several years at Jefferson Barracks in St. Louis. From there he established the fortress that still bears his name.

His career received a boost in 1834 when he was appointed to command of the entire southwestern United States and ordered to negotiate peace treaties with the hostile tribes of modern-day Oklahoma. Before he could complete this assignment, he was stricken by illness and died on 21 July 1834 at Cross Timbers, Indian Territory.

Originally buried at his home in Delhi, New York, he was reinterred at Fort Leavenworth in 1902. A large monument of Barre granite was erected at his gravesite in Section 2 of the cemetery. Atop the monument is the sculpture of an eagle reposing on a cairn.

Through the years the fort served as a staging area for troops on their way west, either to fight the Mexican War or to quell uprisings among the Plains Indians. Both the Santa Fe and Oregon Trails border the national cemetery. Many Indian treaties were signed at the fort, some of which were actually kept, and when the Territory of Kansas was organized in 1854, Fort Leavenworth became the temporary capital.

In 1881 General William T. Sherman selected Fort Leavenworth as the location of what eventually developed into the U.S. Army Command and General Staff College. For generations it has also served a less desirable but necessary function as the U.S. Army's maximum security stockade for felons and other offenders.

The first interment made in what became the national cemetery was of Captain James Allen of the First U.S. Dragoons on 23 August 1846. Seven Confederate prisoners of war who died in captivity were also laid to rest here. Several Medal of Honor winners lie buried here, including Captain Harry Bell, U.S. Volunteers. He was decorated for valor in action in the Philippines in 1899. Another private monument in the cemetery commemorates the life and deeds of Colonel Edward Hatch, U.S. Army. A cavalry leader under Sherman in the Civil War, he later campaigned against the Apaches in Arizona and was chairman of the peace commission to end the Ute uprising in 1879. Though he survived fifty-three Civil War battles and skirmishes and several Indian campaigns, he met his untimely end at the age of fifty-seven when thrown from a carriage.

Initially, Fort Leavenworth comprised only fourteen acres but incremental expansion brought it to the current size of thirty-six acres. As of 31 December 1976 there had been 16,742 American veterans buried there, including 1,589 unknowns. Except for special cases or previously reserved plots, committals are no longer conducted here. Those requiring burial space are now handled at the large Leavenworth National Cemetery nearby.

FORT SCOTT NATIONAL CEMETERY

Fort Scott, Kansas

Like many modern towns of the Midwest, Fort Scott, Kansas owes its name and location to a U.S. Army post. Fort Scott, lying on the Kansas-Missouri border south of Kansas City, was established in 1842 as protection for the many settlers and traders traversing the immigration routes of the area. Its name memorializes General Winfield Scott, hero of the Mexican War and various Indian wars, and is generally regarded as one of the finest military tacticians this nation has produced.

Fort Scott was garrisoned until 1855 when it was abandoned. And in those days, when the army abandoned a post, it did it right. The palisades were torn down and the lumber sold; the buildings were auctioned off. However, the outbreak of the Civil War once again made the strategic site desirable for a base. Reestablished hastily, the fort became a support and staging area for Union troops operating in Missouri and as far south as the Red River in Texas.

For a brief period after the conflict, the fort was used as a trans-shipment center for displaced Indians on their way to western reservations. But the tides of settlement passed it by and it was abandoned for good a few years later. By then, however, the survival of the surrounding community was assured.

On 15 November 1862, part of the nearby Presbyterian Cemetery was designated the Fort Scott National Cemetery. After the Civil War many reinterments were made here from old Fort Lincoln, Kansas and isolated battlefields in the area. The first recorded burial here was of army Captain Alexander Morrow, who died on 1 July 1851. Also resting here are the remains of many unknown Union and Confederate war dead. Two soldiers executed for capital offenses can be found at Fort Scott--a most unusual situation. In this century such individuals are no longer considered eligible for interment in a national cemetery.

Perhaps the most noteworthy veteran here is Eugene F. Ware. A captain of the Seventh Iowa Cavalry, he became one of midwestern America's foremost poets. His best-known creation is "John Brown." He also possesses one of the most unique gravestones anywhere, a large sandstone boulder he chose prior to his demise.

Other Union veterans here are from many of the Indian regiments during the Civil War. These men rest beneath tombstones bearing such colorful names as "Young Chicken," "Deep-in-Water," "Set-them-Up" and "Stick-out-Belly." Presumably these reflected character traits; hopefully their characters were not as inauspicious as some of the names suggest.

The 10.5-acre Fort Scott National Cemetery is expected to provide service until at least the year 2000, if not longer. It will hold about seven thousand gravesites when filled.

LEAVENWORTH NATIONAL CEMETERY

Leavenworth, Kansas

Away, I'm bound away,
Across the wide Missouri.

So goes the refrain of the popular ballad which filled thousands of hearty pioneer throats as these men and women poured into Kansas Territory in the 1840s and 1850s. And while they did cross the river, they did not leave its influence. Old Misery flowed at the very doorstep of Leavenworth; the Missouri River then, as now, was the second mightiest river on the North American continent. In fact, on occasion it flowed over that doorstep. Floods were a major problem for the entire area until a generation ago when various dams and reclamation projects finally eased the threat.

But difficulties of weather and water were only some of the travails undergone by the denizens of Leavenworth in their history. Just across the river lay Missouri, and Leavenworth became a major battleground between pro and anti-slavery forces in the decade before the Civil War. With the exception of Lawrence (forty miles to the west) which was sacked and burned in July 1863 by Quantrill's raiders, few parts of "Bleeding Kansas" shed its blood more copiously than Leavenworth.

Just to the north is St. Joseph, Missouri. From this terminus in 1860 the riders of the Pony Express set out on their perilous trip to Sacramento, California. It was also here in a small home that America's most legendary bad man, Jesse James, met his end at the hands of a treacherous cohort on 3 April 1882.

However, it was the burgeoning metropolis of Kansas City twenty-five miles to the south, and the Missouri Pacific Railroad which served it, that put Leavenworth on the map. In 1884 the citizens donated 640 acres of land on the bluffs above the river for the Western Home of Disabled Volunteer Soldiers. In 1886 Thomas Brennan, appropriately enough a former member of the Seventh Kansas Regiment, became the first interment there. Since then veterans of every American struggle have been buried there. In the 1930s a huge V.A. hospital was established to serve Kansas City and surrounding environs and it remains among the largest in the nation.

The cemetery contains a number of unusual features. A giant

obelisk erected over the grave of Colonel C.W. Wadsworth commemorates all American war dead. Another marker stands over the gravesite of a dozen Indians whose remains were unearthed in the construction of the hospital. How and when they came to their end at this location will forever remain a conundrum. In the older, original thirty-seven-acre part of the cemetery are many private markers unlike the standard white markers decreed by later edict. Clustered about the Wadsworth Obelisk are a number of quite impressive headstones.

The undulating topography and tree-studded hills of the area are typically midwestern. In the old section of the cemetery rest fifteen thousand decedents. However, with the proposed closing of Fort Leavenworth National Cemetery just to the north, a major expansion is beginning which will expand this cemetery to some 130 acres capable of receiving over forty thousand gravesites in toto. The master plan calls for a six-acre lake as part of the scenic considerations. With this project completed in the 1980s, Leavenworth National Cemetery is expected to provide service to area veterans until well into the twenty-first century.

Grave Excavation
Leavenworth National Cemetery
--Department of Veterans Affairs photo

CAMP NELSON NATIONAL CEMETERY

Nicholasville, Kentucky

Located seven miles south of the town of Nicholasville on U.S. Route 27, Camp Nelson is the only installation of its type still available in the state providing burial space for the large veteran populations of Kentucky's metropolitan areas along the Ohio River to the north. Like all national cemeteries located in the border regions of the United States, Camp Nelson had its origins in the American Civil War. Most Kentuckians sought to avoid being embroiled in the struggle, but it became a state divided despite all efforts. It was in such border states that the greatest familial and community heartaches occurred due to different loyalties. According to military records, ninety thousand Kentuckians served the Union cause and another forty thousand bore arms for the Confederacy.

Though no major battles were fought in the immediate vicinity, the site was chosen as a recruiting and training area in Jessamine County in 1863. It stretched for two miles along the turnpike towards Nicholasville and had one of the more heavily fortified perimeters in the country. First referred to as Fort Bramlette, it was renamed in honor of Union General William "Bull" Nelson following his demise and is now registered as a national historic site.

Nelson was one of the strangest apparitions of the American Civil War. He stood six feet four and weighed three hundred pounds, reputedly little of it fat. He had served as a naval midshipman in the Mexican War from 1846 to 1848 and was a long-time friend of Abraham Lincoln. In September 1861 he was commissioned a brigadier general to arm and train loyal Kentucky men as a home guard. He served at the Battle of Shiloh, in the advance on Corinth, Mississippi and was wounded in action at Richmond, Kentucky in August 1862. Then promoted to major general, he was given command of the Army of Kentucky. While organizing this force in Louisville, he was killed by a Union officer named Jefferson C. Davis in a personal dispute in a local hotel lobby on 29 September 1862. For reasons now obscured by time, Davis was not prosecuted for the incident. Presumably he was no relation to the Confederate president, but he certainly rendered the Southern cause a considerable service. At the time of his death, Nelson was marked by superior officers as one of the Union's finest officers and a valuable leader almost certain to achieve army stardom.

The huge grounds at Camp Nelson originally contained two separate graveyards, one at the site of a smallpox hospital. The 379 men buried here were subsequently reinterred to the second location, now the actual national cemetery. This included the old post cemetery in which 1,183 Union men had been buried by the end of the fighting. The first known interment is of James Sexton, First Kentucky Cavalry, who apparently was killed in a skirmish on 14 October 1861.

Within weeks of Lee's surrender at Appomattox, a massive reinterment effort was underway for the reclamation of Union war dead. Camp Nelson received them from all over the state. In 1958 the Perryville National Cemetery was closed and its 1,245 unknown soldiers were transferred here over a period of nearly a decade.

In the years since, American veterans of every subsequent war through the Vietnam conflict have found a final resting place at Camp Nelson. The 19.75-acre facility should remain open indefinitely. Through 31 December 1975, total committals numbered approximately 5,900. The director here is also responsible for the administration of the other national cemeteries in central Kentucky located at Danville, Lexington and Perryville, which are inactive.

CAVE HILL NATIONAL CEMETERY

Louisville, Kentucky

Though Kentucky contains many Civil War cemeteries, the only one located within the city of Louisville itself is Cave Hill. Louisville today is one of the major metropolitan areas along the Ohio River. Home of the fabled Churchill Downs race grounds, which features the annual Kentucky Derby, Louisville is within a stone's throw from the nation's treasure house at Fort Knox.

Because of its location, Louisville was a much-sought prize in the Civil War. Numerous Confederate attempts to capture the city and assure Kentuckian adherence to the Southern cause had to be defeated during the first two years of conflict. A dozen battles and innumerable skirmishes against Southern raiders were waged to the south.

Shortly after the commencement of hostilities, the Union high command realized the city was a key to control of the Ohio River. On 21 September 1861 Major Robert Anderson, of Fort Sumter fame, established a Union headquarters here. He was supplanted by William T. Sherman, who was soon ousted when he had the temerity to say that it would take over two hundred thousand men to win the war in the West. He was replaced by General Don Carlos Buell, whose projections were considerably lower. Unfortunately, so was his ability. Sherman later got his two hundred thousand man army and played a significant part in winning the Civil War.

The first burial in the four-acre Cave Hill National Cemetery occurred as early as 1861. After the war it was primarily used for reinterments of fallen Union warriors. Approximately twenty-five hundred Americans lie here, a few of them veterans of subsequent conflicts.

However, with the establishment of nearby Zachary Taylor National Cemetery, Cave Hill was rendered useless. It has been inactive for more than a generation. Even the exact date of its closing is hazy. It is administered by the cemetery director of the facility at the Zachary Taylor Memorial.

DANVILLE NATIONAL CEMETERY

Danville, Kentucky

Located just south of the major loop of the Kentucky River, the small town of Danville possesses a national cemetery which, like too many others, has generally been bypassed as population and industrial growth occur elsewhere. To the east lies beautiful, elongated Cumberland Mountain Forest and the city of Richmond, site of a major Union defeat at the hands of Confederate General E. Kirby Smith during his Kentucky Campaign of 1862. Indeed, the final engagement of this campaign occurred just twenty miles west of Danville at Perryville, when Union hegemony over the state was established once and for all.

Danville National Cemetery was originally opened in 1863. Evidently it was a collection point for Union dead who fell in the hundreds of skirmishes, ambushes and cavalry raids that occurred statewide throughout most of the Civil War. While information is sketchy, it seems most of those Union war dead interred here were original burials in the site. This is vouchsafed by the fact that only 13 of the 396 men whose remains were committed here are unknowns. Most post-war reinterment efforts were directed at Camp Nelson or other larger installations in the state. Today, unfortunately, information on the men buried here has become as lost in time as the cemetery itself. The small plot is but .31 acres in extent. Though a few gravesites remain available, Danville National Cemetery has been inactive for nearly a century. It is administered by the cemetery director of Camp Nelson National Cemetery, Nicholasville, Kentucky.

LEBANON NATIONAL CEMETERY

Lebanon, Kentucky

During the Civil War, Lebanon was a terminus on a major branch spur of the Louisville and Nashville Railroad. Just east of the city at Perryville on 8 October 1862, General Braxton Bragg was repulsed in the last Confederate attempt to maintain hegemony over western Kentucky. Equidistant to the west lies Hodgenville, Kentucky, birthplace of Union President Abraham Lincoln.

Railway Battery

As most towns in central Kentucky, Lebanon escaped the worst aspects of the struggle for most of its duration. But the halcyon days ended in July 1863, during General John Morgan's Ohio Raid. Moving north to stage a diversion during the Knoxville Campaign, Morgan crossed the area on his route to Ohio with twenty-five hundred picked Confederate troops. Repulsed in crossing the Green River, Morgan swept down on Lebanon on the morning of 5 July 1863. Awaiting him was Colonel C.S. Hanson and the Twentieth Kentucky Regiment of the Union army. A long, hot engagement ensued before the Northern troops were driven from town. Morgan captured four hundred prisoners and large quantities of stores and medicines.

However, though he did eventually invade Ohio, the delay incurred by the Battle of Lebanon cost Morgan his chance of success. Harried by innumerable Union forces, he was finally defeated and captured at New Lisbon, Ohio on 26 July. Though he did escape from the Union prison where he was held and returned south, he was slain by Union cavalry the following year near Greeneville, Tennessee.

Lebanon National Cemetery was established in 1867 as part of the huge expansion program authorized by the U.S. government. Within a few years 277 unknown Union soldiers lay at rest here, reinterred from Lebanon and other locations--Bardstown, Crab Orchard, Green River and Campbellsville. Though Kentucky had seen few major battles, there had been dozens of raids and skirmishes and these had proven just as deadly to the men who fell there.

While the small Lebanon National Cemetery is primarily considered a Civil War site, and its one plaque contains the words of Lincoln's Gettysburg Address, it has provided burial space for many American veterans of subsequent wars. In fact, it is one of the few national cemeteries of Civil War vintage to contain more recent interments than Union soldiers.

On 16 June 1966, Pfc. Ray Pendygraft became the first interment of a Vietnam casualty. Since then, a dozen others have been made. As of 30 June 1974, the cemetery was nearing capacity. Because of this, a local veterans' group purchased two acres of land adjacent to the cemetery and it appears expansion will occur, thus assuring Kentucky veterans of continuing interment space if they so desire, though it is believed another expansion might be necessary by the year 2000.

LEXINGTON NATIONAL CEMETERY

Lexington, Kentucky

Lexington National Cemetery is a part of the Greater Lexington Cemetery Complex first established in 1849. With its picturesque lakes and sunken gardens, Lexington Cemetery is considered one of the most beautiful cemeteries in the nation. It is one of a handful of such facilities listed on the National Register of Historic Places.

The cemetery was created in 1849 by public-spirited citizens as a result of cholera epidemics sweeping the area. Comprising 170 acres in a plot of land known as Boswell's Woods, the cemetery has been in operation ever since. The segment dedicated as a national cemetery lies in the southwestern part bordering the Leestown Pike and is less than ten percent of the overall facility.

Set in the rich Bluegrass country of central Kentucky, Lexington lies one hundred miles east of Louisville where it was a major terminus of the Kentucky Central Railroad, especially during the Civil War. Though the Confederates had been forced to evacuate the state early in the war, some action did occur around Lexington.

The most notable incident was Confederate raider John Morgan's last foray into the state in 1864. Near Mount Sterling twenty miles east, Morgan captured 380 Union prisoners on 9 June 1864. However, rapid Union pursuit destroyed the garrison he left there and ran him to earth north of Lexington at Cynthiana. Crushed here on 11 June, Morgan retreated to Virginia and his days of value to the Confederacy were ended.

Many of those in Lexington National Cemetery were reinterred from Union gravesites in the above areas as well as others. One of these was the battlefield at Richmond, Kentucky to the south. Here, in August 1862, a Union force was defeated by a Confederate force under General Kirby Smith during an abortive Confederate attempt to re-establish control over eastern Kentucky.

Many Civil War leaders and other distinguished Americans lie either in the national cemetery itself or in the main section adjacent to it. One of the best-known is Henry Clay. A member of Congress for twenty-seven years and secretary of state for four, "Harry of the West" is principally remembered for sponsoring the Missouri Compromise of 1850. Though it deferred civil strife for a decade, it made it more dreadful when it came by establishing the principle of admitting one state to the Union "free" for one "slave." This, of course, was unworkable and caused "Bleeding Kansas" and other such bloody battlegrounds.

He is commemorated by an impressive 120-foot column which towers over his sarcophagus.

Also interred here is John C. Breckenridge, youngest man ever to serve as vice president of the United States and later secretary of war for the Confederacy. John H. Morgan, "Thunderbolt of the Confederacy" who was killed in 1864, also lies here in a family plot.

Other military figures are Confederate General Roger Hanson and Union General Gordon Granger, one-time commander of the Army of the Cumberland. Found here is Colonel James Morrison, Revolutionary War hero and founder of Morrison College at Transylvania University. Lt. Hugh McKee, U.S.N., a hero of the Mexican War lies here, a casualty of the little-known Korean Incident of 1870 to 1871.

In 1875, an admirable example of Victorian architecture was erected in the national cemetery by a group of Southern women in honor of Confederate dead. In 1893 a subsequent memorial was raised to all Confederate dead of the Civil War here and elsewhere.

The huge Lexington Cemetery and its concomitant national cemetery remains one of the largest in the state. It is believed they will be able to provide service to American veterans for many generations.

MILL SPRINGS NATIONAL CEMETERY

Nancy, Kentucky

Now forgotten in the larger conflict, at the time it was fought, the Battle of Mill Springs (often referred to as Logan Cross Roads) was one of the most crucial conflicts of the Civil War. It brought two of the most colorful, flamboyant commanders of that war into head-on collision.

The first of these was General George H. Thomas, Union army. An 1840 graduate of West Point, he had seen service in the Seminole Wars and frontier duty, and won two brevets for distinguished service in the Mexican conflict of 1846 to 1848. Though a Virginian by birth, he remained loyal to the Union despite that state's secession in 1861. Throughout his career, he achieved a formidable array of nicknames, but is primarily remembered as the savior of the Army of the Cumberland in 1863, where he became for all time "The Rock of Chickamauga."

The other man in question was General Felix Zollicoffer, C.S.A. A newspaper editor by trade, he had also fought in the Seminole War and eventually become a political power in the Whig Party in Tennessee. Possessing an exasperating, mercurial personality, he actually fought a duel while serving in the U.S. Congress. Appointed a general in the Confederate army on 9 July 1861, he was charged with defending eastern Tennessee. However, his peculiar personality led to the defeat of the Southern cause there and his own strange demise.

Early in the war, Zollicoffer occupied the Cumberland Gap and contented himself with skirmishing against Thomas as Union troops recovered eastern Kentucky. In October 1861 he routed another Union force under Schoepf at Wildcat Mountain, and this apparently gave him a false sense of invincibility. Emboldened by his success, he moved north in November and entrenched near Logan Cross Roads, nearly seventy miles from the Gap. Union forces immediately concentrated to smash his exposed army. When General George Crittenden arrived to take overall command of the Southern forces, he realized instinctively that his best method of protecting the Gap was a withdrawal. But it was too late. He was forced to fight along the Cumberland whether he wanted to or not.

In a desperate attempt to retrieve the situation left him by Zollicoffer's ill-advised offensive, he launched an assault against the forces of Thomas south of Logan Cross Roads at dawn on 19 January

1862. At first, the Confederate attack made progress and the Union troops began to retreat. Then, as both sides sought to stabilize their lines, a lull occurred and one of the strangest events of the Civil War transpired.

Colonel S.S. Fry, commander of the Fourth Kentucky Regiment, Union army, rode to a flank to reconnoiter. As he spoke with another officer, a stranger appeared and shot and wounded Fry's horse. Colonel Fry and several soldiers who witnessed the incident, opened fire and killed the intruder. He was later identified as Zollicoffer. How he got there, why he did it and what he thought he was doing will remain a conundrum forever.

The death of Zollicoffer threw the Southerners into disarray. A Union counterattack, led by the Ninth Ohio, soon drove them from the field in a stirring bayonet charge. Thomas later reported sustaining 246 casualties, which seems low. Confederate losses must have been twice as high. In addition, the Northerners captured numerous guns, caissons, war supplies and over one thousand horses and mules when they overran the Confederate encampment.

The Union triumph at Mill Springs opened the door to eastern Tennessee. Grant and his subordinates could plan their assault on Chattanooga, and subsequently on Atlanta, without any concern for a potential Confederate envelopment. Zollicoffer's rashness and bravado had shortened the war considerably by eliminating the only viable Southern army in the area.

The small Mill Springs National Cemetery, three and one-half acres in size, was established in 1862 as a final resting place for those Union troops which fell in the battle and elsewhere. Numerous reinterments from other locations occurred after the cessation of hostilities.

No Confederate dead were brought here. In another plot about a mile away, the location known as Zollicoffer Park was created. It was the first resting place of the general and 165 of his men who fell at Mill Springs. Though they remain there to this day, Zollicoffer was reinterred shortly after the struggle ended and rests today in a private cemetery in Nashville.

Though technically still active, this national cemetery has not had any interments (except for special cases) since the Korean War era.

PERRYVILLE NATIONAL CEMETERY

Perryville, Kentucky

The defeat of Confederate forces under General Felix Zollicoffer at Mill Springs in January 1862 effectively resolved the issue of Union control of Kentucky. However, the confusion and incomplete information at the time did not allow area commanders to immediately digest that fact and thousands more men on both sides would die before the Southerners admitted defeat. The largest of these later campaigns culminated in the battle of Perryville in October 1862.

In the summer of 1862, the Confederate commander in the West, General E. Kirby Smith, launched a coordinated offensive with General Braxton Bragg to prevent a Union advance into middle Tennessee. Both Southern increments proceeded north, cleverly feinting in various directions and winning a series of victories over dispersed Union forces. This included Smith's destruction of an untested Union army at Richmond, Kentucky on 30 August 1862 in which he took over four thousand prisoners.

By the time Smith and Bragg joined forces south of Lexington in October 1862, however, Union commander Don Carlos Buell had regrouped and reinforced at Louisville. He then moved south with sixty thousand men in four separate columns. For several days, both sides skirmished vigorously with each other as a major engagement shaped-up near Perryville.

At dawn on 8 October 1862, a Union division seeking to secure water sources for their comrades collided with Confederate cavalry, and the decisive battle was joined. At first, the more experienced Confederates were successful and threw the Northern forces into disarray. However, counterattacks by the divisions under General Philip H. Sheridan and others managed to restore the line and repulse Smith's sledgehammer blows.

Due apparently to irregular geographical acoustics, Buell and his headquarters staff were not aware the battle was on until it was over. Thus, when the Southerners retreated, he lost a magnificent opportunity to win a total triumph. Many months of long, convoluted and bloody campaigning would be required for the Union army to capture Atlanta. Buell would not be there to see it. His dismal performance led to his replacement by General William S. Rosecrans. Both sides claimed victory but it was Smith who had to withdraw. Never again would the Confederacy harbor serious thoughts of extending its sway over the country of the bluegrass.

Smith lost thirty-three hundred men, while Buell reported forty-two hundred casualties. Perryville National Cemetery was established to provide burial space for the men who fell here, as well as reinterments from the scenes of innumerable other skirmishes and clashes in the state. The location is fifty miles due south of the capital of Frankfort and is surrounded by other, small Civil War era national burial grounds--Danville to the east, Lebanon to the west and Camp Nelson to the north. Few Confederate war dead were buried here, although some ex-Southern soldiers who passed on in later years may have been accommodated.

Due to a lack of use, Perryville National Cemetery has been inactive for some years now. In fact, though still maintained on the register of national cemeteries, it no longer contains remains. Beginning in 1958, all were transferred to Camp Nelson National Cemetery, Nicholasville, Kentucky and is administered by the director there. All that remains at the 4.3-acre Perryville installation is a monument dedicated to the 1,245 unknown Union men who previously rested here. However, the land has been technically returned to the state of Kentucky. It is not certain what its future use might be.

ZACHARY TAYLOR NATIONAL CEMETERY

Louisville, Kentucky

"Old Rough and Ready." It is perhaps one of the most accurate descriptions ever applied to an American leader. Zachary Taylor, twelfth president of the United States, was born in 1784 in Orange County, Virginia. Immigrating to Kentucky with his parents at an early age, he spent most of his life in military pursuits or as a Louisiana planter. He had absolutely no political interests or experience, yet, before his death, he would become one of the most popular American chief executives in his century.

He spent most of his life in the military. A chronicle of his career is a virtual textbook of military Americana. Beginning with the War of 1812, he fought the Seminoles in Florida, crushed the Black Hawk Revolt in Illinois and was a victorious general in the Mexican War of 1846 to 1848. He won a series of triumphs here against superior Mexican forces which culminated in the smashing of Santa Ana at Buena Vista, a battle that ended all Mexican threats to Texas. He was one of the few American military men to ever have a gold medal struck in his honor by order of Congress.

Though totally lacking political ambition, his military successes and general popularity proved enough to gain him the Whig nomination for president in 1848, a contest he won handily over several opponents. However, his administration was short-lived. He succumbed to a typhus epidemic on 9 July 1850, one of many who died in the plague as it swept through the nation's capital. He was succeeded by Vice President Millard Fillmore, a far from incompetent man, but one who was so overshadowed by Taylor that few remember him today.

The second president of the United States to die in office, Taylor was initially buried in the family home in Louisville, where fifty members of several generations of Taylors rest today. The plot is now within the confines of the national cemetery and is maintained by the U.S. government.

In 1926 Taylor and his wife were reinterred to a Roman-style mausoleum in what was to become the national cemetery. A fifty-foot granite shaft surmounted by a figure of the former president is nearby. It was erected in 1883 by citizens of his state in appreciation of his national service. On 10 May 1928 some 16.4 acres surrounding the mausoleum were set aside by Congress and designated the Zachary Taylor National Cemetery.

As of 30 June 1968, 8,647 interments had been made. Included in these are many mass burials from World War II. There are no less than 340 such sites containing the remains of almost fifteen hundred men. The largest single burial was of twenty-three American war dead. The cemetery remains open to future committals, though probably will be filled by the year 2000 when all of the projected ten thousand gravesites will be used. The director here is also responsible for the administration of Cave Hill National Cemetery, which is another Louisville location.

ALEXANDRIA NATIONAL CEMETERY

Alexandria, Louisiana

Located in the north-central part of the state, Alexandria is almost midway between the capital of Baton Rouge and the town of Nachitoches; Nachitoches is the oldest settlement in the state, founded four years before New Orleans in 1714 as a French trading post. Here in the center of the state, where the red clay of the East begins to meld into the rich, black delta earth of the Mississippi, one will find some of the oldest ruins in the nation. The Marksville Prehistoric Indian Park contains a cultural display of the art and life of the first Americans long before the white man ever came to the continent.

Alexandria came to national prominence during the Civil War. Alexandria and the Red River on whose south bank Alexandria is located became a symbol of Union frustration in that conflict. More men fell here on both sides in two bungled campaigns, yet accomplished less in the long run, than in any other action of what awesome, sanguinary struggle.

By November 1862 New Orleans had long since been captured by Union forces under Admiral David Farragut and Grant was rapidly closing in on Vicksburg to the north. It was then that the first Red

Levee at New Orleans

River Campaign began under Union General N.P. Banks when he occupied Baton Rouge and branched out through central Louisiana. In the spring of 1863, alarmed by the turn of events, Confederate leaders gave command of the Trans-Mississippi Region to General E.

Kirby Smith, issuing orders for him to block Banks' attempts to reach Texas and thus split the harried Confederacy even further.

Banks was unwilling to assault the Confederate bastion at Port Hudson without securing his flanks, and thus he sent a large force up Bayou Teche and Atchafalaya towards Alexandria, smashing the scattered forces of General Richard Taylor as they went. However, the Southern forces escaped one trap after another and Kirby Smith continued to maintain a viable command even after Banks occupied Alexandria and turned northeast to clear Port Hudson to insure the free flow of Union commerce on the Mississippi.

By the spring of 1864, Alexandria had once again been abandoned to the Confederates. It was then that international politics began to dictate Union policy. Fearing the threat posed by the French who were supporting Maximilian in Mexico, President Lincoln determined that military operations must be undertaken at once to raise the Federal flag over some part of Texas. Grant, Sherman and Banks all disagreed but a second Red River Campaign was eventually ordered. Though designed as a three-pronged assault, Banks eventually found himself on his own.

Despite this, he managed to seize Fort De Russey, a mud fortification on the river south of Alexandria, on 14 March 1864. Occupation of the city followed two days later. But then things began to turn sour. Outnumbered Confederate forces under General Richard Taylor whirled on pursuing Union columns near the Texas border and sent them reeling. The Battle of Sabine Cross Roads on 8 April 1865 decided the campaign. Union endeavors to occupy Texas were ended until long after Lee's surrender at Appomattox.

However, for several weeks thereafter, both sides traded meaningless victories in a desultory campaign that ended with the repulse of a Confederate attempt to reach Baton Rouge at Yellow Bayou on 18 May 1864. By then Alexandria was once again a Confederate base.

Alexandria National Cemetery, actually located in the neighboring city of Pineville, was originally established in 1866 to provide a central spot for the reinterment of Union war dead from the Louisiana campaigns. And there was much digging to be done at places like Sabine, Pleasant Hill, Fort De Russy, Yellow Bayou, Henderson's Hill, Monett's Ferry, Fort Bisland, Irish Bend and a host of other minor sites where ambushes and skirmishes had added to the conflict's grim toll of carnage. Thousands of Union men eventually found a final resting place here. Though exact records are lacking, it appears some Confederate fallen were subsequently entombed here in later years as passions cooled. No known count of the unidentified personnel buried here is available but, as was usual in such cases, the number must be staggering in proportion to the total interred.

However, Alexandria National Cemetery has since provided a final resting place for American servicemen of every twentieth century conflict fought by this nation through Vietnam. It remains open at the present time.

BATON ROUGE NATIONAL CEMETERY

Baton Rouge, Louisiana

Union forces first occupied this city during the Civil War on 12 May 1862, shortly after the capture of New Orleans by Admiral David Farragut. When attempts to reach the Confederate bastion at Vicksburg failed, the area became a major Union staging and supply base for the remainder of the conflict.

By the end of July 1862, Confederate forces under John C. Breckinridge, formerly vice president under James Buchanan, had been gathered to expel the invaders. In a savage collision on 5 August they failed, but not before several hundred men perished on each side. Only the fire of Union gunboats on the Mississippi allowed the spirited Southern assaults to be stemmed. In addition, the Confederate ram *Arkansas* had been disabled and captured, thereby removing the last obstacle to Union control of the "Big Muddy."

Breckinridge and his men fell back on Port Hudson and turned it into a massive fortification in their attempt to protect the Southern flank of Vicksburg. Not until the next summer, after a long, costly siege did Union General N.P. Banks manage to conquer it.

By 1865 tens of thousands of Union soldiers and sailors had passed through the Baton Rouge area. In addition to battle casualties, which were of course quite numerous, yellow fever, malaria and other causes exacted a grim toll of the occupying forces. In the days after the cessation of hostilities, Baton Rouge became the site of a national cemetery designed to provide a final resting place for the thousands of veterans reinterred from all over the region.

Now located at 220 North 19th Street, Baton Rouge National Cemetery contains the remains of several thousand such men. Exact statistics are lacking but it is evident that a goodly percentage are unknowns. Servicemen of twentieth century conflicts have also found interment space here. Unfortunately, space limitations have forced a closure of the site in recent years. However, with burial sites still available at Alexandria National Cemetery and the newly expanded location at Port Hudson, survivors of local veterans currently have no cause for alarm.

CHALMETTE NATIONAL HISTORIC PARK

Arabi, Louisiana

Few locales in the country are more rich historically or diverse culturally than New Orleans. Yet despite this, its greatest claim to fame is neither architecture, nor Mardi Gras nor river trade. Mention "New Orleans" and most Americans will think of the epic conflict waged there at the end of the War of 1812 between the forces of General Andrew "Old Hickory" Jackson and those of British General Edward Pakenham.

Just to the east of New Orleans proper, along the banks of the Mississippi River, lies the old Chalmette Plantation. On this stretch of rich, delta soil one of the most famous victories in American history was won.

In December 1814 some 7,500 British soldiers, veterans of Wellington's Peninsula War in Spain against Napoleon, landed south of New Orleans. General Pakenham immediately began to march on the city itself after pausing to establish a base camp at Lake Borgne. If he could capture the metropolis, England could control much of the Mississippi Valley, undermine the American economy and impede U.S. westward expansion. His victory would also stiffen British morale, sagging because of the war. The campaign against New Orleans was one of three prongs in the great offensive the British had launched against the infant American republic. The other two thrusts had been foiled on Lake Champlain and Chesapeake Bay. In many ways, the New Orleans offensive was Britain's last hope for a clearcut triumph in a struggle which had cost it much blood and treasure and hampered many operations against Napoleonic France.

On the night of 23 December, Jackson launched an attack against Pakenham, supported by the sloop *Caroline*, seven miles south of the city. Though Jackson shook the British commander slightly, he was unable to halt the advance. Therefore, Jackson retreated to the dry Rodriguez Canal at Chalmette and threw up a breastwork of logs, kegs and mud. His flanks were protected by a swamp to the north and the river to the south. Behind this primitive abatis Jackson and his four thousand squirrel hunters awaited the pride of the British army.

And there was not long to wait. When a bombardment failed to dislodge the Americans, Pakenham resolved on a morning assault through the fog of 8 January 1815. Whether or not there were truly "a hundred of them beating on the drums," as the song "Battle of New

Orleans" says, is problematical. But the advance must have appeared impressive to the homespun militia preparing to meet it.

Pakenham led the main assault against the northern flank while Highlanders under General Keene struck the center, and more troops under Colonel Rennie hammered at the southern anchor of the canal near Jackson's headquarters at the Macarty Plantation. Incredibly, the conflict was over in half an hour. Thirteen Americans had fallen. When the British withdrew, two thousand red-coated figures lay sprawled on the field.

It was one of the most horrendous, if gallant, blunders in British history. However, since Pakenham had the good taste to fall with his men, recriminations in Whitehall were muted. And, of course, it had little effect on the outcome of the war. The Treaty of Ghent had been signed two weeks previously. But the conflict did establish Andrew Jackson as a national hero.

Today Chalmette has changed somewhat due to the constant ravages of the mighty Mississippi. Jackson's headquarters and the original Chalmette Plantation, as well as the southern end of the abatis attacked by Colonel Rennie, are all under water. Modern superhighways now traverse what was impassable swamp in 1815. However, the site is still recognizable.

The visitor center is now located in the old Beauregard Home, a beautiful plantation edifice and a remarkable example of French Louisiana architecture. A one-hundred-foot monument was started by the state of Louisiana in 1855 and completed by the federal government in 1907. It stands near the visitor center at the western extremity of the battlefield.

Chalmette National Cemetery comprises less than ten percent of the 140 acres of the park and lies in a long rectangle along the eastern edge of the area. In fact, it was on this very ground that Pakenham's troops formed up for the assault.

It is perhaps surprising, but of those buried in the cemetery here, only four are identified as veterans of the War of 1812. Only one British serviceman lies here and he is a casualty of World War II, when the nations were allies. Most of those interred here were Union soldiers from the many hospitals in the area during the Civil War, but American veterans of every later war through Vietnam also rest in Chalmette National Cemetery. Regrettably, it was closed in 1955 to all but war dead, and this too ceased after Vietnam when space was exhausted.

Like other national historic sites, Chalmette is administered by the Department of the Interior.

PORT HUDSON NATIONAL CEMETERY

Zachary, Louisiana

Port Hudson lies at the terminus of an old railroad spur running into northeast Louisiana and on the eastern bank of a great loop of the Mississippi River. Twenty-five miles above Baton Rouge, Port Hudson became a natural Confederate staging base for operations against the capital city during the Civil War.

Following occupation of Baton Rouge by Union troops in May 1862, all available Southern forces began to converge on Port Hudson. Confederate commander General John C. Breckinridge, until 1856 vice president of the United States, knew he had to act quickly before the invaders became too strong to be expelled. When his gallant but abortive assault was repulsed in August 1862, Breckinridge fell back on Port Hudson in an attempt to dominate the river at that spot, thus covering the flank of the bastion at Vicksburg. Within months, feverish efforts had turned the locale into a veritable Fortress Mississippia.

The first challenge did not occur until 14 March 1863 when Union naval forces under Admiral Farragut subjected the fortifications to heavy bombardment on their way up the river to Vicksburg. However, Farragut was unable to do any substantial damage and suffered the sinking of one gunboat, which blew up with heavy loss of life. Later, from 8-10 May, as a preliminary campaign on behalf of advancing Union troops under General N.P. Banks, gunboats finally managed to destroy the Confederate batteries along the river. Even so, over seven thousand Southern troops grimly awaited the arrival of the Army of the Gulf.

On 26 May the first encounter occurred on the Bayou Sara Road. Within days, the defenders were locked up in their lines. Several Union assaults were bloodily thrown back, and Banks reluctantly began an investment of the position. A siege every bit as bitter and sanguinary as that of Vicksburg ensued. In fact, the deprivation here may well have been worse. By the time the Confederates surrendered on 9 July, five days after the northern bastion fell, one besieged officer noted in his diary that all beef, mules, dogs and rats had been consumed.

The action cost the Union over three thousand casualties. Confederate losses were seventy-two hundred, including five thousand captives, as well as a mountain of war-making material. More importantly, Lincoln's dream of the Father of Waters flowing unfettered to the sea was now a reality.

Established shortly after the cessation of hostilities, Port Hudson National Cemetery is actually located in the town of Zachary. Of fairly small size originally, it was designed only to provide burial space for those Northern soldiers who perished at the siege as well as those reinterred from other sites up and down the river.

However, upon assuming responsibility for the National Cemetery System in 1973, the Veterans Administration realized that providing interment space for veterans would be one of its greatest challenges for the rest of the century. Therefore, Port Hudson was one of those sites chosen for expansion to help meet that need. This supplemental development was accomplished in a timely manner and, as of 1 June 1979, the installation was once again open to committal services. Strategically placed, it can serve the populations of Arkansas, Alabama, Mississippi, eastern Texas and Louisiana. Hopefully, it will remain active at least through the first several decades of the twenty-first century.

TOGUS NATIONAL CEMETERY

Togus, Maine

Unlike the rest of New England, Maine offers wide contrasts. Across its northern hinterlands lies a tangled mass of forested uplands interspersed with innumerable rivers and lakes. But it is the rock-girded coast that enchants most vacationers.

Three major rivers drain the interior--the Androscoggin, Kennebec and Penobscot. For centuries they have provided cheap transport for traders, farmers and lumberjacks. "Devil's Half Acre," a lurid stretch of Bangor known for its doubtful pastimes and enervating recreational pursuits, is now but a memory.

Togus National Cemetery is located in the midst of these thrifty, independent-minded people. Just to the south of the capital of Augusta, it is perfectly situated to serve the urban centers of Maine.

At the mouth of the Kennebec River, only a short drive to the coast, one will find Fort Popham, the military installation of the first English attempt to colonize the area in 1607. Just up the sound lies Bath. In addition to possessing one of the finest maritime museums on earth, it is the home of Bath Iron Works, long one of the premier producers of small warships for the U.S. Navy.

One hundred miles further south along U.S. Route 95 is the town of Saco, set in the heart of the area ravaged by the first major Indian wars of American history. French-led Abenaki warriors engaged in deadly, if desultory, conflict with the local settlers for over half a century.

East of Portland, at the mouth of Casco Bay, lies small Eagle Island, summer home of fabled Arctic explorer Admiral Robert E. Peary. Nearby Kennebunkport is home to a large Franciscan monastery, one of the rarest edifices in Puritan New England, and now to President George Bush as well.

Just across the southern border with New Hampshire lies the town of Portsmouth. In addition to being the adopted home of Revolutionary War hero John Paul Jones, it is today the home of the U.S. Navy's Atlantic submarine force. Its large contingent of retired personnel and other veterans has made the placement of Togus even more strategic.

Maine has been heavily represented in the U.S. armed forces over the years. During the Civil War, the Seventeenth Maine fought in every major engagement from Fredericksburg to Appomattox. The much-publicized Twentieth Maine also distinguished itself at Gettysburg. Two of its former commanders went on to higher echelons and became among the more capable generals of the Union army. The First Maine Heavy Artillery has the dubious distinction of ranking first on the register of casualties of the 2,047 regiments of the Union army. This fact is more remarkable since the First Maine fought only during the last ten months of the war.

Many veterans of both world wars made the establishment of Togus V.A. Medical Center and its cemetery mandatory. Following the birth of the Veterans Administration in the 1930s, it has provided interment space for hundreds of former servicemen. Unfortunately, the cemetery has been closed to future activity due to lack of space. Expansion has been planned for many years but seems doubtful now because of the new regional cemeteries opened in the 1980s at Indiantown Gap, Pennsylvania; Bourne, Massachusetts; and Long Island.

ANNAPOLIS NATIONAL CEMETERY

Annapolis, Maryland

The name "Annapolis" brings visions of the U.S. Naval Academy to the average American. And for over one and a half centuries some of our greatest and most legendary military leaders have matriculated there. Among those recognized as great naval captains of history are Admirals David Farragut and Chester Nimitz.

However, Annapolis is the site of some of America's earliest and most revealing history. Founded in the early seventeenth century, it has been capital of Maryland since 1694. An entire downtown district is a registered historic site, containing the State House and other facilities. Along its waterfront, which was established in the eighteenth century, are located the Tobacco Prise House, Revolutionary War barracks and still-maintained historic "victualling installations" for shipping. Just to the south near the town of Port Tobacco the world's greatest loose-leaf tobacco sales can be viewed on any weekday. Port Tobacco itself is now nearly abandoned but its town square contains perhaps the oldest well on the continent. John Smith mentioned filling his ship's casks from it as early as 1608 and it provides potable refreshment today.

But even before Annapolis was founded, significant American history was being made. In 1635 Virginia colonial secretary William Claiborne established a trading post on Kent Island on land claimed by Lord Baltimore, founder of the Maryland colony. When the dispute was resolved in favor of Lord Baltimore, Claiborne, in the best pioneering traditions, seized the island anyway. Naval engagements between extemporized "fleets" from the colonies occurred in Chesapeake Bay. Only direct intervention by the crown prevented a war between Catholic Maryland and Protestant Virginia.

In September 1781, American troops embarked on French ships at Annapolis for transport south to Virginia during Washington's campaign to defeat Cornwallis. Landing a few days later at Williamsburg, these troops soon sealed the fall of the British Empire in the New World.

During the Civil War, a special Department of Annapolis was constituted in 1861. It was designed to protect the terrain for twenty miles on each side of the railroad between Annapolis and Washington. Initially commanded by General Benjamin F. Butler, it was merged into the Department of Pennsylvania a few months later.

About the same time, one of the nation's most famous sailing craft came to the Naval Academy as a training ship. The yacht *America*, which had won the famed America's Cup from the British Royal Yacht Club in 1851, had been used as a Confederate despatch boat and was found scuttled in a South Carolina river by the Union South Atlantic Squadron. It was raised and brought to Annapolis as a training bark, subsequently defending the cup in 1870. Three years later, Butler purchased it as a private yacht, but in 1921 it was permanently moored at the academy where it remains today.

Annapolis National Cemetery is naturally identified with the naval academy. No precise figures are available, but it is known that many graduates of the facility who achieved high rank in their careers are interred here. The installation has been closed for many years due to limited size. No expansion is foreseen for the future to add to the few thousand people buried there already.

ANTIETAM NATIONAL BATTLEFIELD

Antietam, Maryland

> Up from the meadows rich with corn
> Clear in the cool September morn
> The clustered spires of Frederick stand
> Green-walled by the hills of Maryland.
>
> Round about it orchards sweep
> Apple and peach trees fruited deep
> Fair as a garden of the Lord
> To the eyes of the famished rebel horde.

So begins John Greenleaf Whittier's epic Civil War poem "Barbara Fritchie." And not through Frederick, Maryland alone did the "rebel horde" come when "Lee marched over the mountain wall."

Having repulsed McClellan's Peninsula Campaign and defeated Union forces under Pope at Second Bull Run, the Confederate leadership resolved to invade the North. Lee's object was to encircle Washington, inflict a severe defeat on Union forces and create overwhelming Northern agitation for peace. Thus, his scattered command poured north over various routes, captured Harper's Ferry and invaded Maryland in September, 1862.

General McClellan

That Lee failed was due more to his fabled "Lost Order," which fell into McClellan's hands, than any military acumen displayed by the Union commander himself. The Confederate forces were eventually blocked near Sharpsburg, Maryland. After a brief clash at South Mountain a few days previously, McClellan launched a general assault against Lee's army along Antietam Creek on 17 September 1862. Some one hundred thousand men were engaged, and a quarter of them fell. It was the bloodiest single day in the history of American warfare. By comparison, the U.S. Army fought in France after the Normandy invasion of World War II for a month before sustaining sixty thousand casualties.

Today it is difficult to determine what strategy the commanders sought to employ. The only thing for certain is that unheard-of locations became a part of American tradition--Roulette House, The Cornfield, Bloody Lane and Burnside's Bridge. At the latter location the Union corps under General Ambrose E. Burnside (whose hairstyle created a new tonsorial fashion for men which still bears his name) sacrificed thousands of lives on both sides to seize a bridge over Antietam Creek. It was later determined the water was so shallow a child could have waded it.

Though neither side could claim victory, and McClellan was soon cashiered from command, Antietam became the justification for Lincoln's Emancipation Proclamation. Once the war became an antislavery crusade, all foreign help for the Southern cause was unthinkable.

Antietam National Cemetery was established in 1865 as a result of the efforts of State Senator L.P. Firey. Contributions were obtained from eighteen Union states to purchase an eleven-acre site. The remains of 4,476 Union soldiers, over one thousand unknown, are buried here. No Confederate dead reside in the cemetery, all being removed to Hagerstown or Frederick, Maryland or Shepherdstown, West Virginia.

American Presidents from Lincoln through Kennedy have visited the battlefield to speak on the lessons to be drawn from the fierce struggle which transpired there. Numerous monuments can be found. Among these is one of the largest in the United States. Called "The Private Soldier," it is known locally as "Simon." It stands forty-five feet high, is composed of twenty-seven separate pieces and weighs 250 tons. Another is that erected to the Twentieth New York Infantry. Its inscription reads, "Erected to our fallen comrades by the survivors of the regiment." The unique part is that this is a translation from the German language. The inscription is in German, the language most of the men who fell at Antietam as part of the regiment truly understood. Many units in blue were almost totally comprised of recent German immigrants and the Twentieth New York was apparently among them.

Since 1933 the cemetery has been administered by the Department of the Interior as part of the larger historic park. It has supplied gravesites to American veterans of all conflicts through Korea. However, lack of space forced its closing in 1953.

BALTIMORE NATIONAL CEMETERY

and

LOUDON PARK NATIONAL CEMETERY

Baltimore, Maryland

Washington was an occupied capital and the White House and other key buildings lay in smoking ruins. Now British troops were trying tenaciously, if unsuccessfully, to rout American militia units from the inappropriately named Godly Woods east of Baltimore. And creeping up the Patapsco River toward Fort McHenry, which was militarily the key to British occupation of Maryland, came a mighty battle fleet under Admiral Sir George Cockburn.

On the morning of 13 September 1814, firing cannons and general bombardment rockets perfected in the Napoleonic Wars, the British armada began to hammer at the American fortress. All day and all night the bombs burst in air and the eerie glow of incendiaries lit the gaudy, nightmarish scene. But the determined defenders answered shot for shot throughout the most spectacular bombardment yet seen on the North American continent. By the dawn's earliest light, several of the attacking vessels were so holed and badly cut-up that Cockburn withdrew.

While being detained on a British transport as he sought to negotiate the release of a prisoner, a Baltimore lawyer named Francis Scott Key witnessed the epic struggle. "My heart sang," Key later observed to friends, and many generations of Americans have joined him in the song which poured forth from his pen.

The brilliant defense of Baltimore denied the enemy a useful staging base in Maryland and brought about an abandonment of the central thrust in their three-pronged attack against American shores in the War of 1812. But it was not the final time in the nation's history that Baltimore would be a battlefield.

At the outbreak of the Civil War, Maryland contained a heavy proportion of Southern sympathizers. On 19 April 1861 Pennsylvania and Massachusetts troops were en route to Baltimore. As horses pulled their cars from one station to another, the caravan was blocked by pro-slavery mobs hurling epithets, bricks, and firing pistols at them. The Union forces detrained to march on to the next terminus, battling the crowd every step of the way. When it finally ended, four soldiers, a dozen members of the mob and several horses were dead. Untold numbers were wounded in what became known as "The Baltimore Riot."

In many ways the historic heart of the city, Charles Square and the Inner Harbor, has changed little to this day. Few areas offer a more interesting and varied look at nineteenth-century Americana.

Anchored at a dock in the Inner Harbor is the U.S.S. *Constellation*. The frigate, launched in 1797, is the oldest warship constructed on these shores extant today. Though no longer in commission, as is the *Constitution* in Boston, the *Constellation* fought in no less than five American conflicts. Some U.S. vessels have gained greater acclaim, but none have ever enjoyed more enduring success.

A few blocks to the northeast lies the former home of Mary Pickersgill. Commonly referred to as the Star Spangled Banner House, it was here in the early days of the nineteenth century that Mary Pickersgill made the largest U.S. flag on record, a mere 1,260 square feet in area.

Nearby is located Mount Vernon Square, one of the most beautiful civic sites in the land. Here is located the first completed monument to George Washington, first unveiled in 1829.

In a small, private cemetery between Baltimore and Fayette Streets in the western section of the city lies the grave of Edgar Allan Poe, America's first great literary light and still deemed the master of Gothic suspense throughout the world. Whether in cinematic or published form, his works remain stupendously popular today. It is often difficult to remember that he has actually been dead since 1849.

Baltimore claims many other tourist attractions. Lexington Market is one of the oldest in the country, first established in 1803. Lloyd Street Synagogue, the third oldest Jewish temple in the United States, is now a museum located at 1100 Baltimore Street. Mount Clare Station, at the corner of Pratt and Poppleton Streets, was the first combination passenger/freight railroad terminus in the country. It was here in 1844 that witnesses saw a telegraph key in operation for the first time. Samuel F.B. Morse's epic message: "What hath God wrought?" changed world communications forevermore. The Baltimore and Ohio Railroad Museum of Transportation possesses the greatest examples of old locomotives and rolling stock anywhere in the world.

Located at 5501 Frederick Avenue, Baltimore National Cemetery lies halfway between the *Constellation* and the Pickersgill Home. Just seventeen blocks down the street, at 3445 Frederick, is its subsidiary, Loudon Park National Cemetery. Both cemeteries are a reflection of the great part played by the city in early American development. In addition, they have provided burial space over the years for the huge number of U.S. veterans, notably retired personnel, who tend to congregate in the vicinity of the nation's capital.

Both cemeteries have been closed for many years. As a result, exact statistical data on individuals or groups interred there is difficult to glean. However, veterans from the War of 1812 and later wars have found their final resting places in these locales. The staff at Baltimore National Cemetery administers both facilities.

FORT SNELLING NATIONAL CEMETERY

Fort Snelling, Minnesota

On 14 July 1939 the Fort Snelling National Cemetery was dedicated to serve the twin metropolitan areas of St. Paul and Minneapolis as well as other locales far removed from existing interment locales. Though the military reservation itself was deactivated by the U.S. Army in 1947, the cemetery continues on its course and is actually undergoing an expansion due to the high numbers of military veterans to be found in the southern Minnesota area.

This is only appropriate because Fort Snelling is one of the oldest installations on American soil. It was established as a temporary post at the junction of the Minnesota and Mississippi rivers in 1805. However, not until 1820 was a permanent fortification, Fort Anthony, constructed by soldiers of the U.S. Fifth Infantry. In 1824 inspector general Winfield S. Scott was so impressed with the post that he renamed it Fort Snelling in honor of its commander, Colonel Josiah Snelling.

With the advent of the Civil War the post became the primary training and assembly area for Union troops in that part of the country. Governor Alexander Ramsey was the first governor to offer President Lincoln state militia to deal with the "secessionist problem." Before the conflict ground to a halt in 1865 some twenty-two thousand Minnesotans would serve in the Union army, a high percentage for what was then an underpopulated, rural environment.

In the ensuing years, Fort Snelling performed as a major recruiting and training depot for the Indian fighting army that ranged across the American plains. It continued in that capacity until 1947. In addition, during World War II a Japanese language school was established there.

On 5 July 1939 the first interment was conducted. The decedent was Captain George H. Mallon, Thirty-third Division, who was awarded the Medal of Honor in the Meuse-Argonne during World War I for heroism which resulted in the capture of one hundred prisoners, eleven machine guns and four howitzers. In the following months, the 680 soldiers interred in the Old Post Cemetery were transferred to Section A of the new national burial facility. Many of these had fallen in campaigns against the Sioux during the latter half of the nineteenth century. As of 31 December 1972, a total of 137 acres had been developed for burials. Approximately fifty-five thousand interments reportedly had been made as of 1987, including over two hundred marked "Unknown." In addition, some fifty-six memorial markers commemorated members of the armed forces whose final resting place was never discovered.

It is estimated the continuing expansion will allow Fort Snelling National Cemetery to provide service to the area until at least the year 2035.

BILOXI NATIONAL CEMETERY

Biloxi, Mississippi

Located near the mouth of the Leaf River, Biloxi is generally protected from the most inclement weather by the coastal islands in the Gulf of Mexico and by the southeastern tip of Louisiana. Equidistant to the west and east of Biloxi are the thriving communities of Gulfport and Pascagoula. Basking in the Gulf twenty-five miles south, and looking like a huge banana, are the Chandeleur Islands, which contain the large Breton National Wildlife Refuge. Twenty miles further south is the delta which marks the mouth of the Mississippi River, one of the most heavily traveled "chokepoints" of seaborne commerce in the world. Every year the "Big Muddy" dumps enough silt and sediment into the Gulf to construct a large island.

While Biloxi and environs have become a major resort area, industry and commerce bloom as well. To the north "King Cotton" and its accompanying textile manufacturing make the port a strategic site for forcing interchange. At Pascagoula will be found Ingalls Shipbuilding Corporation. A subsidiary of Litton Systems, it has become a conglomerate of commercial and naval ship construction. Many of the amphibious assault and logistical support vessels that will be used by the U.S. Navy to fulfill its obligations for the remainder of the twentieth century have come down these slipways.

But even in paradise difficulties can arise. No amount of protection can prevent the ravages of such natural debacles as Hurricane Camille, which hammered Biloxi and the Gulf Coast in 1969. Biloxi and her sister cities were some of the worst hit locales in America's most infamous storm.

To the north sits historic De Soto National Forest. The unfortunate Spanish explorer passed through the vicinity of Biloxi in 1542 after his unsuccessful pursuit of riches in Florida. During the great enforced anabasis known as "The Trail of Tears," Seminole Indians were herded through the area on their way to what is now Oklahoma.

Biloxi escaped the worst of the Civil War. However, Admiral Farragut's Gulf Squadron effectively closed the port as it did all others and trade virtually ceased to exist. Ship Island, located but a few miles off Biloxi in Mississippi Sound, was captured by the Union navy in September 1861. It became Farragut's primary blockade base and served as the staging area for his conquest of New Orleans in 1862.

For many years Biloxi has possessed one of the largest Veterans Administration Medical Centers in the deep South. The burial grounds adjacent to it officially became a national cemetery with the passage of the National Cemetery Act of 1973. Along with Mobile and Pensacola to the east, Biloxi is one of the facilities located along the Gulf Coast designed to serve the vast veteran population to be found in this burgeoning area of the South. Most of its interments have been American servicemen of both world wars. Biloxi National Cemetery is open to future committals at the present time. But according to Department of Veterans Affairs estimates, the constant pressures of space limitations indicate that inevitable closure of the twenty-five-acre site will occur before the year 2000.

CORINTH NATIONAL CEMETERY

Corinth, Mississippi

Corinth National Cemetery is situated in Alcorn County, about three-quarters of a mile from the courthouse of Corinth and one and a half miles from the intersection of major highway arteries 72 and 45. One of the more peaceful and serene locations of its type east of the Mississippi, Corinth is another of those cemeteries in principally a Civil War location.

No area was more significant than Corinth during the Vicksburg Campaign of Ulysses S. Grant. From Corinth in April 1862 Confederate General A.S. Johnston rode north with forty-four thousand men to hurl Grant back from his base at Shiloh, Tennessee. Johnston was killed in the struggle waged there and Grant remained firmly entrenched.

General Halleck

Following this battle, supreme Union commander Henry W. Halleck arrived to supervise preparations to take the strategic base at Corinth. Starting south on 29 April, Halleck advanced with one hundred ten thousand men, while new Confederate commander Beauregard could muster but thirty thousand to oppose him.

However, the Southern command realized the importance of the base and had no intention of conceding it to the enemy. For this reason, many skirmishes and battles occurred as Halleck slowly forced his way south. Finally, he surrounded Corinth and was ready to commence a bombardment. Beauregard managed to extricate his command and fled south down the Mobile and Ohio Railroad.

With Grant's continuing threat to Vicksburg, the Confederates attempted to launch a counter-strike in the fall of 1862. Troops under Generals Sterling Price and Earl Van Dorn began to concentrate at Iuka, southeast of Corinth. Routing a small Union force, they occupied Iuka in September 1862. A tentative counterattack by Union commander Rosecrans was repulsed at the Battle of Iuka on 19 September, though the Confederates sustained heavier casualties. Despite this, Price sought to follow up the victory with an assault on Corinth itself. This was thrown back in a heated battle in early October 1862 and Union control over the area was never threatened again. However, fighting would continue in the area sporadically throughout the war and thousands of men would fall on both sides.

As a memorial to those who died in battle in the area, a national cemetery was authorized for Corinth by Quartermaster General Montgomery C. Meigs in 1862. Remains of Union soldiers were reinterred from Iuka, Holly Springs, Farmingdale and other battlefields of northern Mississippi. These original burials represented no less than 273 Union regiments from fifteen states. As far as is known, only three Confederate war dead were laid to rest here. By 1870 over fifty-seven hundred men had been brought here to spend eternity in this last post.

Like many Civil War locations, the twenty-acre cemetery has provided burial space for American veterans of all later wars. As of the late 1980s, about 7,000 interments had been made. Burial space is expected to be available beyond the year 2000.

NATCHEZ NATIONAL CEMETERY

Natchez, Mississippi

Some called it the "Devil's Spine," to others it was the "Spawn of Evil." But by whatever name, the old Natchez Trace, which terminated on the Mississippi River at the city which bore its name, was the primary route of travel and expansion from the eastern seaboard into Louisiana Territory during the late eighteenth and early nineteenth centuries. Here such infamous highwaymen as the Brothers Harpe and their murderous ilk held sway for many years. Here too, in the earliest days of the nineteenth century, Aaron Burr's scheme to carve out a great empire from the American West was betrayed to authorities.

But generations before the first American settlers began to make inroads into the area, Natchez was already a historic site. Early in the eighteenth century it was known as Fort Rosalie, one of the first French settlements on the lower Mississippi. For many years the French maintained their precarious foothold by supporting the various Indians in wars against each other. However, this perfidy eventually registered on the powerful Natchez tribe. On 28 November 1729 Fort Rosalie became the site of one of the worst butcheries in American history. Sweeping down on the fort, the Natchez warriors massacred two hundred fifty settlers and soldiers and carried three hundred women and children into captivity. Though the French finally defeated and virtually exterminated the Natchez, their tenuous hold on the area was broken forever.

At the outbreak of the Civil War, Natchez was a thriving river community. Though there was comparatively little fighting in the vicinity, major campaigns raged to the north at Vicksburg and to the south in Louisiana. For this reason, Quartermaster General Montgomery C. Meigs ordered the establishment of a national cemetery in the town.

A lovely site was chosen on a prominent bluff overlooking the river. The twelve-acre location was purchased by the government in January 1867 for $1,800. Reinterment work on fallen Union soldiers from up and down the river began almost immediately. But, as usual, original hasty burials and lack of identification tags made it impossible to establish who most of them were. Sometimes only a few buttons or strips of blue cloth showed them to be Union dead. Despite this, by 1871 over three thousand men had been buried in the cemetery, though only three hundred of them had known identities. Most of these came from "The Gardens," an old Natchez home which had been a Union hospital.

Among those interred here are two men who served under Admiral David G. Farragut, America's great seafarer. William Preston had been quartermaster of Farragut's flagship, U.S.S. *Hartford*, during the capture of New Orleans in 1862. Landsman Wilson Brown, a Natchez native who remained loyal to the Union, conducted himself so meritoriously on the *Hartford* during Farragut's 1864 capture of Mobile Bay that he won the Medal of Honor. At his death in 1900 he was quietly buried in his home town.

Since those dark days of American history, Natchez National Cemetery has provided burial space for veterans of subsequent wars. As of 31 March 1965 a total of 4,330 remains had been committed. Of these 2,786 are of unknowns. Interments are not frequent and the cemetery should remain open beyond the year 2000.

VICKSBURG NATIONAL MILITARY PARK

Vicksburg, Mississippi

"Vicksburg is the key," expounded Abraham Lincoln, speaking of the major Confederate strongpoint on the Mississippi River. And, indeed, he was correct. No area on this continent has been the cause of greater expenditure of blood and treasure.

Between Illinois and the Mississippi Delta, "The Big Muddy" meanders for almost one thousand miles. Control of it by the Union would effectively hew the Confederacy in half and make the shipment of supplies to the main battlegrounds of the East all but impossible.

In October 1862, Ulysses S. Grant was made commander of the Department of Tennessee and given the charge of opening the river. That same month, Confederate General John C. Pemberton, himself a West Point graduate, was appointed to command of area Confederate forces and given the task of preventing such a feat.

Grant's Headquarters at Vicksburg

For many months Grant's initial operations, known as the Bayou Expeditions, foundered dismally. By the spring of 1863, constantly criticized over his losses, Grant knew he must obtain victory at the lowest possible cost in casualties. Therefore, he divided his army into three divisions and moved through the Louisiana delta country to establish himself twenty-five miles south of Vicksburg at Grand Gulf. On the night of 16 April 1863 the Union riverine navy under Admiral David D. Porter staged its famous run-by of the Vicksburg batteries from north to south and reached Grand Gulf. Grant now had both his army and the means of ferrying it across the river south of the Confederate citadel.

On 29 April, Grant leaped the river and began his huge campaign of encirclement. Winning triumphs at Port Gibson, Champion Hill, Jackson and Big Black River, the Union leader soon had the prey surrounded. Then, assuming Confederate morale was broken, he assaulted the fortress with disastrous results on 19 and 22 May. Reluctantly, Grant began siege warfare. Union engineers dug numerous trenches of approach, and vicious battles raged over redoubts and other positions. Foot by foot, the Union "Gophers" closed in as Grant began to dig out the defenders of the key bastion on the Confederacy's lifeline.

Inside the beleaguered fortress, time was running out on Pemberton. His soldiers were eating mules and ground peas for rations. By the end of June, his forces were in such sad shape he could not even sorty in an attempt to cut free. On 4 July 1863 the Confederates marched out and stacked their arms. The greatest Union war objective in the West had been accomplished. When Port Hudson, Louisiana fell five days later, Lincoln could truly state, "The Mississippi now goes unvexed to the sea."

The loss of Vicksburg, coupled with Lee's defeat at Gettysburg the day before, marked the beginning of the end. Confederate Chief of Ordnance, Josiah Gorgas, confided to his diary: "Events have succeeded one another with alarming rapidity. A brief month ago we were apparently on the point of success. All looked bright. It seems incredible that human power could effect such change in such a short space. The Confederacy totters to its destruction."

Located in the northern section of the military park, Vicksburg National Cemetery, forty-one acres in size, lies on land occupied by Sherman's XV Corps during the fighting. In terms of Civil War burials, it is the final resting place of seventeen thousand Union soldiers. Originally established in 1866, Union reinterments were made from three states--Arkansas, Mississippi and Louisiana. However, record keeping was so haphazard and so many grave markers were used as firewood during the brutal winter of 1864, that few of them remain identified today. Approximately thirteen thousand of these men are listed as unknown. The only higher percentage of unknowns in any national cemetery is at the former Union prison at Salisbury, North Carolina.

Since the cemetery was established under an act of Congress for those men who died in the service of the country, it only applied to Union dead. Fallen Confederates were buried in the Vicksburg city cemetery. However, later modification was allowed and approximately thirteen hundred veterans of later wars, including some Confederates, were interred there. The remains of only two known Confederate war dead are buried there, Pvt. Reuben White of Texas and Sgt. C.B. Brantley of Arkansas. How they slipped in remains a conundrum to historians of the site.

One member of the Royal Australian Air Force who perished in World War II was accorded interment at Vicksburg. So also were four former park superintendents.

Vicksburg National Park is administered by the Department of the Interior. It has been closed due to lack of space since 1961. However, though the cemetery is no longer in service, the park itself remains one of the pre-eminent historic sites in the United States.

JEFFERSON BARRACKS NATIONAL CEMETERY

St. Louis, Missouri

Jefferson Barracks is located about thirteen miles south of downtown St. Louis on the rolling bluffs overlooking the Mississippi River. The cemetery derives its name from the barracks, brought about as a direct result of the great territorial expansion after the Louisiana Purchase in 1803. Many members of the U.S. Army who were destined for greater fame served duty tours here--Jefferson Davis, Robert E. Lee, Ulysses S. Grant, William T. Sherman and others. A small post cemetery was set aside in 1826 and the first known interment occurred the following year.

Jefferson Davis

During the Civil War, the barracks were the major supply and distribution depot during the Union campaigns in the West. The barracks also served as an administrative center for the massive hospital complex in the St. Louis area. By 1863, hundreds of Union dead had made an expansion of the old post cemetery mandatory.

Jefferson Barracks became a national cemetery in 1866, and in 1868, Quartermaster General Montgomery C. Meigs noted that 8,601 committals had already been carried out. Reinterments from area battlefields and local church cemeteries eventually raised the number of Union men who lie here to 12,000, a total exceeded by only a handful of locations in the United States. Among these were 470 who died of disease on Arsenal Island in the river opposite St. Louis. Known as "Smallpox Island," there was little hope of escape for the men interned there.

American veterans of every war lie at rest here. The man with the earliest known service is Private Richard Gentry of Virginia. His headstone bears the inscription, "Present at the capture of Cornwallis at Yorktown." Some 1,140 members of the once-awesome Confederate army also found their final resting place here. Most perished in captivity while held in prisons in the St. Louis area or at the penitentiary fifty miles north at Alton, Illinois. In 1904 the mainly unidentifiable remains located in the old post cemetery were reinterred to the national cemetery. The Daughters of the American Revolution installed a large red boulder adorned with a bronze plaque to commemorate them. There are 3,255 Americans buried here who are known but to God.

Also, some five hundred group burials have occurred of men who could not be separately identified. The largest is of 123 men who died in a Japanese massacre on Palawan Island in the Philippines in 1944 while being held as prisoners of war. In another instance, 41 members of the Marine Corps, victims of a helicopter crash in Vietnam in 1968, were buried in a mass grave in Section 81.

In addition to the D.A.R. boulder, two other notable monuments stand in the cemetery. One commemorates 175 men of the U.S. Colored Troops who perished in an epidemic shortly after the Civil War. The most impressive is a gigantic bronze female figure entitled "Memory." Originally installed by the state of Minnesota in memory of the 164 Union soldiers from that state who perished in the Civil War, it has since become applicable to all those Americans who lie here.

As of 30 June 1972, a total of 53,047 interments had been made at Jefferson Barracks National Cemetery. However, the 307-acre site, one of the nation's largest, should provide service indefinitely. The cemetery director is also charged with the administration of Alton National Cemetery, Alton, Illinois.

JEFFERSON CITY NATIONAL CEMETERY

Jefferson City, Missouri

No area was more thoroughly or bloodily split by the American Civil War than the state of Missouri. Indeed, for many of the local citizens, the war began in 1855 with the struggle over slavery in neighboring Kansas. For a decade, Missouri roughnecks and bushwhackers engaged in savage, if desultory, warfare against pro-Union "Redlegs" under such men as Senator Jim Lane. The notorious raiders of William Quantrill have become literary and cinematic legends. But they were only one group of guerrillas in this merciless, barbaric struggle.

Before it was all over, vast stretches of central and western Missouri were depopulated. The problem was exacerbated when many hard-core Southerners refused to accept the verdict of history and fled to Mexico with General J.O. Shelby. Though most of them eventually returned home, this hegira offers excellent testimony to the intensity and hatred of the period.

The most infamous incident was the so-called Centralia Massacre of 27 September 1864. That morning, "Bloody Bill" Anderson, a virulent opponent of all things "Yankee," led his band of bushwhackers into the town fifty miles north of Jefferson City. They promptly shot up the place, terrified the citizens and waylaid a passing stagecoach. The passengers were robbed and two of them killed, apparently for concealing valuables. One of them was a teenaged boy killed in his mother's arms. Shortly thereafter, the outlaws captured a train which had the bad luck to stop at the station. From this they ordered twenty-four unarmed, wounded Union troops being sent home to be mustered out, and Anderson had them executed.

After a few other scattered atrocities, Anderson led his "troops" to the backwoods from which they had come, secure in the knowledge of a job well done. However, within an hour they were pursued by three companies of the Thirty-ninth Missouri Infantry under Major A.E.V. Johnson. This Union force was mounted on mules and plow-horses, and the advantage was to the guerrillas in both mounts and armament. Under these circumstances, Johnson should have exercised discretion.

But when he caught the half-drunken raiders three miles from town, he deployed for the attack. The guerrillas charged, slaughtering his force, pursuing the remnant clear back to Centralia. Only when they reached town did the survivors rally and throw them back. Of the 147 men in Johnson's command, he and 124 others paid the ultimate price for his folly. When the dead soldiers were later discovered mutilated, this further embittered the already ferocious North-South conflict. Nor did Anderson's death a few weeks later change anything.

When the war ended, many Centralia casualties and those from other areas were removed to a two-acre cemetery in Jefferson City which had become designated a national site. Though the first interment occurred here in 1861, the small location remained open until lack of space closed it in 1969. It is laid out in thirteen small sections and is surrounded on three sides by major thoroughfares in the heart of the city. Approximately one thousand American veterans, including those of twentieth-century wars, rest here.

SPRINGFIELD NATIONAL CEMETERY

Springfield, Missouri

The establishment of the national cemeteries of Missouri poignantly exhibited the division inherent in the Civil War for the border states. Nowhere was this more true than in Missouri. Here innumerable factions and fanatics separated Union from Confederate, relative from family, friend from friend.

On 10 August 1861, one of the earliest battles of the struggle occurred in southwestern Missouri at Wilson's Creek. General Nathaniel Lyon, one of the fastest-rising young Union commanders, had moved south to repel Confederate forces attempting to reassert shaky Southern sentiment in the state. He found himself outnumbered two to one by enemy troops under General Sterling Price, former governor of Missouri, but he made his stand anyway. A confused and savage battle ensued. Lyon was killed leading a Union charge to restore his line. When the smoke cleared, both sides had lost over a thousand men. Tactically a Confederate victory, it was a major strategic success for the Union. Price withdrew and with him went the last Southern dreams of making Missouri an integral part of the Confederacy. Not that this ended or alleviated the internecine strife and plunder in Missouri. That continued throughout the bitter four-year struggle.

In 1867 Springfield National Cemetery was established to include five acres of land purchased from the city. Additional acquisitions through 1911 brought it to its present size of almost fourteen acres. In the interim, the Confederate Cemetery Association of Missouri had developed two adjacent acres for Confederate veterans. In 1911 these became part of the national cemetery, with the proviso that this section be held for Southern men who had served The Lost Cause. However, in 1945 all such restrictions were removed.

Earliest burials included Union dead from Wilson's Creek and the battlefields at Forsyth, Newtonia, Carthage and Pea Ridge, Arkansas--all sites of combats during later Confederate attempts to wrest control of the state from the Union. All battles after Pea Ridge in March 1862 were little more than Southern harassment raids. By 1868 over 1,500 Union war dead had been reinterred at Springfield, of which 795 were identifiable, a remarkable effort in light of post-war reinterment trends.

Many monuments are found here. The Union Monument is a twenty-foot granite spire topped by a Union soldier. Erected in 1870, it was a bequest from a local physician who wished to honor the Union men who fell in the defense of Springfield on 8 January 1863. Though General Lyon himself does not lie here, a ten-foot edifice was raised in his honor by the citizens of Springfield. One Confederate monument has a Southern soldier on its crown with a bronze replica of the Confederate battle flag on three sides, and a portrait of Sterling Price on its front. Yet another memorial rests at Grave 245, the final resting place of one Henry Walters, a former partisan ranger with John S. Mosby, the "Gray Ghost of the Confederacy."

The last interment of a Civil War veteran, a Confederate, was made here on 12 June 1939. But both before and since, the cemetery has provided interment space for American veterans of other wars. As of January 1988, about 7,500 committals are reported, of which 760 are known but to God. Springfield National Cemetery remains open at the present time.

CUSTER BATTLEFIELD NATIONAL MONUMENT

Crow Agency, Montana

According to some authorities, more words have been written about the Battle of Little Bighorn than any other single event in American history. And certainly, coming as it did at the height of America's Centennial celebration, few events have ever made a greater impact on public consciousness, with the possible exception of Pearl Harbor. That a great and powerful nation found it so difficult to deal with a handful of "ragtag aborigines" was more than most editorial writers of the time could bear to contemplate. But in reality, the Indian wars had been won. The Little Bighorn was a last, abusive, thumbing of the nose at the U.S. Army by a defeated foe.

From 1854 to 1876 there had been numerous conflicts with the Sioux Indians on the northern plains. Slowly, but inexorably, they had been driven onto reservations at Pine Ridge and elsewhere. The stand at the Little Bighorn was a last, truculent refusal to accept the white man's authority and a defiant, unrealistic attempt to re-establish the Indian way of life.

This last and bloodiest of Sioux Wars had erupted following the discovery of gold in the Black Hills. The U.S. Army had lacked sufficient strength in the area to seriously chastise the hostiles. All that changed in the spring of 1876. The plan was to surround the Indians somewhere around the Big Horn River with soldiers on three sides and the Wolf Mountains at their back. It was felt they would immediately capitulate once flight was denied them. And this was the misconception that led Custer to his doom.

Colonel George Armstrong Custer, leading the U.S. Seventh Cavalry, commanded the center column; his duty was to drive the hostiles into the trap. It is fashionable today to denigrate Custer personally, professionally and ethically. Undeniably, his character flaws were legion, but he was one of the finest cavalry commanders ever enlisted by the U.S. Army. His demolition of the command of General Jubal Early at Waynesboro at the close of the Civil War is considered perhaps the finest and best-conducted cavalry charge ever staged in North America. For a decade of campaigning against Indians, he had shown a propensity for getting into tight spots, but he had always escaped them, emerging victorious. Merely "Custer's Luck" say critics--it eventually ran out at the Little Bighorn. Possibly so.

At any rate, on Sunday, 25 June 1876, this "flamboyant, reckless boy" led his command into the valley of the Little Bighorn where two-thirds of them lie today. Contrary to myth and legend, he did not violate his orders. Once the hostiles clearly knew of his whereabouts, he decided to attack, a decision consistent with the prevailing belief that the enemy would seek to escape if given opportunity. And he had every reason to believe the Seventh Cavalry would cover itself in glory again.

So he committed the cardinal military sin of dividing his force without knowing the strength and disposition of his enemy; he rushed blindly forward, attempting to cut off the retreat of an enemy whose only intention was to stand and fight. When it was over, he and every man in companies C, E, F, I and L lay dead on Battle Ridge above the Indian encampment along the river. Allegedly there was an escape route left open to the east for some time before the Indians could close it. Perhaps Custer never saw it. Perhaps he was just too proud to run. Whatever the reason, the resulting debacle became one of the most earthshaking and controversial affairs of nineteenth-century America.

In the long run, the outcome at the Little Bighorn had no effect on the ultimate fate of the Sioux nation. Within a few months the army had returned in even stronger numbers and destroyed them as a tribal power. Only a few survivors under Sitting Bull fled to Canada. But even he returned to accept reservation life in 1881.

Sitting Bull

On 1 August 1879, shortly after the fighting in the area ended, General Order No. 78 designated the site of the battle as a national cemetery. Today it lies thirty miles southeast of Billings, Montana. The eight-acre location is completely enclosed in the national park, now administered by the Department of the Interior.

Approximately four thousand veterans lie here, including those of World War I and II, Korea and Vietnam. Surprisingly, few of the men who fell with Custer are buried here. Most of them are entombed in a common grave beneath the monument on the northern end of Battle Ridge where the so-called Last Stand was made. The body of Custer was returned to West Point. A few other officers were interred at Arlington National Cemetery. Only Lt. John Crittenden and a few skeletal remains of Custer's men found much later reside in the national cemetery.

However, those buried there include decedents of many famous Indian battles. When a number of old posts were abandoned in the area, many fallen troopers were reinterred here. These include those who fell in the Fetterman Massacre of 1868 in Wyoming and elsewhere. Major Marcus Reno, Custer's second in command and the man later court-martialled for the disaster, died in 1889 and lies here. Two of the Indian scouts who fell on Battle Ridge are buried here, Goes Ahead and Curley. The cemetery was officially closed to future interments in 1978. It remains one of the most interesting and colorful sites on American soil.

FORT MCPHERSON NATIONAL CEMETERY

Maxwell, Nebraska

Originally built in September 1863, the fort was designed to provide protection for settlers trekking westward along the Platte River on what was called the Mormon Trail, and to guard construction gangs working on nearby railroads. It was christened "Fort McKean" and was even known briefly as the Post of Cottonwood Springs. However, the current name was applied on 20 February 1866.

It commemorates Major General James Birdseye McPherson, one of the most brilliant tacticians of the Union army. He played a crucial role under Grant in capturing Vicksburg in 1863 and later became one of Sherman's more dynamic commanders during the Atlanta Campaign of 1864. He was killed shortly before the fall of the city on 22 July 1864.

By 1873, development of Nebraska had diminished the needs of protection for the citizenry considerably. On 3 March of that year Fort McPherson took on a new role of importance when a 107-acre tract was designated as a national cemetery. It became one of many sites established to accommodate Union veterans who found the locations in the East inaccessible. Hundreds of Union veterans were subsequently interred here but, as far as is known, no Confederates.

Death came in many ways on the frontier and some of the earlier burials characterize the people and their times. Among these are the twenty-eight men killed near Fort Laramie, Wyoming in 1854. Sioux Indians had appropriated a cow from a passing wagon train and a Lt. Grattan and his men were sent to a nearby village to retrieve it. Somehow violence flared. A Sioux chief named Brave Bear was killed and the entire army detachment perished in the "Grattan Massacre." Their bodies were reinterred along with many others at Fort Laramie in 1891.

Many other members of America's Indian fighting army are buried here. So are many famous trappers and Indian scouts. Baptiste Garnier, known as Little Bat, was a noteworthy scout for General Crook who was murdered in the 1880s at Crawford, Nebraska and was later reinterred from Fort Robinson. Moses Milner, better known as California Joe, is buried nearby. Originally a hunter along the North Platte River, he fought in the Mexican War, went to California for the gold rush and scouted for Custer at the Battle of the Washita in 1868. In 1876, while journeying from one camp to another, he was apparently killed by

Sioux warriors. He too was reinterred from Fort Robinson. Others buried here are the Pawnee scout Spotted Horse and two former cemetery superintendents, Patrick O'Rourke and Benjamin Baker, both of whom had served with distinction in the Union army.

The last Civil War veteran buried here was Pvt. Cyrus Fox of the Seventh Iowa Infantry. His interment took place on 12 June 1942. Ironically enough, he had served at Vicksburg under the man whose name the national cemetery bears.

Fort McPherson is one of the leading cemeteries in handling unknown decedents in group burials. At least eighty-one of these have taken place. Also, three Medal of Honor winners are buried here, including two who displayed great gallantry in the Indian Wars, and one from Vietnam.

Current data indicate that the installation is about one-third filled. Therefore, the facility will probably remain open until the next century.

BEVERLY NATIONAL CEMETERY

Beverly, New Jersey

Beverly National Cemetery is situated in Edgewater Park township in Burlington County, New Jersey. Once known as the hamlet of Dunks Ferry, it was the center of troop movements during the Revolutionary War. Located on the Delaware River near Philadelphia, it was also bisected by the Camden and Amboy Railroad and served as a recruiting station for local troops in the Civil War.

Just to the north lies the town of Trenton, site of one of the most important conflicts in American history. While there are few better means of insuring military success than personal leadership, there are also few great examples of it. One of the best was that supplied at Trenton by George Washington during the darkest days of the American quest for freedom.

In the summer of 1776, British General Howe had invaded New York and driven the vastly outnumbered Washington across New Jersey after three sharp battles. By that winter, Howe had occupied New Jersey, and Washington was freezing on the far side of the Delaware attempting to protect Philadelphia. However, it was obvious to Washington that Howe could capture it in the spring. Never again--not even the following winter at Valley Forge--would American fortunes sink so low.

Because of this, Washington opted for a daring gamble to restore the balance of power. He crossed the river on Christmas Eve 1776 to fall on the southern anchor of the British lines at Trenton. There, in a brilliant dawn assault, he smashed the force of German-speaking recruits referred to by the generic term "Hessians." Howe quickly moved to entrap Washington in New Jersey and thereby end the rebellion once and for all. But Washington outmaneuvered him and fell on the main British depot at Princeton a few days later. He was back across the river, having killed or taken prisoner two thousand British troops, before the befuddled Howe even located him. Grudgingly, the British general withdrew to New York and planned an ambitious, three-pronged attack which led to Burgoyne's debacle the next year at Saratoga.

In ten short days, Washington's outstanding personal leadership had fanned the dying embers of revolution into a bright blaze. He hardly seems one of the Great Captains of History but this bold accomplishment has rarely received its due. If Samuel Adams was the true father of his country, Washington certainly qualified as the midwife on that wintry night when he sallied forth across the Delaware. Frederick the Great of Prussia, who knew a thing or two about military affairs, even went so far as to categorize this operation as one of the most intrepid in history. At any rate, few military operations have ever been more important.

Washington Crossing the Delaware

The name Beverly was applied to the area of the national cemetery in 1848, so losing its more unique and bucolic designation, Dunk's Ferry. During the Civil War a major hospital was created in the area. At least 140 Union soldiers who died there were buried across the road on land owned by a local citizen named Weyman. He later donated this to the government as a soldiers' cemetery in August 1864.

Though the original tract was but one acre, the cemetery was expanded until its current size of sixty-nine acres was reached. Like Arlington, Beverly National Cemetery contains veterans of every principal American conflict. It maintains a distinguished service section, including three men who were posthumously awarded the Medal of Honor, two from Korea and one from World War II. As of April 1980 a total of 39,162 interments had been made. The cemetery is now closed due to committal of all space, though a number of previously reserved gravesites have been filled, bringing the number to nearly forty thousand.

FINN'S POINT NATIONAL CEMETERY

Salem, New Jersey

Salem, New Jersey lies on the southern coast of the state at the head of Delaware Bay. Just to the northwest across the Delaware River lies heavily populated Wilmington, Delaware, while to the southeast is Cape May. During the early part of this century its wireless station was one of the key radio transmitters in monitoring ocean traffic on the transatlantic route. To the north is the heartland of New Jersey, scene of some of the most important battles of the American Revolution.

But it was not the historic or scenic virtues of the location that brought about the establishment of Finn's Point National Cemetery. Rather, as in all too many cases in the East, it was the American Civil War that made the site imperative.

On Pea Patch Island in the Delaware River, about one and a half miles from the current cemetery, broods infamous Fort Delaware. During the Civil War it was one of the largest Confederate prisons in the north, and beyond doubt the most hated and feared in the South. With the influx of prisoners after the Battle of Gettysburg in the summer of 1863, the situation became intolerable. The death rate during the following winter, spawned by overcrowding and dreadful sanitation and food problems, became staggering. Space for a cemetery lacking on the island itself, all Confederate dead possible were taken to the vicinity of old Finn's Point Battery, which was established in 1837 for the protection of Philadelphia on land which had formerly been a Swedish colony in the New World and from which the name derived. By the end of hostilities, some 2,436 members of the Confederate armed forces had been interred there.

In addition, a few others and their Union guards who had succumbed to various causes had been briefly interred on the island when winter inclemencies made water travel impossible. These men were later transferred to the site.

In 1875, Governor James L. Kemper of Virginia informed the secretary of war of a resolution of the Virginia General Assembly that the site was in deplorable condition and needed to be improved, either by government or private parties. As a result, Adjutant General E.D. Townsend declared that the location would henceforth be a part of the National Cemetery System. After considerable renovation, lending credence to Kemper's complaints, the cemetery was officially opened the following year.

Finn's Point contains some of the most notable grave markers in the country. Initially, Confederate prisoners were buried in long trenches and their identities lost. Consequently, no rows of marble markers indicate their resting place. Instead, above them grow evergreen trees--perhaps a memorial the men would appreciate even more. The interments total 2,704, including 135 Union men and veterans of subsequent struggles through World War I.

Two monuments have been raised also. In 1879 the U.S. government erected a marble edifice to the Union men here and a Grecian cupola was added in later years. In 1910 one of the largest monuments in the nation was erected of white granite and reinforced concrete. Towering eighty-five feet, the structure commemorates the Confederate dead here, and bronze tablets affixed to its base list every name.

Except for interments to be made in reserved gravesites, the 4.5-acre location is closed to future activity.

FORT BAYARD NATIONAL CEMETERY

Fort Bayard, New Mexico

Established in August 1866, Fort Bayard is located about ten miles east of Silver City, New Mexico. Major N.H. Davis, assistant inspector-general of the Military District of Arizona, was so inspired by the site at the foot of the Santa Rita Mountains, that his strong recommendation led his commander, General James Carleton, to order immediate construction.

The post was named in memory of Union General George D. Bayard. An 1856 graduate of West Point, Bayard had been severely wounded in the face by a poisoned arrow while fighting Indians, and had later become an instructor at his alma mater. Taking command of the First Pennsylvania Cavalry during the Civil War, he had helped oppose Jackson's Shenandoah Valley Campaign in the spring of 1862, and had served elsewhere. While leading the cavalry brigade of the Left Grand Division, Army of the Potomac, he was mortally wounded during Burnsides' debacle at Fredericksburg, Virginia and died on 14 December 1862.

The post which came to bear his name was situated to protect the Pinos Altos mining district against the Apaches, and substantial evidence of such a need was already in hand. In 1861 a giant Apache chieftain, nearly six and a half feet tall, entered the gold mining camp of Pinos Altos to inform the prospectors there that they were trespassing on Indian land. They acknowledged the rectitude of this claim by flogging him before kicking him out of camp. The scars on his back never healed, and the Indian wore a red shirt thereafter to hide them. Mangas Coloradas became one of the most implacable foes the U.S. Army encountered during the Plains Indian Wars. He returned in force to Pinos Altos and massacred every man, woman and child in sight. This act did not remove the scars, but presumably assuaged the pain.

Fort Bayard, along with a dozen other installations in southern Arizona and New Mexico, became a garrison fortification in what became a generation-long conflict against various Apache leaders. The fighting involved pursuit, stealth and ambush in the craggy hills and steep canyons of the Southwest. A tactic was born in which troops trained their horses to lie on the ground and serve as living breastworks for their riders during combat. Most cavalry regiments used the trick but none mastered it any better, through necessity, than the men of the U.S. Sixth Cavalry of Fort Bayard in the 1880s.

Not that it was all "glorious" Indian campaigning. Soldiers often put in a twelve-hour day, much of it comprised of stable cleaning, telegraph building, road construction and other activities not likely to maintain troop morale. One disgruntled soldier in the Dakotas was speaking for every soldier at Fort Bayard and elsewhere when he wrote, "None but a menial cur would stand the usage of a soldier in the Army today!"

All this notwithstanding, enough men managed to survive the ordeal to keep Fort Bayard a viable military post until it was abandoned in January 1900. At that time, the buildings were transferred to the surgeon general and a hospital was established on the reservation. Today it remains a Department of Veterans Affairs facility.

Though not large by the standards of the system, 14.8-acre Fort Bayard National Cemetery remains open. Its comparatively isolated locale has undoubtedly contributed to this. As with most V.A. locations, original interments were restricted to those who had succumbed in government hospitals. However, with the National Cemetery Act of 1973, all such limitations have been lifted.

SANTA FE NATIONAL CEMETERY

Santa Fe, New Mexico

The area now comprising New Mexico was settled in the sixteenth century by the Spanish. The savage Zuni Indian revolt halted expansion for some time, but immigrants were soon pouring into the upper Rio Grande Valley again. Santa Fe was founded in 1609. The first overland trade from the East was undertaken by French brothers named Mallet in 1739. Soon a steady stream of freight wagons and frontiersmen traveled the Santa Fe Trail as the United States began to move west.

American troops occupied Santa Fe in 1846 during the Mexican War. Old Fort Marcy was headquarters for General S.W. Kearny prior to his California expedition. A Mexican-stimulated uprising of Indians at Taos in January 1847 brought the death of the first American governor of the territory, Charles Bent, but did not shake U.S. control of the Santa Fe area.

Early in the Civil War, however, a threat developed. Confederate forces under General Sibley resolved to capture Santa Fe, feeling that this would heighten Southern prestige and stop the flow of gold from California. Capturing Santa Fe was a forlorn hope at best but a sharp campaign developed as Sibley was opposed by Union forces under General E.R.S. Canby.

General Canby

Initially successful at Valverde in February 1862, Sibley did temporarily occupy Santa Fe. But he was subsequently routed at Glorieta by a combination of Union troops and Colorado mountain men. By the end of the year he was driven from the territory and back into Texas. Comparative peace reigned in the area for the duration of the Civil War.

By 1870 the remains of nearly three hundred thousand Union veterans were interred in various national cemeteries. And other terms of new legislation made all Union veterans eligible. Because of this, new cemeteries were authorized in other parts of the nation. Westward expansion made Santa Fe one of these.

Established in 1875, Santa Fe National Cemetery was constructed on ground donated by Bishop John B. Lamy of the Roman Catholic Church. Later expansion brought the locale to its current size of thirty-five acres. Many veterans of the Civil War, Indian conflicts and other campaigns were buried here. Among those reinterred were Governor Bent from Fort Marcy and army soldiers from the post cemeteries of famed locations such as Fort Apache, Fort Grant and Fort Wingate. The remains of five Confederate soldiers from Texas cavalry units are identified as well. These have since been joined by veterans of every major American conflict since the Civil War.

Among the noted personages resting here are Patrick J. Hurley, secretary of war to President Hoover and ambassador to China from 1944 to 1945; and Lt. Col. Oliver La Farge, who served in the Army Air Corps during World War II. His book *Laughing Boy*, a study of an Indian youth caught between tribal tradition and modern society, won the Pulitzer Prize for literature in 1930.

As of 1985, approximately eight thousand burials had been made at Santa Fe National Cemetery (495 unknowns). It is still open for veterans' interments.

BATH NATIONAL CEMETERY

Bath, New York

Situated near Lakes Cayuga, Seneca and the other bodies of water which comprise upstate New York's famed Finger Lakes, Bath lies amid some of America's most impressive scenery and figures in its earliest as well as its most contemporary history. Nearby Taughannock Falls is a lavish example of such a natural phenomenon and forms part of the waters of Lake Cayuga, above which Cornell University is located. One hundred miles to the west lies the grandaddy of all spillways, Niagara Falls, long synonymous for the American honeymoon. For those inclined more to outdoor pursuits, the Watkins Glen Grand Prix is held every year at the town of the same name at the foot of Lake Seneca. To the east, after a leisurely drive, one encounters Cooperstown, New York, home of the Baseball Hall of Fame and one of the meccas of the professional sports movement in this country. To the south is Elmira, New York, site of another national cemetery built around one of the largest Confederate prison camps of the Civil War.

The Wounded Herkimer

But perhaps the most significant aspect of New York history lies to the north, and in the events which transpired there in 1777. On 25 July of that momentous year, British Colonel St. Leger arrived at

Oswego with a large band of British troops and Iroquois Indians. Attempting to stage a diversion for Burgoyne's Albany Campaign to the east, St. Leger promptly besieged Fort Stanwix, now Rome, New York. American General Nicholas Herkimer rushed to the rescue with eight hundred militiamen. On 8 August he was ambushed by Tories and Indians six miles from the fort at Oriskany. Herkimer, though mortally wounded, led his men in resisting attack after attack, although nearly half the Americans were killed. The Americans retreated, but returned within days, ejecting St. Leger from New York soil; then American forces concentrated against Burgoyne. Soon the Patriots had won the epic Battle of Saratoga, an event which insured French support and made inevitable the success of the American Revolution.

Bath National Cemetery and its concomitant V.A. Medical Center, is situated on a hill overlooking the scenic community of Bath, New York. It was officially dedicated 25 December 1879. Since then, American veterans of every war through Vietnam have been interred here and over eighty-six hundred have been provided with burial space.

The most dominant feature of the cemetery is a forty-foot granite monument erected in 1892 by the state of New York in honor of all soldiers and sailors from within its boundaries who gave their lives during the Civil War. Prior to June 1974, burial here was restricted to those who had died in V.A. installations. But in 1974, all such limitations were removed. At Bath the committal service generally includes military honors rendered by residents of the V.A. Domiciliary located here.

Bath National Cemetery is presently open. Interments average about 140 per year.

CYPRESS HILLS NATIONAL CEMETERY

Brooklyn, New York

Cypress Hills, dating from the earliest days of the Civil War, was established to provide burial space for the veterans of the numerous New York regiments who were returned home for interment after falling in battle. Located near Highland Park and the Ridgewood Reservoir, the cemetery lies just south of the Interborough Parkway in what is today the Woodhaven section of Brooklyn. A few miles southeast sits famed Aqueduct Race Track and John F. Kennedy International Airport.

Though numerous historical sites are to be found in Greater New York, Cypress Hills National Cemetery is irrevocably associated with the Civil War and its attendant carnage. In fact, one of the worst battles of the era was waged in New York. And it was not against Confederate forces either!

In August 1862 Abraham Lincoln issued a call for some three hundred thousand men to serve the Union army. If the state quotas could not be filled via volunteers, all governors were expected to commence conscription to make good the deficiencies. This produced minor disturbances in Ohio, Vermont, Boston and elsewhere, but nothing like the New York City Draft Riots of July 1863.

Since this was the first time in history that Americans had been subjected to unwilling service to their country, Governor Seymour of New York added to his problems when he challenged the constitutionality of the procedure. When the first names were chosen on 11 July and published in the papers, large mobs ran rampant through the streets. Local authorities could not end the rioting. The mobs, soon totaling fifty thousand, terrorized the city for several days. Before it was over, damage to property amounted to one and one-half million dollars, a staggering total by nineteenth-century standards. The mobs had also murdered and mutilated several dozen people, mainly blacks. Troops finally quelled the revolt and restored order on 16 July, at the cost of twelve hundred rioters' lives. Most reports indicate that those killed were typically criminals and other assorted trouble-makers and idlers. However, the devastation remains a black eye to America's pride.

The average New Yorker did, however, know his enemy during the Civil War. Very few states provided more heroic regiments for the Army of the Potomac. Among these was the illustrious Sixty-ninth

Infantry, known as the Irish Brigade. It fought in every action from the Peninsula Campaign to Appomattox. In Bloody Lane at Antietam no less than eight of its color bearers were shot down. At Fredericksburg the brigade lost over half its men in two short hours. But perhaps the most famous New York unit was the First Zouaves. Primarily composed of former firemen, it patterned its dress on the scarlet and blue uniforms of the French infantry. The First Zouaves was one of the few units to distinguish itself at Bull Run in July 1861.

Zouaves

The available gravesites at Cypress Hills were basically filled by former Union veterans and American casualties of World War I. In 1936 the Long Island National Cemetery had to be developed to replace it. Ten times the size of Cypress Hills, it remains one of the largest in the national system. Cypress Hills has been closed for many years since surrounding land use forced rejection of all surveys designed to expand it. It is the only national burial ground within the city of New York.

LONG ISLAND NATIONAL CEMETERY

Farmingdale, New York

Long Island National Cemetery, established in 1936, is one of many not specifically associated with a historical or cultural site. Rather, it reflects the rapid urbanization of American society. Of course, there are many notable sites within a short drive. Not far to the north lies one of America's greatest aviaries, the Roosevelt Bird Sanctuary. Bethpage State Park is only miles away. To the southeast is Fire Island amidst the Great South Bay, one of the foremost water-sports areas in the New York vicinity. Only twenty-five miles to the east, around Upton, Long Island, lies Brookhaven Laboratory, a prime local employer and a pioneer industry in the radiation field.

This urban sprawl brought about the creation of the cemetery. In the wake of World War I, some five million new veterans were eligible for interment in national cemeteries, and it became obvious that those existing sites in large cities would be unable to provide service for even a small percentage of them. Nowhere was this more critical than the New York area. Cypress Hills National Cemetery, founded in 1862 in Brooklyn, was rather small and had few unoccupied gravesites. Recognizing the problem, Congress authorized purchase of 175 acres of land in Suffolk County, and additional acquisitions in 1951 brought the cemetery to its current size of 364 acres.

The first burial occurred on 16 March 1937. An average of fifty-three per month was reached soon thereafter. The cemetery has long been a national leader in number of committals in any fiscal year. From 1970 to 1971 an incredible 11,602 interments were made. On 1 November 1963 former World War II Pfc. Ernest Palmer became the 100,000th committal there.

Numerous reinterments of Civil War dead from army posts in Rhode Island and Maine have been made and over one hundred veterans of that struggle rest in the cemetery. Unlike most national cemeteries, Long Island contains the graves of German (thirty-seven) and Italian (fifty-six) prisoners of war. All died from various causes in American captivity. Since the United States signed the Geneva Accord, which stated that prisoners would receive decent burial, all were entombed in graves at Long Island.

Presently seven winners of the Medal of Honor rest in the cemetery. Among these are Lt. Bernard Ray, U.S.A., who fell in the Huertgen Forest, Germany in 1944 and Sgt. J.R. Julian, USMC, who died during the capture of Iwo Jima in 1945. There are numerous mass graves of American veterans who died together but could not be identified.

Annual observances are conducted by the Gold Star Mothers, Jewish War Veterans, Annual Military Field Mass and Pearl Harbor Memorial Service groups. Few national cemeteries more greatly represent the shared traditions of the American people or their international image as a melting pot than that located at Long Island, New York. The exhaustion of space at this installation made the much larger site at Calverton, L.I. necessary. This site was placed farther east in order to also serve Rhode Island, Connecticut and areas besides New York City. It opened in 1983 and has 600+ acres.

WOODLAWN NATIONAL CEMETERY

Elmira, New York

Elmira lies along the banks of the Chemung River just north of the Pennsylvania border. Some of upstate New York's largest population centers, such as Binghamton and Ithaca, sit just to the north and east. One hundred and fifty miles to the northwest lies the major urban sprawl of Buffalo.

Like many locations in the National Cemetery System, the facility at Elmira owes its existence to the American Civil War. In May 1864, after the halting of all prisoner exchanges, it became obvious that existing facilities were inadequate. Elmira and other sites were chosen for prison camps, and a suitable location was established by enclosing the local barracks along the Chemung River with a high wall.

But the buildings were unable to house more than half the ten thousand prisoners held here. The rest lived in tents, exposed to the terrible winter storms which swept across the state from the Great Lakes. Food was sparse and unpalatable. Medical services, when available, were poor. Consequently, the death rate was nearly five percent per month!

Of those Confederate enlisted men held prisoner, 3,343 remain forever interred in what has become Woodlawn National Cemetery. In a separate area lie 140 Union prison guards, all of whom succumbed to disease or other non-combat causes.

Officially designated a national cemetery in 1874, Woodlawn was enlisted to provide burial space for the myriad Union veterans from those regiments recruited in upstate New York. Thousands of remains were returned home following the cessation of hostilities, including some from the most honored regiments in the Union army. Among these were the 121st and 126th New York Infantry, the former having fought at every major battle from Fredericksburg through Appomattox while the latter had stemmed Pickett's Charge along the Cemetery Ridge at Gettysburg. Another famous regional unit was the Eighth New York Heavy Artillery, organized at Lockport, between Buffalo and Rochester. In only ten months of action, from Spotsylvania to Lee's final surrender, the unit sustained one thousand casualties.

Many of these veterans found their final resting place at Woodlawn, as have the veterans of subsequent American conflicts. However, the 7.6-acre site lacked any space for expansion and it was closed for that reason on 26 May 1969 with all gravesites committed. There are two notable monuments at the location. One commemorates those Confederate soldiers who perished in captivity, the other is in tribute to all American veterans who rest here. One Medal of Honor recipient lies here, Richard Dewert, U.S.N.

The current cemetery director also administers the Bath National Cemetery, Bath, New York.

NEW BERN NATIONAL CEMETERY

New Bern, North Carolina

New Bern sits at the head of the Neuse River near huge Croatan National Forest. Like most of those areas along the coast of the American South, it figures prominently in our nation's history.

The palatial residence of Governor William Tryon, last royal ruler of the state, is on display here. Carefully restored, it is one of the most prestigious examples of colonial life. Not far to the north, along Albemarle Sound, is the so-called Lost Colony. Established in 1585, the colony was England's first effort to settle the area. When supply ships returned a few years later, there was no sign of life, yet none of death either. The only thing ever found was the mysterious inscription "Croatoan" chiseled in the bark of a tree.

To the east, bordering Pimlico Sound, lies the string of islands known as the Outer Banks. For generations, the area has been called the graveyard of the Atlantic. By the dawn of this century, hundreds of sailing craft had met their end here. Modern navigational aids such as Hatteras Lighthouse have alleviated the danger, but every year new vessels are added to the ghastly maritime scroll. On the northernmost of these islands, Roanoke, one will find the Kill Devil Hills. From here in 1903 Orville and Wilbur Wright conducted the first successful manned flight in history.

New Bern today remains a part of progressive Carolina society. Its strategic location has made it the hub of a number of military bases, notably those of the U.S. Marine Corps. Wildlife refuges and campsites abound, and Cape Lookout National Seashore is within a short drive.

But as with all national cemeteries in the South, the one at New Bern is a direct result of the American Civil War. Less than one hundred miles west near Goldsboro lies Bentonville Battlefield. It was here that the Confederacy made its last stand under General Joseph Johnston as Sherman's juggernaut rolled north from Savannah during the waning days of the struggle. New Bern itself, though a prosperous port in the 1860s, never had a chance to serve the Southern cause. Union forces knocked it from the war quickly.

In October 1861, Union General Ambrose E. Burnside gained approval of a plan to seize the area as a major blockade base for the South Atlantic Squadron. He set sail in February 1862 with the largest amphibious armada yet mustered by the U.S. Navy. It contained his flagship, nineteen war vessels and sixty-five ersatz transports. On 8 February he seized Roanoke Island after a stiff fight and then pressed on to capture New Bern on 14 March. Union losses were but 471 men. Burnside went on to bigger and better, if temporary, things as Union commander in chief, though his command ended after the debacle at Fredericksburg.

However, Union forces maintained command of the area for the duration of the war. Established in 1867, New Bern National Cemetery provided a final resting place for the Union men who died in the vicinity. Battle casualties were rare after the initial campaign. The major problems were disease and drownings. A severe yellow fever epidemic in 1864 killed far more Union troops than fighting in the area, and these troops, too, are interred here. Of the original 2,300 burial here, 1,091 were of unknowns.

The soldiers interred here represent twenty different states, including North Carolina which had many men serving the Union cause. Four states have erected monuments to their war dead. Since then, veterans of every conflict through Vietnam have been buried here. The 7.7-acre facility is the largest national cemetery in the state. It should remain open some years. By the date of projected closing in the early 1990s, interments should total about five thousand.

RALEIGH NATIONAL CEMETERY

Raleigh, North Carolina

The state capital of North Carolina bears the name of Sir Walter Raleigh, one of England's visionary colonizers during the time of Queen Elizabeth I. Though he eventually fell from favor and was executed in the Tower of London, Raleigh greatly influenced the American South in two ways. First, he initiated the tobacco industry. And then, he created a sense of local community that in some respects led to a provincial outlook.

Indeed, no area is prouder of its southern heritage than the central North Carolina district around Raleigh. Civil War mortars and other artifacts decorate the grounds of the capitol building. From 1861 to 1865 saltpeter for gunpowder was even stored in the rotunda. An impressive statue in front of the main entrance commemorates Andrew Jackson, James K. Polk and Andrew Johnson, the three native North Carolinians who achieved the presidency of the United States.

Few cities in the nation are more closely surrounded by major educational institutions than Raleigh. Duke and North Carolina State lie with a few miles of the state capitol, the latter being the first to operate a nuclear reactor for medical and other research.

Just one hundred miles south is a bulwark of the American defense establishment. Fort Bragg, North Carolina, honoring the popular and successful Confederate general of that name, is a training base and staging bastion for American paratroop warfare.

Raleigh contains some of the most modern architecture in the United States. The J.S. Dorton Arena, with its roof composed of two ninety-foot parabolic arches, is one of the more futuristic structures in this nation.

And the city's progressive attitude does not stop there. One of the dynamic metropolises of the South, it is a major transshipment point on the Atlantic and East Carolina Railroad. Industry and agriculture boom, an economic situation that did not apply to the South prior to 1861, and was one of the sources of conflict with the North.

Raleigh National Cemetery was officially opened in 1865. Among its earliest interments were reburials of Union dead from the battlefield of Averasboro near Greensboro, North Carolina and from other locales in the state. Under the name "Camp Green" the site was used by the Union army as an occupation post during reconstruction. It was not abandoned until 1875. By then, the old post burial ground, now Section 10 in the national cemetery, had combined with the Civil War interments to create an area large enough to warrant making the location a permanent facility.

Seven acres in size, Raleigh National Cemetery remains open to interments, but is expected to have space exhausted by 1995. Four memorial markers are there, all dedicated to unrecovered American remains. Sp1c. William M. Bryant, U.S.A., a Medal of Honor recipient, also lies here, as do a number of American veterans who fell in twentieth-century wars. The cemetery is among the most eye-pleasing, being divided into twenty-five symmetrical burial sections with a centrally located speaker's rostrum.

SALISBURY NATIONAL CEMETERY

Salisbury, North Carolina

A few miles east of Raleigh, the North Carolina Piedmont rises, rolling westward to the escarpments of the Blue Ridge Mountains. Lying almost halfway between is the small town of Salisbury. Situated just off Interstate 85, it is strategically located midway between the larger communities of Greensboro and Charlotte. Consequently, it has reaped many economic benefits from the burgeoning population centers of inland Carolina. And, like most areas of the American South, Salisbury is rich in history dating even prior to the Civil War.

Near Charlotte to the south lies the birthplace of President James K. Polk. Under his aggressive stewardship, the U.S. defeated Mexico in the 1840s to annex most of what became the American Southwest. He also was able to resolve the Oregon controversy with Britain in this nation's favor.

To the north of Greensboro lie two of the country's earliest battlegrounds. In the eighteenth century, a group of truculent frontiersmen renounced taxation and all other manifestations of royal rule. These "Regulators," as they termed themselves, consistently ignored the edicts of Governor William Tryon. Eventually, this worthy dispatched a militia force to Greensboro which crushed the revolt at Alamance Creek on 16 May 1771. But this was merely the harbinger of a greater struggle to come--the American Revolution. One of the most significant battlefields of that conflict is also found near Greensboro.

When the American Revolution came, the South inevitably found itself embroiled. In 1778 bitter warfare commenced between Patriot and Tory. Finally, after his evacuation from Philadelphia, British General Clinton was ordered to conquer the Carolinas. It proved an impossible task. Clinton had never been a loser and he had no intention of starting now. He threw over his command to Lord Charles Cornwallis and withdrew to New York. His successor was soon compelled to abandon the Carolinas. The event which forced this abandonment occurred on 15 March 1781 at Guilford Courthouse near Greensboro. He attacked American militia under General Nathaniel Greene and, though winning the field, could claim only a Pyrrhic victory. After Cornwallis and the bulk of his army decamped to Virginia for their rendezvous with destiny at Yorktown, it was Greene who competently eliminated the last vestiges of British authority from the Carolinas.

Sir Henry Clinton

During the Civil War, Salisbury's central location on the Western and North Carolina railroads made it the logical site of a Confederate prison camp. The one established here was a simple stockade on the order of Andersonville in which as many prisoners as possible could be watched in an open space by just a few guards. Naturally, all too many of these captives perished from a variety of causes, a total of 3,419 men.

Not until 12 April 1865 was the city captured and the prisoners liberated by Union General Stoneman and his cavalry raiding from Knoxville, Tennessee. By then the scroll was so long, all records had been lost. Thus, the Salisbury National Cemetery contains the highest number of unknown Union dead of any such facility. Over ninety-nine percent of the prisoners who died there are known but to God.

Union war dead comprise the majority of interments made here. However, in the succeeding years, the locale has provided burial space for American servicemen of all later wars. It remains open at the present time.

WILMINGTON NATIONAL CEMETERY

Wilmington, North Carolina

Wilmington sits at the head of the Cape Fear River several miles inland from Onslow Bay. It is now, as it has always been, a major transshipment port for seaborne commerce. And the roots of its involvement in American history go far back in time.

Some twenty miles north of the city lies the Moores Creek National Military Park. At the time of the outbreak of the American Revolution, Carolina Tories sought the immediate intervention of regular British forces. Such aid was promised provided they could seize the port at Wilmington as a route of supply. Thus, in February 1776, some eighteen hundred Royalists converged on the community. They were blocked at the bridge over this tributary of Cape Fear and soundly defeated on 27 February. This victory of Patriot militia was for many years the only major battle waged in the American South.

Its proximity to the battlefields of Virginia made Wilmington one of the Confederacy's main blockade ports during the Civil War. Indeed, the small community of Carolina Beach on the peninsula to the south, contains the Blockade Runner Museum, a tribute to Southern gallantry during the nation's internecine struggle.

Wilmington remained the pre-eminent Southern port until 1865, primarily due to the fact that Fort Fisher at the mouth of the Cape Fear River protected its only route of approach. For four years it was a festering sore in the craw of the Union South Atlantic Squadron.

In December 1864, with the siege operations around Richmond beginning in earnest, Union Commander in Chief Ulysses S. Grant ordered the capture of what he described as "the last gateway between the Confederate States and the outside world." General Benjamin F. Butler took personal command of the assault that took place on 27 December. Cynics have claimed that was the reason for the abject failure which followed. At any rate, despite such novelties as exploding "powder ships" to demoralize the defenders, Union forces were repulsed even though covered by heavy supporting fire from a Union fleet.

Understandably dissatisfied with the results, Grant then ordered General A.H. Terry to try it again. This time they left the flamboyant Butler at home. On 13 January 1865 Terry landed most of his eight thousand troops on the peninsula north of the fort where they were opposed by a Southern division sent as reinforcements by Lee. After two days of sanguinary assaults and naval bombardments, the fortress capitulated on 15 January.

As if the location had not caused enough trouble, the next morning two drunken sailors in search of booty entered an ammunition bunker with uncovered torches. The resulting explosion killed or wounded over one hundred more men. But the issue had been resolved despite the secondary tragedy. Fort Fisher was Union, the mouth of Cape Fear was closed and Lee no longer had a worthwhile port through which he could obtain war supplies from foreign soil.

A few weeks later, as Sherman and his "Bummers" stormed north in their Carolina Campaign, Union forces under Schofield occupied Wilmington on 22 February. A few weeks after this, the Confederacy's lost cause came to an end.

The large number of Union war dead resulting from these various campaigns made Wilmington National Cemetery a necessity and it was opened in 1866. Several thousand Civil War veterans found their final resting place in this centrally located reinterment center. Exact statistics are unavailable but the percentage of unknowns here, as elsewhere, is high. Since then, it has provided burial space for American veterans who served a united cause in later conflicts. It is presently open, but with the many veteran interments currently facing the system, it cannot be predicted how much longer this will be so. Current information indicates interments will cease within a year, except for active duty fatalities, which should be accommodated for some years yet.

DAYTON NATIONAL CEMETERY

Dayton, Ohio

Dayton National Cemetery is one of many facilities whose presence reflects the burgeoning population of modern American society. The city is a major transshipment point on various railroad lines in southern Ohio, the most crucial being the Dayton and Michigan Railroad and the Atlantic and Great Western Railroad, both of which were heavily traversed during the Civil War. One hundred miles east lies the state capitol at Columbus. An equal distance south on the Ohio River is the small community of Point Pleasant, hometown of one Ulysses S. Grant, born 27 April 1822--a stunning example of a local-boy-made-good.

Shortly after the great internal conflict of 1861 to 1865, Dayton became the site of a National Asylum for Disabled Soldiers and Seamen. Its large hospital complex was taken over and expanded by the Veterans Administration in 1930 and its burial grounds became the Dayton National Cemetery on 21 July of that year. Since then it has served the population of southern Ohio, proving invaluable because the closest other facilities are the small and nearly filled Civil War cemeteries of Kentucky.

The first interment occurred here on 11 September 1877 when the remains of Union Civil War veteran Cornelius Solly were committed. Ten years later, a lavishly-carved monument was erected. It is composed of a ten-foot statue of a soldier at parade rest atop a forty-eight-foot column. Around its base are four smaller figures commemorating the infantry, cavalry, artillery and navy. It is thought the model for the statue was George Washington Fair, a Civil War veteran of Dayton who also modeled for a larger but similar monument in Riverview Park.

A number of interesting American veterans are at rest here at Dayton. One of these is George Geiger. He served in the Forty-seventh Ohio Infantry during the Civil War and remained on active duty where he eventually served with the U.S. Seventh Cavalry. On 25 June 1876 he won the Medal of Honor for heroism while serving under Major Marcus Reno at the epic battle at the Little Bighorn River in Montana. He and his men staged a diversion and offered covering fire to medical personnel seeking water for their wounded comrades the night after Custer's battalion had been destroyed to the north and Reno's command was being besieged by overwhelming numbers of warriors.

Another veteran buried here is Major General M.R. Patrick. A native of New York, he led a lengthy and distinguished career that saw service in the Seminole Wars of 1835 to 1842, the Mexican War and the Civil War, where he finished as provost general of the Army of the Potomac and later became governor of the soldier's home at Dayton from 1880 until his death in 1888.

Two other veterans, known as much for their athletic ability as for their military service, can be found here. Louis Margolis enjoyed a boxing career in his youth as "Kayo Mars." Edmund Magner once played infield for the New York Yankees in 1911.

As of 1980 there have been 24,850 interments in the sixty-nine-acre Dayton National Cemetery. It is presently open, and should continue to serve the area into the twenty-first century.

FORT GIBSON NATIONAL CEMETERY

Fort Gibson, Oklahoma

On they came ... for nearly fifteen years. Across the dry, windy plains of Arkansas and across the swampy, malaria-ridden coasts of the deep South, thousands of Indians and their families were herded to what became known as Indian Territory. In what was one of the worst examples of avarice and self-aggrandizement in American history, the Five Civilized Tribes were uprooted from their homelands east of the Mississippi and resettled by force. Seeking to gain ownership of the lands they occupied, white settlers prevailed upon President Andrew Jackson to remove their red competitors. When the Supreme Court ruled such an action was illegal, Jackson noted the decision with the words: "They [the judges] have made their decision. Now let them enforce it." The hegira went on.

The Choctaws, the Chickasaws, the Cherokees, the Creeks and, finally, the Seminoles were ejected. Except for a few of the latter, who fled into the Everglades under a chieftain named Billy Bowlegs and have survived as a viable tribal entity, all traces of Indian civilization in the South were eradicated. Authorities differ as to statistics, but at least eighty-seven thousand people were relocated despite their protests. Perhaps as many as ten percent perished along the way--mostly women, children and the elderly. Little wonder the exodus is remembered in Indian folklore as "The Trail of Tears."

During the Civil War, as many as two thousand Indians fell fighting for both armies. This active participation in the affairs of the white man heralded the demise of all political power and sense of identity for many of them because of bitter divisions in their own ranks. This fighting over different sides in the white man's war led too many to lose their tribal views and sense of purpose as Indians. Many became in a sense "white men." Only by rigorous efforts in this century have the various tribes been able to survive as recognizable ethnic groups.

From Lake O' the Cherokees to the north to the Arbuckle National Recreational Park to the southwest, Oklahoma retains relics of this Trail of Tears to the present day. Among those sites still maintained is the cabin of Sequoyah, developer of the Cherokee alphabet. The town of Muskogee hosts the Five Civilized Tribes Museum, one of the main reasons that Indian folklore has not totally evaporated in the area.

When the emigrants arrived, waiting for them was the guard garrison from Fort Gibson. Located between Muskogee and Tahlequah, the post is the oldest military installation in Oklahoma. First established on 28 April 1824, Fort Gibson was occupied by troops from Fort Smith, Arkansas. Located on the left bank of the Neosho River, it was named for a General Gibson, then commissary general of the army. The immediate reason for its construction was the massacre of white trappers by Osage Indians in 1823.

Temporarily abandoned twice, the fort was occupied by Confederates with the outbreak of Civil War. After the Battle of Round Mountain in November 1861, a Union force under Colonel William A. Phillips recaptured the fort. Among his troops were the Third Indian Home Guards, composed mainly of Cherokees from the Tahlequah area. New construction followed, including formidable earthworks to protect all routes of approach. General James F. Blunt, commander of the Military District of Kansas, later used it as a base to repulse a last Southern thrust in July 1863. After this, Indian Territory remained firmly within Union control.

Fort Gibson was dissolved as a military post in 1871. Though maintained as a quartermaster's depot, it was fully abandoned in 1890. With the exception of the national cemetery, its land was transferred to the Department of the Interior. Subsequently, many post buildings were torn down while others were converted into private homes.

Fort Gibson National Cemetery, established as a small post burial grounds in 1824, remained as such throughout the Civil War. However, in 1866, reinterments of Union soldiers from areas of Oklahoma and elsewhere forced the installation to be enlarged somewhat. Though never large by the standards of the National Cemetery System, Fort Gibson has provided final resting places for American veterans to the present day. It should remain open for the foreseeable future. It is expected to be exhausted by the turn of the century. Studies have been made to convert and enlarge the facilities at either Old Fort Rend near Oklahoma City or the still-active army base at Fort Sill. But no decision has been made, and the idea seems to have been abandoned.

Veterans of every American conflict since the Revolutionary War are at rest here. However, perhaps two of its more interesting denizens never served that cause. One is Diana Rogers, wife of Sam Houston, buried under her Cherokee name of Talihini. The other is "Billy Bowlegs," the Seminole chieftain who led the last uprising of his people in Florida before they were deported in 1852.

ROSEBURG NATIONAL CEMETERY

Roseburg, Oregon

Roseburg lies south of the most agriculturally productive part of Oregon. The Willamette River, irrigating some of the most luscious fruit orchards in the world, extends to within fifty miles of the city of Eugene to the north. To the south lies Grant's Pass and the isolated Rogue River. To the west is Coos Bay, known for wildlife and fishing. To the east, amid the splendor of the Cascade Mountains, lies Crater Lake National Park, containing the deepest lake in the United States (1,932 feet).

This part of the American Northwest is no stranger to history either. Southern Oregon saw as much Indian strife during the last century as most parts of the Great Plains. Though not as famous as the later Modoc War, the last stand of the Cayuse Indians along the Rogue River in 1855 and 1856 was a drama replete with historical stereotypes.

For some years, Captain Andrew J. Smith, gruff but fair commander of nearby Fort Lane, had labored mightily to keep the peace and had interceded on behalf of the Indians and the local settlers alike. But in 1855, due to deteriorating relations, Smith removed many of the Indian men to the fort. Before their women and children could join them, local settlers stormed the Indian village and killed twenty-three of them. Needless to say, the fighting then became general. Before it was over, General John E. Wool, Pacific Department Commander, was led to observe, "It has become a contest of extermination."

In May 1856, the Indians agreed to surrender to Smith at Big Meadows along the Rogue River. However, when Smith arrived with an army detachment, misunderstandings occurred which turned the Surrender at Big Meadows into the Battle of Big Meadows. For three days, Smith's outnumbered soldiers held off the assaulting red men. Chief Old John spent most of his time hurling threats and epithets at Smith, all of which were thoughtfully translated for Smith by Old John's female interpreters. Finally, in the nick of time, another army unit under Captain C.C. Augur came charging to the rescue. Well ... not charging exactly, since the infantry was mounted on mules, but the expression is no doubt adequate by Hollywood standards.

Eventually the conflict petered out and the Cayuses became but one more tribe which ceased to exist as a viable entity. The development of southern Oregon then proceeded apace. Many of its volunteers later saw service in the West during the Civil War.

Roseburg National Cemetery is part of the Department of Veterans Affairs complex in the area. During the early part of the century it was the Oregon Soldiers Home for disabled and homeless veterans of the Civil War and subsequent American conflicts. It was taken over by the U.S. government in 1932 as part of the huge V. A. expansion of the era. In 1975 it officially became a national cemetery.

At present the cemetery contains 3.3 acres of burial ground. As of May 1980 there had been 2,323 interments. It is still open to receive burials, but as of the early 1980s was closed to interments except for special circumstances--all interment activity has since been transferred to the huge new site at Willamette near Portland.

WHITE CITY NATIONAL CEMETERY

Eagle Point, Oregon

Nestled in the scenic, hilly terrain north of Medford, Oregon, White City Veterans Domicilary allows an excellent vista. Not only is lush Willamette Valley visible, but so is territory rich in American history.

The United States first became aware of Oregon when it seemed to face the loss of Oregon to Canadian settlers. In 1828 an emigration society was organized in Massachusetts under H. Jackson Kelley. By 1831 the first conscious effort to settle and secure the area was underway. Soon Fort Vancouver, far to the south of Medford, became the terminus of the Oregon Trail, symbolic of a westward expansion which would continue unabated for three-quarters of a century. Not until 1854 were the last difficulties pertaining to American annexation ironed out with the Canadians, and war with Britain averted. As an army officer here, George W. Pickett, who commanded the final charge at Gettysburg, started a brief spate of shooting with Canada. It was called "The Pig War" (probably because they suffered most of the casualties) and precipitated the cry of "fifty-four forty or fight!"

However, even before that year, arriving settlers had begun the inevitable clash of cultures with the Indians. In this case, they were a small tribe (never more than three hundred) called the Modocs. Unfortunately, this band was led by men of considerable vision and recalcitrance. These Indians generally wore a hang-dog expression which belied a dynamic, aggressive spirit, as manifested in the names applied to their leaders--Hooker Jim, Bogus Charley and Shagnasty Jim. However, the most virulently opposed to reservation life was a young man named Kintpuash, known to history as Captain Jack.

Prior to 1870 there were a few clashes with army troops in which the Modocs fared poorly. They would then return to their lodges along Lost River north of Tule Lake to ponder the repercussions of arousing the wrath of the bluecoats.

Obviously, an explosion was unavoidable. Continued agitation by settlers for the Indians' removal to the Klamath Reservation provided the impetus. At dawn on 29 November 1872, a troop of cavalry entered Captain Jack's village; there was an exchange of rifle fire. The Indians scattered and the Modoc War was on!

Leaving a trail of destruction behind them, the Indians fled north of Tule Lake to the garish, twisted lava beds they called "Land of the

Burnt-Out Fires." Here troops closed in and attacked. But the "Battle of the Stronghold" of 16 January 1873 was a debacle. The army was repulsed with heavy losses. As far as could be determined no soldier even saw a Modoc.

The campaign not exactly moving on greased wheels, diplomacy was considered as an alternative plan. At first, progress was made. Then an incident occurred which doomed the Modocs. Convinced that General E.R.S. Canby was toying with him, Captain Jack and several followers treacherously killed him and several peace negotiators under a flag of truce on the morning of 11 April 1873. Though it took six more months of bitter fighting, the ultimate fate of Captain Jack and his people was assured. He and several of the more bloodthirsty Indians went to the gallows. Canby became the only general killed in the Indian wars.

Here, where Captain Jack once roamed and fought, the White City Veterans Domiciliary sits in the rugged, green mountains of southern Oregon. Many permanently disabled and/or homeless American veterans make their home here.

In 1952 a cemetery was established on land acquired from the Department of the Navy. It is located about one mile northeast of Eagle Point, Oregon and about six miles from the domicile itself. Composed of forty-three acres, much of it remains as yet undeveloped. Only about 7.16 acres are in use as burial areas. As of April 1980 a total of 1,393 interments had been made. It is, of course, still open to interments.

WILLAMETTE NATIONAL CEMETERY

Portland, Oregon

On 29 December 1941, the Seventy-seventh Congress approved and President Roosevelt signed an authorization directing the secretary of war to acquire lands in the vicinity of Portland, Oregon for the site of a national cemetery. With the conclusion of World War II, the state of Oregon donated 102 acres, and Multnomah and Clackamas counties donated 100 more for the development of the project. Today the cemetery has developed about 79 of those acres around a central administration area and ceremonial ground. Other land will be opened over the years as necessary. This is because the sloping terrain requires much grading and landscaping.

The cemetery is currently located on the edge of urban development, about ten miles from city center. It is located on the northeastern flank of Mount Scott, an eminence rising one thousand feet above the valley floor, and it provides excellent vistas during clear weather. Mounts St. Helens, Adams, Hood and Rainier are often visible at the same time. The Columbia and Willamette Rivers stretch across the flatlands below. The only drawback, albeit temporary, is that freeway construction makes access to the site difficult.

However, for those who manage to arrive on the slopes of Mt. Scott, a rewarding visual and historical experience awaits. Originally designed to serve both Oregon and Washington, the cemetery is located in an area rich in history.

Directly across the Columbia River sits old Fort Vancouver. Established in 1824 by the Hudson Bay Company, it served as their regional headquarters for years before being abandoned. During the 1840s and 1850s it was the terminus of the legendary Oregon Trail. From here thousands of pioneers branched out, founding some of the most fertile farming areas in the nation. Among the more famous frontiersmen to spend time at the fort was mountain man Jedediah Smith. U.S. troops occasionally used the fort as a staging area in their operations against the Palouse, Cayuse and Yakima Indians in the 1850s. These wars, while among the least known, were also the most savagely contested in American history. A young army officer named Ulysses S. Grant would pass through the fort on his way north to the Tacoma area where he fought a losing battle with the bottle. Eventually he had to resign his commission, though, as most concede, he would later experience a professional comeback of some magnitude.

Just one hundred miles west, where the mighty Columbia reaches the Pacific, lies Fort Clatsop. In 1806 the expedition of Lewis and Clark rested here for some weeks before commencing the homeward trek.

To the east lies The Dalles, Oregon, one of American's most attractive cities. And just beyond is Lake Umatilla and Pendleton, site of the Pendleton Round-Up, one of America's greatest yearly rodeo extravaganzas. To the southeast is Willamette National Forest, one of the largest and greenest in the nation. From the heights of Pacific Crest Trail, one can see from Portland to powerful Bonneville Dam on the eastern Columbia.

However, until quite recently, the national cemetery has not been a part of this natural beauty. It was a policy for many years to remove all vegetation from developed burial areas. This denuding of plant material produced a barren, windswept look that lacked privacy and serenity. Inclement weather also makes cemetery management difficult. However, a master plan was adopted in 1975 which will hopefully soften some of the terrain's more unpalatable views.

The size of the cemetery should allow it to remain active until well into the twenty-first century. On 14 February 1951 Pvt. B.C. Van Ausdeln, a veteran of World War I, became the first committal in Willamette National Cemetery. He was the first of the approximately one hundred thirty thousand American veterans who will one day rest on the slopes of Mount Scott. It is presently only ten percent filled.

GETTYSBURG NATIONAL BATTLEFIELD PARK

Gettysburg, Pennsylvania

On the afternoon of 19 November 1863, a tall bearded figure, stooped by the responsibilities of a long and brutal Civil War, rose from his seat on a platform and strode toward the podium. Abraham Lincoln had come to dedicate the Soldiers National Cemetery at Gettysburg with a few short remarks. The following day a major New York newspaper printed in entirety the remarks of Edward Everett, whose lengthy speech had preceded Mr. Lincoln's and ended its coverage of the event with the observation: "The President also spoke." Rarely in journalistic history has a tabloid so grievously misinterpreted the relevance and tenor of any ceremony. For the words with which Lincoln began were, "Four score and seven years ago ..."

A story has been told through the years about the siege of Vicksburg. As Union artillery shells traced crimson arcs through the night sky and screamed into the shattered town, a woman attempted to comfort her children with the assurance that God would protect them. "But, Mama," wailed her small daughter, "I'm afraid God has done been kilt too." Though perhaps apocryphal, no possible anecdote could be more appropriate for what happened here at this small farming community during the first three days of July 1863. Nearly one hundred seventy-five thousand Americans met here in the most cataclysmic collision on the North American continent. Before it was over, nearly thirty percent of them had been killed, maimed, captured or driven insane in these peaceful, wooded dells of southern Pennsylvania.

But, as Abraham Lincoln hoped, it may not have been in vain. Many historians claim the American Civil War was the one conflict this nation had to fight. And like all wars, this one had a decisive battle--Gettysburg. Perhaps this, of all battles Americans have ever waged, was the one that truly had to be.

In June 1863, after frustrating the latest Union offensive on Richmond the month before, Robert E. Lee led the greatest army he was ever to command on its climactic invasion of the North. He was hoping that a substantial victory on Northern soil would strengthen the anti-war sentiment there and might even encourage British intervention on behalf of the South. In effect, as Lee drove through Maryland, he was looking for the Confederacy's Saratoga.

The campaign led to numerous conflicts before the ultimate verdict was rendered at Gettysburg. Various Union reconnaissance missions led to clashes at Franklin Crossing and Brandy Station. Confederate General Ewell's advance through the Shenandoah Valley led to Berryhill, Martinsburg and Winchester. Cavalry flank actions were fought at Aldie, Middleburg and Upperville. J.E.B. Stuart's raid through Maryland led to conflicts at Fairfax, Westminster, Hanover and Carlile. Union abandonment of exposed positions in the Shenandoah led to struggles at Greencastle, McConnellsburg and Sporting Hill. Minor actions occurred at Frying Pan, Virginia; Seneca, Maryland and Low Creek, West Virginia. To the south, Union diversionary thrusts at Richmond brought conflicts at Baltimore Cross Roads and South Anna. Thus, long before 1 July, thousands of casualties had been sustained by each side.

The quintessential American struggle of all time began on the morning that Confederate troops moved into Gettysburg to capture a supply of shoes and met Union cavalry under General Buford. What followed is described militarily as a "meeting engagement." In the final analysis, it was one of the battles that shaped the course of human history.

That first day, both sides rushed pellmell into battle. By sundown Lee had turned the Union right along the north of Seminary Ridge and forced them to withdraw eastward across the valley to the heights of Cemetery Ridge. On the second day, Lee's sledgehammer blows sought to turn the Union southern flank along Cemetery Ridge. New names were added to the lexicon of American valor and butchery--Little Round Top, Big Round Top, Peach Orchard, Wheat Field and Devil's Den; these were tactically important, bitterly contested battle sites.

Though his troops had held for two straight days, Union Commander in Chief, General George B. Meade, so lacked confidence about a third day's action that only a formal council of war convinced him to stand and fight. Reasoning that Lee had already struck both flanks, Meade now assumed his opponent would hit the center of his line, aiming for the crucial breakthrough.

The morning of 3 July 1863 dawned oppressively hot. Confederate General James Longstreet, unenthusiastically accepting command of the assault, formed his troops directly in front of the Union entrenchments on Cemetery Ridge. These three divisions were under Pettigrew, Pickett and Trimble. Just why what followed came to be known as Pickett's Charge remains a conundrum. He was neither the overall commander nor was his division the largest involved. It may be because his men were the only ones to actually puncture the Union lines--if just barely.

At 1:45 P.M., after a massive artillery bombardment, fifteen thousand Confederate troops charged across half a mile of exposed valley, over the Emmitsburg Road and hurled themselves onto the Union breastworks. A few troops under Armistead, of Picketts division, actually made it to Union lines. But Armistead quickly fell and the 150 men with him were killed or taken prisoner. And so, at 2:15 P.M. "the high tide of the Confederacy" swelled above the ghastly valley between the two ridges, crested against the unyielding blue-clad lines and receded on a blood-red tide.

The survivors stumbled back to their lines to be met by a sorrowing Lee. Their beloved Marse Robert had tears in his eyes as he muttered again and again, "My fault. All my fault." When he retreated the following day, Lee must have suspected the last chance for Southern independence had been eradicated forever on the slopes of Cemetery Ridge.

The Army of Northern Virginia incurred 28,063 casualties in the battle, while Meade lost 23,049. Within weeks, the Union would make good its losses. But Lee's army had its heart torn asunder and it would never be the same.

Today the town of Gettysburg is as peaceful as it was prior to the Civil War. But neither it nor the nation of which it is a part will ever be the same. The town is surrounded on three sides by over three thousand acres of the Gettysburg National Park. It is an area which contains more monuments than any other in the United States. Thirty-one miles of roads twist and turn through it. Ninety-three miles of fences preserve the old battle lines. The ultra-modern visitor's center is dominated by the Gettysburg Cyclorama, painted in 1881 by Paul Phillipoteaux.

Of all the monuments here, perhaps the most symbolic and beautifully done is the memorial raised to the First Minnesota Regiment. Atop it a soldier, bayonet fixed, charges forward to repulse a Confederate breakthrough in Trostle Woods on the second day of the fighting. The First Minnesota was successful. But in fifteen horrid minutes eighty-two percent of its men fell, most never to rise again.

Gettysburg National Cemetery lies in a semicircle on the heights of Cemetery Ridge. It is adjacent to the old burial grounds which gave the locale its name at the time of the struggle. When Lincoln dedicated the installation, most of the thousands of Union dead who perished on the field were already interred here. This was not true, however, of the Southerners. Photographer Matthew Brady had taken a shot of a dead Confederate in Devil's Den after the battle. Four months later he found the skeletal remains of the man still unmoved. With the cessation of hostilities all Confederate dead which could be found were returned home. A few remains which turned up later may have been buried here, but records are sketchy.

Gettysburg National Cemetery is no longer open to interments. It was primarily established to serve those men who died here, and few burials occurred after the Civil War. About six thousand American veterans have found their final resting place in the facility.

Today, young children cavort over the grounds, including Devil's Den where photographer Brady's Confederate lay dead for so many months. Talking excitedly, the children clamor and wonder what it was like here on those terrible days in July 1863. It is fortunate that they will never know.

The Declaration of Independence

PHILADELPHIA NATIONAL CEMETERY

Philadelphia, Pennsylvania

On 19 April 1775, unceasing and ever-increasing differences between England and her American colonies flared into open warfare. That morning, seven hundred British infantry under Major Pitcairn marched to Concord, Massachusetts to destroy American war supplies stocked there. They were intercepted on Lexington Common by local militiamen. These hearty lads ignored Pitcairn's command to disperse and, inevitably, a battle ensued. Driving the farmers off, the British marched on to Concord, destroyed what supplies they could locate and headed back for Boston, harassed every step of the way by rapidly growing numbers of "Minutemen." British volleys kept them at bay but could not drive them off. By the time Pitcairn's footsore command reached the port city, the dusty route was dotted with fallen red-clad forms. It was not a large action, even by eighteenth-century standards. But it was enough. From the crucible of revolution would be born the United States.

Minuteman, Ready at a Moment's Notice

Over a year later, during a lull in the fighting, forty-eight men met in Philadelphia to consider a resolution drafted by a young Virginian named Thomas Jefferson. They rigorously cut the manuscript by three quarters until the original eighteen hundred word work was unrecognizable. What emerged they all felt they could sign. Thus, when the morning of Thursday, 4 July 1776 dawned fair and breezy, they sallied forth from what became known as Liberty Hall on the banks of the Delaware River and read the document, which began with the words, "When in the course of human events ..." Among its more stirring propositions is the belief that all men are created equal and that this truth is self-evident.

Well, maybe so. And then again, maybe not. King George III of England had no quarrel with the proposal, merely with its geopolitical applications. His mother once told him: "George, be king!" He had no intention of letting her down, even if it meant he had to be more equal than others. Americans might have declared their independence in a town he could not locate on the map, but with the military muscle George III commanded, their winning it would be a different matter.

Only fifteen months after the brave declaration was released, British General Howe landed at the mouth of the Delaware River with eighteen thousand troops and marched on Philadelphia. For some reason, the capture and defense of the city of independence had achieved a mystical importance to commanders on both sides. On 11 September 1777 Howe smashed aside Washington's smaller army. A few nights later, his troops wiped out an American brigade at Paoli in a night bayonet assault. On 26 September the scarlet and gold columns occupied Philadelphia. On 4 October Washington's desperate attempt to expel them was repulsed at Germantown. Yet, despite all prognostications, the Americans remained grimly tenacious. If Howe was startled that the revolt did not collapse, he was no more surprised than many Americans. But not even the horrid winter at Valley Forge extinguished the embers of the Patriots' love of liberty.

Eventually, of course, England was unable to sustain the drain of blood and treasure. In 1781 Cornwallis threw in the towel at Yorktown and American independence became a reality. Philadelphia became the mother of independence.

Philadelphia has also been something of a cultural mecca over the years. The local John Bartram House is the first botanical garden in the United States. "Mill Grove," the home of French artist John J. Audubon in the early 1800s, is found here.

During the Civil War, numerous Union hospitals sprang up in the area. Hundreds of Union sick and wounded required burial space when the benefits of nineteenth-century medical science betrayed them. Also, Pennsylvania supplied dozens of combat regiments to the Union army. Among these was the Eighty-third Pennsylvania Infantry, recruited in Philadelphia and Chester County. It fought in every major battle from the Peninsula Campaign through Appomattox. Two of its commanders were killed in action, and only one other Union regiment had more losses in the entire war. Another unit was the 140th Pennsylvania Infantry. Also representative of Philadelphia regiments, this unit suffered the loss of seventeen percent of its men, ranking fourth on the regimental casualty list of the Union army. The dead of these and other units, when brought home, made the establishment of a national burial ground imperative.

Philadelphia National Cemetery sits at the corner of Haines Street and Limekiln Pike in what is today a large urban area. Most of the early interments were of Union war veterans. Records remain sketchy as to the date burials commenced but the location became a national cemetery officially in 1885. Four major monuments are included in the 13.3-acre facility, including, oddly, two to Confederates, and one each to Revolutionary and Mexican War veterans. Some individuals who died long after those earlier struggles may also rest here. Since the bloody internal conflict of 1861 to 1865, the site has supplied burial space for veterans of later wars as well.

Unfortunately, surrounding land use made any expansion impossible. In 1962 the cemetery was closed to future committals. However, the need has been alleviated with the development of Indiantown Gap National Cemetery in Annville, Pennsylvania, halfway between Philadelphia and Pittsburgh.

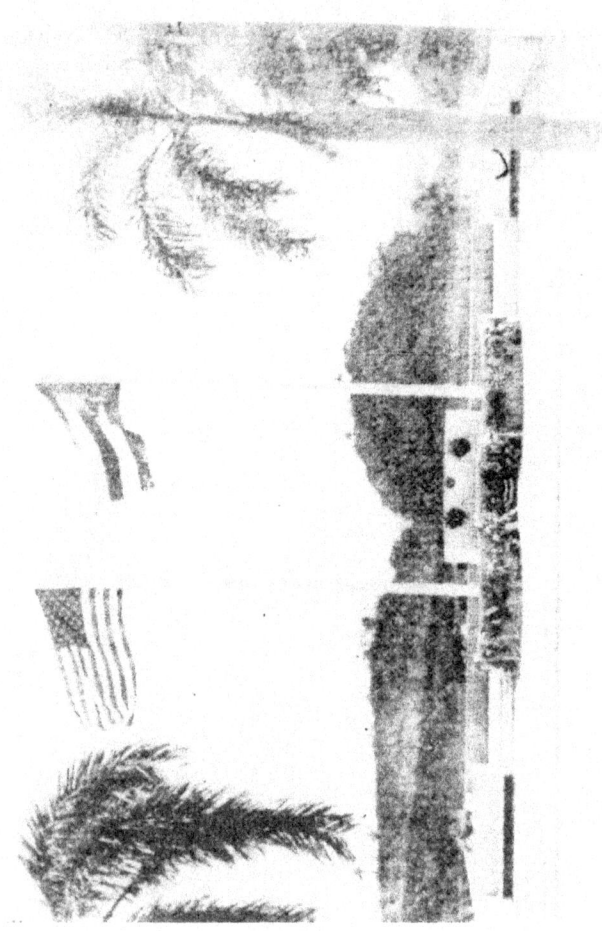

Flag Plaza at Bayamon, Puerto Rico
--*V.A. photo*

PUERTO RICO NATIONAL CEMETERY

Bayamon, Puerto Rico

Located in Bayamon, a quickly expanding sub-center of the metropolis of San Juan, the Puerto Rico National Cemetery is the only one outside of the United States proper. As such, it was intended as a final resting place and monument to the large numbers of Puerto Rican veterans who have served in every American war since 1918. It also occupies a unique position in the culture of the island. The national cemetery is simultaneously a symbol of American presence and the island's commonwealth status; it is a hallmark of Puerto Rico's participation in the events which shaped modern history.

And Puerto Rico has occupied such a post before. It was once one of the foremost linchpins of the Spanish Empire in the New World. In 1519 the conquistadors came. Having ridden in blood through Mexico, destroying Indian civilization in their greedy quest, they continued their search for wealth here. Even the name, meaning "rich port," was an example of Spanish obsession with and belief in the fabulous riches they sought, and the certainty that they lay just over the next mountain, just on the next island.

The San Juan area is the possessor of some of the most priceless and earliest of Spanish American history. Just a few miles from Bayamon are the ruins of Caparra, the first European settlement of any size in the Caribbean. San Juan was founded a century before the *Mayflower* reached Plymouth Rock. It spilled over the island on which it sits to create the suburb of Santurce generations ago. Unlike much of the Spanish Empire of old, Puerto Rico and its citizens have been adamant in preserving the sites and treasures of their past.

One of the most notable is La Gortaleza. In 1621 it became the residence of the governor and remains so today. It is the oldest, continuously occupied building in the Caribbean.

Nearby lies El Convento, one of the oldest convents in the New World. A high-born widow, Dona Ana de Lanzos, donated the facility to the crown in mid-sixteenth century. For three hundred years, barefooted Carmelite nuns padded through its corridors pondering the mysteries of eternity. However, Spanish rulers, beginning with Philip IV, refused to aid it in any way, unwilling to create a precedent for such a drain on the royal treasury. Therefore, shortly after the Spanish were expelled, the convent was found to have declined to an alarming extent. In 1959, Robert Woolworth purchased and reconstructed it. Today the edifice is both a museum and the El Convento Hotel, one of the leading tourist hostelries.

Towering 140 feet above the entrance to San Juan Bay squats the brooding fortress of El Morro, for centuries the guardian of commerce in and out of the port. For most of that time, San Juan was a major collection point for the annual flota or Spanish treasure fleet. Galleons would enter the area through Galleon Passage in the Windward Islands and split up to garner the fabulous wealth of Spain prior to reforming at Havana. It was near here on Silver Shoals, just to the north, that several of these vessels were wrecked. A young entrepreneur from the English colony of Massachusetts, one William Phips, staged one of the most successful salvages in human history. Aided more by determination than anything else, he raised virtually the entire silver bullion cargo of one of these ships. It was an act which gave him such favor with the Crown that he later served as governor of the colony and died one of America's wealthiest men.

However, El Morro proved all but invincible. True, a Dutch fleet managed to invade the port in 1628 and put the torch to it, but the fortress repulsed numerous other assaults. Once it even defeated the pillage attempt of Sir Francis Drake and his corsairs.

San Juan today is in the midst of a land boom. Gleaming new apartments are rapidly replacing the teeming slums which once dominated the area. No longer are suburbs known by such derogatory, if eloquent, names as "El Fanguito" (the Mud Hole).

The only thing most Americans know of Puerto Rico is that it has long supplied a flood of immigrants to New York and the East Coast. However, by 1965 the trend had been reversed and emigration was becoming a bit of a problem. Today it is a prosperous and self-governing commonwealth of 3,437 square miles and two and a half million people.

Puerto Rico National Cemetery, established soon after the Spanish-American War, is a successful attempt to reflect the duality of the Puerto Rican experience; Puerto Ricans are independent people ethnically and philosophically, yet highly Americanized, and proud of that. Nowhere else will one find a cemetery with so many graves decorated by so many flowers on so many occasions. San Juan families make it one of the most visited cemeteries on earth. Puerto Ricans are as proud of the cause these men served as the land from which they sprang.

However, by 1976, the developed burial areas were exhausted. Potential expansion was limited because of surrounding land use, but efficient use of the remaining area by a master plan created in 1975, allowed the site to remain open. Thus, it became one of the first facilities to employ the mausoleum concept and use of columbarium to facilitate maximum land use. A new flag plaza was also added to increase the attractiveness of the cemetery. It is now eighty acres in extent and hopefully will extend burial space to Puerto Rican veterans into the twenty-first century.

BEAUFORT NATIONAL CEMETERY

Beaufort, South Carolina

Beaufort, South Carolina is known today for its sailing regattas and beautiful old homes, and has one of the two U.S. national cemeteries in the state; the other national cemetery is located in Florence. Situated near the coast fifty miles below Charleston, Beaufort is not only rich in American history but continues as a viable part of the national scene.

Beaufort Marine Corps Air Station, Parris Island Marine Recruit Depot, and a large Naval Hospital testify to the military influence in the area. Just to the south, across Port Royal Sound, lies the burgeoning vacation conglomerate of Hilton Head. The low-lying coastal area between Charleston and Savannah, with Beaufort at its heart, has become a retirement mecca for American servicemen and their dependents.

But, as in the case of so many areas in the American South, it was the horrendous Civil War that brought the establishment of a national cemetery to this location. Early in the struggle, Port Royal Sound was guarded by Forts Beauregard and Walker, and the denizens of Beaufort assumed they would spare the area the worst traumas of the Union blockade. It was a forlorn hope. On 7 November 1861 Admiral Samuel Du Pont bombarded and captured the forts and seized Hilton Head Island with the loss of only thirty-one men. It subsequently became a major Union blockade base. During the war some twelve thousand Union troops effectively sealed the area as a Southern port. And, in April 1862 at Fort Pulaski, guardian of Savannah twenty miles to the south, Union gunboats captured yet another Confederate coastal defense fortification in a demonstration of the ineffectiveness of masonry against rifled cannon.

In short, Beaufort existed in the shadow of the blockaders throughout the long struggle, though for a time it was spared the worst ravages of the conflict.

However, Sherman's advancing troops during their epic march to the sea at Savannah was a portent of things to come. Union forces under J.P. Hatch sortied from Hilton Head in an attempt to link with Sherman's army and ease the path of conquest. But three miles south of Grahamville, South Carolina a Georgia militia force under General G.W. Smith defeated him and forced a Union withdrawal to their base. This victory at Honey Hill on 30 November 1864 was the last one for

Confederate troops in the war.

Unfortunately, this did nothing to halt the steamroller Sherman had launched and he was able to present Savannah to Lincoln as a Christmas present. When he finally turned north to join Grant in Virginia, his army easily brushed aside scattered, if fanatical, Southern resistance, captured Beaufort and forced Confederate evacuation of Charleston on 17 February 1865. For Beaufort the war was over.

Some 117 Confederate soldiers killed in these operations were interred at Beaufort National Cemetery with their more numerous Union brethren. As early as 1863 President Lincoln had designated a national cemetery site at the location because of the vast number of Union dead through military action and natural causes on Hilton Head Island. Some 7,000 Union dead eventually were reinterred from this and other locations to Beaufort National Cemetery. This includes 4,019 whose identities were somehow lost during transfer and became simply unknowns.

Not until 1866, however, was the twenty-nine-acre site officially purchased by the U.S. government. The price was $75.00, a real estate bargain even by pre-inflation standards.

The cemetery enjoys one of the most unique patterns in the National Cemetery System. Laid out like a fan, its oyster-shelled roads are like the spokes of a wheel, with the iron entrance gates forming the tie hub. An attractive four-foot-high brick wall completely surrounds the burial ground.

A monument to all Union soldiers was funded and erected by a Charleston woman, Mrs. L.P. Potter, in the interests of future understanding and peace. The inscription reads, "Immortality to hundreds of the defenders of America." Since then, thousands have joined that number. Some four thousand American veterans of later struggles are also interred here. When the grounds are completely filled, nearly twenty thousand former servicemen and war dead will rest here. Mrs. Potter's words will make a fitting epitaph for them all. The facility is expected to be exhausted by the year 2000.

FLORENCE NATIONAL CEMETERY

Florence, South Carolina

Set in the north-central part of the state, Florence is one of two national cemeteries in South Carolina. It is located in a region which contains as much history as any part of the American South. One hundred miles west lies the state capital of Columbia, ravaged by Union troops under Sherman in 1865. In the same direction, but closer, lies Camden. Here on 16 January 1780, American troops under General Horatio Gates were crushed by the British and fled all the way to Virginia without halting. Though Gates had managed to appropriate much of the credit for Burgoyne's defeat at Saratoga, he proved unequal to the task of actual command. His debacle at Camden helped prolong the Revolutionary War for eighteen months.

Camp Scene of Marion's ("The Swamp Fox") Men

One hundred and fifty miles south lies the port of Charleston. It was here in December 1860 that the first secession convention was held and South Carolina became the first state to leave the Union. Here too the war began when General P.G.T. Beauregard opened his bombardment of Fort Sumter. Just to the north of the city lies Francis Marion National Forest named after the Revolutionary War hero who sallied forth from here to wreak havoc on British forces under Tarleton and others. For many bleak months the legendary "Swamp Fox" was the only man who kept the flame of liberty burning in the American South.

Just to the north of Florence lies the city of Darlington. Today it is one of the meccas of American stock car racing.

Florence's central position on the Northeastern Railroad running north and south, and the Wilmington and Manchester Railroad running east and west made it a natural site for a Confederate prison camp during the Civil War. Though never as large as Andersonville, it was built on the same pattern. Basically an open stockade, it left the captives vulnerable to inclement weather as well as dietary deficiencies and lack of sanitation. Because of its role as the site of a prison camp, the U.S. government designated Florence as a location for a national cemetery.

In late 1864 Florence became grossly overcrowded with captives transferred from Andersonville as the South abandoned that facility with the approach of Sherman. By February 1865, however, as that worthy pushed north from Savannah spreading fire and sword along the way, it became obvious there was no place left to hide the Union prisoners, and those who had survived the overcrowding (and myriad of other problems) at Florence were soon liberated.

Most of the 2,802 interred at Florence National Cemetery are Union soldiers who died in captivity and are unknowns. However, one person is identified. She became the only woman to die in a Confederate prison camp. Florena Budwin had joined the army to remain with her husband and they had been captured together. Not until her demise was her sex discovered by physicians.

Sections B and D of the six-acre cemetery are committed to the gravesites of all these unknown Union soldiers. The cemetery remains open at present and has received American veterans of every conflict since 1865, but is expected to be closed within a year or so.

BLACK HILLS NATIONAL CEMETERY

Sturgis, South Dakota

"Gold at the grass roots!" That was the cry when the precious metal was discovered in the Black Hills in 1874. Soon a cavalry column under George A. Custer entered the area to determine the actual quantity of this heralded find. The U.S. government knew that a prospective gold rush by fortune seekers would invariably lead to a war with the Sioux Indians, who regarded the area as a sacred ground.

Custer's report allayed no fears in Washington. Some insinuated he had looked at the area with a jaundiced eye in his glowing reports of the wealth to be found there. Be that as it may, the resulting gold rush was on. Thousands of miners poured into the area. Many did get rich. Many more were killed and scalped after tragic encounters with the Sioux. By the end of this chapter of American history, the yellow metal had spawned the largest and bloodiest Indian war of the northern plains. Custer would live to regret his part in it, though admittedly not for long. To this day some say the hoof-beats of Custer's horsemen can still be heard echoing in the Black Hills. Obviously the story is apocryphal, but as they say, if it ain't true, it oughta be!

In 1947, local Congressman Francis Case and area veterans organizations succeeded in gaining approval for the establishment of a national cemetery in the area. It was to be located on the South Dakota Military Reservation near historic old Fort Meade. The site was dedicated on 3 October 1948 as Fort Meade National Cemetery. But the name was changed the following year to Black Hills in order to avoid confusion with the active military installation at Fort Meade, Maryland.

The first interments had been made on 27 September 1948, and a total of seven remains had been committed prior to the opening ceremony. All were of World War II decedents. Since then, some five thousand American veterans of post-Civil War service have been laid to rest within the cemetery boundaries.

Among the most notable is Sgt. Charles Windolph, Troop H, Seventh U.S. Cavalry. On 25 June 1876, while serving under Captain Frederick Benteen at Custer's debacle along the Little Bighorn River, Windolph was awarded the Medal of Honor for courageous action in aiding wounded comrades. After his retirement from the army, he worked for a local mining company until his death in 1950 at the age of ninety-nine. By then he had seen the Civil War, Indian Wars,

Spanish-American War, and World Wars I and II pass into American history. Perhaps witnessing the unbelievable changes in his native land during his century of life brought his demise as much as anything--the world he had been a part of was gone forever.

Another man to be found here is Major General Richard C. Ellsworth. A 1935 graduate of West Point, he became one of the most decorated American fliers of World War II. While serving as commanding officer of Rapid City Air Force Base in 1953, he was killed in an airplane crash over Newfoundland. The base was renamed Ellsworth Air Force Base in his honor.

There are one hundred memorial markers at Black Hills, erected in honor of American servicemen whose final resting place was never determined. On 30 May 1967 an Avenue of Flags was dedicated here by veterans from Sturgis. It contains flags solicited from next of kin of those interred here.

Black Hills National Cemetery is a 106-acre parcel of land. At first glance it appears excessive for that part of the country, but the northern plains states have always provided a high percentage of American servicemen. Over the next few generations its size may prove none too large for area needs.

FORT MEADE NATIONAL CEMETERY

Fort Meade, South Dakota

Fort Meade National Cemetery and its attendant cavalry museum are perhaps the only examples extant of an old frontier post as it appeared during the height of American territorial expansion and the Indian wars which ensued. War Department records indicate that a temporary camp was established on 1 July 1878 near Bear Butte a few miles from what would become Sturgis, South Dakota. It was christened Camp Sturgis, in honor of a young lieutenant who had fallen with Custer at the Little Bighorn in 1876.

However, a permanent facility with an area of twelve square miles was soon built at Butte Creek and the temporary fort was abandoned. The new encampment was known as Camp Ruhlen before being renamed Fort Meade on 31 December 1878, in honor of General George C. Meade, victor of Gettysburg. However, young Sturgis was not forgotten. The town which sprang up a few miles away retained his name.

Long fabled in literary and cinematic efforts, the old cavalry mount "Comanche" was kept at Fort Meade for many years, and was long considered the only living thing to emerge from Custer's fall. This view, of course, ignores the fact that innumerable Indians managed to survive Little Big Horn, but, be that as it may, the old charger lived here in gilded splendor for many years. Finally taken to Fort Riley, Kansas, he was turned over to a taxidermist after his demise and can still be viewed in an area museum. By the time Fort Meade was established, most of the fighting against the Sioux was over. Thus, it is possible that a horse was the most famous individual to ever occupy a billet here.

Fort Meade also lays claim to being the first army garrison to adopt "The Star Spangled Banner." Colonel C.H. Carlton, assuming command in 1892, decreed that it be played at retreat and that all those in hearing range would remove their hats. The War Department soon issued instructions in a similar vein to all military posts. Carlton's choice was vindicated in March 1931 when President Herbert Hoover signed into law the establishment of the "Banner" as the national anthem.

The 1.6-acre national cemetery here is a virtual time-capsule of American pioneering days. The first interment occurred on 24 September 1878. A list supplied by the nearby V.A. Medical Center indicates that some two hundred adults and children lie here. Many are unknown--and were at the time. "Lucy, Child, Sioux Indian"; "Child of Civilian Refugee"--such epitaphs abound. But others are identified. Sgt. Albert Knaak, Eighth Cavalry, won the Medal of Honor in 1868 in Arizona for courage in various scouting expeditions against the Apaches. He was but one of ninety-one men of that regiment to receive the nation's highest honor for valor during the Indian wars. Also located here is a magnificent private marker over the grave of Pvt. Frank Weg, Seventh Cavalry. It is one of the most impressive markers to be found in any cemetery, and this gives rise to a nagging, unanswerable question. What made a cavalry soldier so important to his comrades that they erected such an elaborate and expensive stone? If Weg's is one of the fanciest stones, Fort Meade also contains one of the most unique. An obelisk in the same section of the burial ground commemorates two members of the Eighth Cavalry who died at Belle Fourche in mortal combat against a beverage containing wood alcohol. One assumes the survivors of the binge raised the monument in shamefaced gratitude for having escaped the same fate.

Fort Meade National Cemetery was officially closed in 1948 with the dedication of the nearby site at Black Hills, and it is administered by the cemetery director there. Though not nearly filled, this location can take a visitor back in time to the way the American West shall, perhaps fortunately, never be again.

V.A. Medical Center at Hot Springs, South Dakota
--*Photo courtesy Karl Borchert, Director of Engineering Services, acting for the V.A.*

HOT SPRINGS NATIONAL CEMETERY

Hot Springs, South Dakota

The northern plains of this continent have been described as a land of savage extremes. South Dakota is no exception, with temperatures ranging from 40 below in the winter to summer highs of 118. The state is sixteenth in size, yet only forty-fifth in population. However, it does enjoy one considerable economic advantage. It ranks first in the nation in the production of what once was referred to as a soft metal subjected to hard usage--gold.

Sitting at the southern extreme of the Black Hills, Hot Springs is located in the very heart of the gold fields. But it is also rich in American history, and the natives are experienced in panning the wealth available via tourism. Indeed, it is doubtful that more sightseeing attractions exist anywhere in the nation than within one hundred miles of this small community.

Approximately that distance to the north lies Custer National Forest, a reserve which is two and one-half million square acres. Nearby is the battlefield of Slim Buttes, an early encounter between cavalry and Sioux. The L-shaped park itself is sandwiched between two of the larger towns in northwestern South Dakota, one named Buffalo, the other, more formally, Bison.

Proceeding south down U.S. Highway 86 until just north of the Belle Fourche Reservoir, one will encounter a spot designated the geographical center of the United States. Only thirty miles further south lies the town of Spearfish, gateway to the Black Hills. It is in the vicinity of Spearfish that most of the more famous tourist attractions are to be found.

To the east at Sturgis is historic Fort Meade, previously discussed. Due south are the twin cities of Lead and Deadwood. The Homestake Mine in the former community has been in profitable operation for a century, annually producing more gold than any other site in the Western hemisphere. However, the rip-roaring boom town of Deadwood has received most of the publicity. In a saloon here on 2 August 1876, fabled gunslinging marshal Wild Bill Hickok was shot dead while playing cards by a cross-eyed, psychotic stablehand named Jack McCall. Today, the old lawman lies in Mt. Moriah Cemetery along with other picturesque frontier characters such as Preacher Smith and Calamity Jane.

One hundred miles east is the Badlands National Monument, famed for its prehistoric animal fossils and subtle, intriguing coloration. Due west of the Badlands, halfway down the length of the Black Hills, lies Mount Rushmore. The granite mountain is impressive by itself, but it is here that one Gutzon Borglum devoted his life to blasting detailed likenesses of Washington, Jefferson, Lincoln and Theodore Roosevelt from its face. The location is probably the most famous natural monument in North America.

Just to the north of Hot Springs is Wind Cave National Park, deriving its name from the curious air currents wafting in and out. Jewel Cave National Monument, also to the north of the city, is a remarkable system of subterranean chambers and galleries producing striking visual effects of kaleidoscopic color.

One hundred miles southeast is Pine Ridge Agency. Here, in 1890, the mighty Sioux made their last stand against the U.S. Army at Wounded Knee Creek, generally considered, though not in fact, the last battle of the Indian wars. The grave of Sitting Bull, whose death stimulated the final confrontation, lies beneath a monument at nearby Mobridge. Even as late as 1972, modern Sioux warriors have battled federal marshals while adamantly asserting their tribal rights.

Hot Springs possesses the largest natural indoor pool in the world. The warm mineral waters are known as Evans Plunge.

Appropriately enough, this small community on the outskirts of so much American history is home to a Department of Veterans Affairs Medical Center. Adjacent to the center lies small Hot Springs National Cemetery. Like most of those originally operated by the Veterans Administration, Hot Springs was restricted for many years to interments only of those servicemen who perished in government hospitals. However, all such limitations were lifted in wake of the National Cemetery Act of 1973. While precise data is unavailable, it appears most of those buried here are veterans of twentieth-century American conflicts. Unfortunately, exhaustion of gravesites has now forced the facility into an inactive status. Despite this, if for no other reason than its proximity to such a myriad of famous attractions and historical sites, Hot Springs must rank as one of the most strategically placed and interesting in the entire system.

The 8.65-acre site was officially closed in 1964, and holds about five thousand gravesites.

CHATTANOOGA NATIONAL CEMETERY

Chattanooga, Tennessee

The city of Chattanooga, situated on the Tennessee River just north of the Georgia border, became one of the principal battle grounds of the Civil War. As far as the Confederates were concerned, it was the key to holding Tennessee. And it was the most direct and logical route of advance on Atlanta for the Union forces.

The Union Army of the Cumberland had slowly fought its way southeast and occupied the city after the Battle of Stones River in 1863. Confederate forces under General Braxton Bragg evacuated it on 4 July 1862 and, despite determined efforts, were never able to eject the Yankee troops again.

However, with the fall of Vicksburg, the Confederate command could easily read Union intentions, and they realized it was now

General George H. Thomas, "The Rock of Chickamauga"
--*National Archives photo*

mandatory to protect Atlanta. On 19-20 September 1863 Bragg's army struck Union forces under General William S. Rosecrans just over the Georgia border at Chickamauga. The Confederates were generally successful and Rosecrans retreated back into Chattanooga--but Bragg was denied the needed victory by the strong stand of the Union corps under General George H. Thomas. Jackson became "Stonewall" after Bull Run, but Thomas made a stand even more important, gaining a nickname even more colorful--"The Rock of Chickamauga."

The still viable Union army fell back into Chattanooga and Bragg could do nothing but besiege it. After battles at Orchard Knob, Missionary Ridge and Lookout Mountain two months later, Grant relieved the city and Sherman soon began his devastating Atlanta Campaign. Chattanooga National Cemetery is a symbol of the sacrifice of the hundreds of men on both sides who came to lie here.

But even before the great Atlanta Campaign, considerable Civil War history was in the making here. Atop a large monument in Section H sits a bronze replica of a railroad locomotive called *The General*. It memorialized the assignment undertaken by Major James Andrews and a unit of Ohio volunteers in 1862. Penetrating deep into Southern lines, they commandeered the locomotive at Big Shanty (Marietta), Georgia one morning in April of that year. Fleeing north, they did their best to destroy bridges and overpasses to sever this vital Confederate supply link to Chattanooga. Immediately discovered, they were pursued by Confederates in the locomotive *Texas*. The "Great Locomotive Chase" ended eighty-seven miles later with Andrews and his Raiders being captured. He and seven others were hanged as spies. The rest of his band was later exchanged for Southern prisoners. These fifteen men were all awarded the Medal of Honor, the first Americans so decorated. Andrews and the others hanged with him rest here at Chattanooga.

Another monument located here was raised shortly after the Civil War by the members of the IV Union Army Corps in memory of their fallen comrades. One of the more unique monuments to be found anywhere in the National Cemetery System was erected here in 1935 by the German government in honor of seventy-eight Germans who died in American prison camps and were interred in this cemetery. Since then, an additional 108 German prisoners from World War II have joined them in the same section.

In addition to Andrews' Raiders, one other Medal of Honor recipient rests in this location. He is Sgt. Ray E. Duke, U.S.A., who gave his life protecting his comrades in Korea in April 1951.

The large Chattanooga National Cemetery presents one of the more fascinating layouts in the entire system. It is surrounded on three sides by railroad tracks, but its many, widely separated and interestingly shaped burial sections make it one of the most aesthetically pleasing in the nation. It remains open for future interments, and should remain so for many years.

FORT DONELSON NATIONAL MILITARY PARK

Dover, Tennessee

Established in 1928 by the Department of the Interior, the Fort Donelson national park, of which the national cemetery is a part, occupies some 544 acres of land on what is one of the most significant battlegrounds of the American Civil War. It was here in early 1862 that Union General Ulysses S. Grant began his campaign to penetrate the Southern cordon defenses by reducing two posts and opening the Cumberland and Tennessee Rivers.

The first step in this strategy began on 6 February 1862 when Grant, aided by riverine naval forces under Flag Officer Andrew H. Foote, besieged Fort Henry on the Tennessee. The structure was a modest-sized, low-lying firebase of but seventeen guns and it was easily captured after Foote's bombardment. Grant promptly moved overland on the more formidable fortifications of Fort Donelson on the Cumberland, ordering Foote's gunboats to backtrack and join him there.

On 14 February the gunboats were repulsed from the fort. This reverse convinced Grant that a wholly new type of river craft would be necessary for the capture of Vicksburg and so it turned out; soon much more heavily armored, slab-sided gunboats made their debut, and two dozen were finally constructed. Despite naval problems, the Union forces invested the site in a howling blizzard that sent temperatures plunging to near-zero.

Confederate commander, General John B. Floyd, now found himself surrounded by an enemy army outnumbering his, two to one. Calling a council of war at which he received an amazing variety of advice, he opted for an attempted breakout south and retirement eastward along the river. He struck on 15 February, but despite initial success, the vacillating Floyd allowed his troops to be thrown back and once again penned-up inside the fortress.

Having served as secretary of war to President Buchanan, Floyd evidently feared immediate execution as a traitor if the fort should fall. Therefore, he threw over command and fled with a few others toward Nashville. He succeeded in his flight, as did a number of other Confederate contingents. But when the position surrendered the following day, some sixteen thousand Southern soldiers were eliminated from the war effort either as casualties or captives.

The Henry-Donelson campaign brought Ulysses S. Grant to national prominence. His demands for unconditional surrender titillated the North and became a policy with him throughout the struggle. More importantly, this Union victory forced the Confederates out of most of Kentucky and much of Tennessee. The route was open down the Mississippi to Vicksburg, and the splitting of the Confederacy in two became just a matter of time.

Fort Donelson National Cemetery became the final resting place for those Union troops who perished in the campaign. In addition, reinterments were made after the war from battlefields throughout the northern and western part of the state. Since then the location has provided burial sites for American veterans of all this nation's later conflicts. The cemetery is open to interments, and should remain so into the next century.

ANDREW JOHNSON NATIONAL HISTORIC SITE

Greeneville, Tennessee

"His faith in the people never wavered." Those words are found inscribed on the monument over the grave of Andrew Johnson, the only American chief executive ever impeached. And perhaps they are a fitting epitaph for one of this nation's most controversial yet admirable presidents.

Johnson's life reflects his belief in democracy. His efforts on behalf of general education and homesteader rights made him the champion of the common man. His term in office classically illustrates that any man worthy of the charge can become president.

His success was a triumph over adversity. Born in Raleigh, North Carolina in 1808, his youth was marked by extreme poverty. After the death of his father, he took over the family support by becoming a tailor's apprentice; they moved to Greeneville in 1826 where he established himself in the trade. Within a few years he owned his own shop. Prosperity ensued.

In 1827 he and his bride were married by a justice of the peace who was a second cousin to one Abraham Lincoln. This family connection spawned what would become a strong, enduring political relationship between Lincoln and Johnson.

To remedy his lack of education, Johnson hired men to read to him as he worked. He also joined a debating society at Greeneville College, an act that made him an adept public speaker, and led to his election as mayor of the town in 1833. His political rise was rapid thereafter, and in 1857 he was sent to the U.S. Senate.

Though a Southerner and a temporary slave holder, he firmly believed in the Union. In December 1860, at the height of the secessionist controversy, he was one of the few Southerners who did not advocate separation for his state. "I intend to stand by the Constitution and insist on compliance with all its guarantees."

Johnson's stand against secession made him popular in the North. His actions led 13,010 "Andy Johnson Democrats" from his state to volunteer for the Union army. He was later appointed advisor to Lincoln for Southern affairs. Elected vice president in 1864, he assumed the highest office upon Lincoln's assassination.

Yet this simple, straightforward man of the people became one of America's most controversial figures. His firm adherence to Lincoln's policy of malice toward none led him to try to alleviate the Southern burdens during reconstruction. Naturally, this led to a struggle with the Radical Republicans who dominated Congress. The struggle between two such diverse and unyielding views could only end one way.

In 1867 he was impeached by the House after he removed Edwin M. Stanton as secretary of war. The trial was held in the spring of 1868 because of his violation of the Tenure of Office Act, a piece of legislation of questionable constitutionality anyway. The impeachment failed when it fell one vote short of the two-thirds needed. Senator Edmund Ross of Kansas, who cast it, and six other Republicans who voted with him, did so at the sacrifice of their political careers. But the cause of peace with justice had prevailed.

Johnson's administration also saw the purchase of Alaska and the stringent application of the Monroe Doctrine to force the French out of Mexico. Elected again to the Senate in 1875, he died within months.

The national cemetery, part of the Andrew Johnson Historic Complex in Greeneville, was opened in 1908. Comprising fifteen acres, it is the final resting place of Americans from every war since 1865. Johnson himself and many members of his family are also interred here. The site, administered by the Department of the Interior, remains open to receive veteran burials. Because of few burials, it is expected to remain open indefinitely.

KNOXVILLE NATIONAL CEMETERY

Knoxville, Tennessee

Located in the east-central part of the state, Knoxville became a major battleground of the Civil War, though ofttimes neglected by historians of that conflict. The Confederate counteroffensive of which it was a part was the last Southern hope of protecting Atlanta from the massive Union forces gathering to the north of Georgia.

Following the indecisive Battle of Stones River (Murfreesboro), Union General Ambrose E. Burnside, recently relieved of command of the Army of the Potomac, was ordered to proceed against Knoxville in March 1863. Contenting himself for months with harassing raids on the city, Burnside finally roused himself to action on 15 August. The small Confederate forces opposing him could offer little resistance and the town was occupied on 12 September. Sending detachments in support of Rosecrans' Chickamauga Campaign, Burnside captured the Cumberland Gap in an uncharacteristic burst of initiative.

However, by November, Rosecrans had not only been defeated at Chickamauga but was also besieged in Chattanooga by Braxton Bragg, himself showing unusual perspicacity and resolution in the field. As a subsidiary to his operations, Bragg sent a Confederate force north under General James Longstreet to link with troops from Virginia and attempt to regain Knoxville. Though numerous minor clashes occurred, Burnside managed to regain the safety of the town's breastworks without a decisive engagement. Lacking the means of pursuing a siege, Longstreet resolved on an attack.

Before ordering the assault, he had his plans checked by a Confederate engineer, one Daniel Leadbetter, a man of whom one disgruntled Confederate wrote, "... being the oldest engineer in the service he was also supposed to be the most efficient." Apparently the Peter Principle was at work here. Leadbetter approved the assault, which was promptly carried out and even more rapidly repulsed with heavy loss.

Following Bragg's failure at Chattanooga, a Union corps under Sherman relieved Knoxville on 5 December. However, Burnside failed to pursue the retiring Longstreet and this slight oversight forced Grant to maintain a large Union army in eastern Tennessee until the following spring.

Burnside was relieved of command at his own request, although it must be conceded that few of his colleagues tried to change his mind. For his part, Longstreet felt so strongly about the dissension among his subordinates, that he eventually leveled charges against three of them. However, the gentlemen in Richmond simply transferred these men to other locales. Thus, the Knoxville Campaign, was perhaps the only one of the Civil War in which absolutely everybody was absolutely dissatisfied with absolutely everything.

Knoxville National Cemetery was established in the days immediately following the cessation of hostilities. Like all facilities of its type in the South, it was designed to provide a final resting place for those Union war dead who fell in the major and minor engagements waged in the area. Hundreds of these were reinterred within the first few months of peace, most of them simply listed as unknown. As far as is known, no Confederate war dead were buried here, though service has been rendered subsequently to several hundred ex-Southern soldiers who died in later years.

Due to its small size, Knoxville has now been closed for some years. Along with the installation at Stones River National Battlefield, it is one of only two of the nine national cemeteries in Tennessee no longer offering gravesites for veteran committals. One known Medal of Honor winner lies here.

Memphis National Cemetery
The Monument to All Dead from the State of Minnesota
--photo courtesy of the author

MEMPHIS NATIONAL CEMETERY

Memphis, Tennessee

Memphis National Cemetery was originally established in 1867 and comprised thirty-three acres. It was chosen by a board of the U.S. Quartermaster Corps chaired by Chaplain William Earnshaw. At that time, it lay seven miles northeast of the city in what is now suburban Memphis.

Records indicate the initial choice of name was "Mississippi River National Cemetery." However, this name was abandoned with the development of many other national burial grounds along the banks of the "Father of Waters." But the name would have been appropriate, because the contest over the Mississippi River was one of the longest and fiercest in American history. And Union veterans were reinterred from locations as far away as Kentucky and Arkansas so that their remains might be laid to rest there.

Memphis fell to Union forces on 6 June 1862 following a river naval battle between Union gunboats and a Confederate mosquito fleet of "cottonclads." With the earlier capture of New Orleans by Admiral Farragut, it became obvious to the Confederates that the assault on both ends of the river was on in earnest. Playing a significant and effective role in this was the Union riverine force of gunboats and floating batteries which ranged up and down the river for months. Though the operations of this naval force are among the least known in American history, they are also among the most fascinating. Some two hundred members of this fleet lie buried here at Memphis.

In addition, the cemetery contains nearly nine thousand unknown Union soldiers, the second highest such concentration of any national cemetery. Only Andersonville National Cemetery betters it.

In April 1865 Memphis National Cemetery was inundated with the largest number of burials any such facility has ever had to sustain at one time. On the night of 26 April 1865 the S.S. *Sultana*, a paddlewheel steamboat, fell victim to a boiler explosion on the Mississippi just above Memphis. Drifting several miles back downstream before sinking, it left seventeen hundred repatriated Union prisoners on their way home dead from burns, scalding or drowning. Almost all of these men entered Memphis National Cemetery as unknowns.

Other exigencies of war brought numerous reinterments from local hospitals which became unknowns as their identities were lost in the shuffle. At one time, general hospitals in and around Memphis could simultaneously care for five thousand Union troops. Death rates from wounds and disease were naturally high, nineteenth-century medicine being what it was.

By 1870 nearly fourteen thousand Union veterans were buried here. This included members of no less than 537 separate regiments. Among the monuments raised here is one erected in 1916 by the state of Minnesota to honor its fallen warriors. It is topped by a bronze figure of a Union soldier, rifle reversed and head bowed in tribute to his less fortunate comrades. Another monument is that of a bronze and granite sarcophagus funded by the state of Illinois to the Union dead. Atop it lies the sculpted figure of a soldier lying in state. Its inscription reads in part: "Upon them therefore, a grateful state bestows its undying affection and the laurel of victory."

Today the cemetery has been expanded to 44.15 acres. As of 1985, over thirty thousand interments had been made, including veterans of all subsequent American wars. At present it remains open to receive eligible veterans, and is expected to be open until the end of the century.

Memphis National Cemetery
The Sarcophagus Dedicated to All Dead from the State of Illinois
--*photo courtesy of the author*

MOUNTAIN HOME NATIONAL CEMETERY

Johnson City, Tennessee

Set in the northeastern corner of the state, Johnson City is only a few miles up Highway 11E from Greeneville, site of the Andrew Johnson Memorial. It is an area rich in natural and human history.

Nearby is massive Cherokee National Forest. In this vicinity the proud Cherokee nation made its last, violent stand against the encroachments of European settlers during the American Revolution. At first their efforts rendered considerable service to the British war effort when they took up the hatchet in 1775. However, in 1776, American militia swept through the area, burning towns, farms and crops from Watauga near Boone Lake in the north to the verdant fastnesses of the Nolichucky River in the south. The Cherokees were forced to abandon their traditional homeland and flee west. But even this did not save them from eventual expulsion to Oklahoma during the nineteenth century.

Less than one hundred miles south of Johnson City, in westernmost North Carolina, lies 6,684 foot high Mount Mitchell, the highest point on the continent east of the Mississippi. To the west lies Morristown, host to the Davy Crockett Museum and set in the heart of the area which spawned the fabled, if coarse, American frontiersman.

In the fall of 1863, a number of sharp clashes occurred as part of the Knoxville Campaign of the Civil War. Though the Confederates were successful as often as not, by the time the smoke cleared at Blountsville, Blue Springs and Rogersville, any thoughts they had entertained of regaining control of the area had been soundly dismissed.

Near Greeneville, one of the great tragedies overtook the Southern cause. On 4 September 1864 famed and beloved cavalry raider General John H. Morgan was killed attempting to escape Union pursuers there.

Mountain Home was established in 1903 as a national asylum for disabled volunteer soldiers. It was the last of those set up according to the act of Congress which authorized them in the wake of the Civil War. It was the asylum's policy to use its attached cemetery strictly for those soldiers who died in the installation. However, all such restrictions have now been removed and all veterans are entitled to burial space since 1973.

The site contains a large monument in Brownlow Circle over the gravesite of Congressman Walter P. Brownlow and his wife. Brownlow was apparently one of those whose activities resulted in the establishment of the home, although records are incomplete about this.

Also interred here is a Union army veteran named George C. Maledon. A special U.S. marshal under Judge Isaac Parker in the Indian Territory, he served as hangman at that worthy's court in Fort Smith Arkansas for many years. If the unpopular and distasteful job bothered him, he never showed it. He dispatched sixty of the seventy-nine men hanged on Parker's orders, and aided the demise of several others who attempted to escape his noose. He lived at the home for many years and was buried there after his death in 1911 at the age of eighty-one.

Mountain Home National Cemetery comprises forty-two acres. Of these, about thirty have been developed for interments. As of 1 June 1980, 6,040 American veterans have found a final resting place here. The facility should remain open well into the twenty-first century.

NASHVILLE NATIONAL CEMETERY

Madison, Tennessee

Following the Union capture of Atlanta in the fall of 1864, what remained of local Confederate forces under General John B. Hood retired northward into eastern Tennessee. Hood apparently felt he could harry Sherman's lines of communications and force him to withdraw from the Georgia city. This plan was negated when the Union leader abandoned all such lines two months later to begin his legendary "March to the Sea." Despite this, Hood maintained himself in Tennessee, apparently with some nebulous plan of awaiting reinforcements from Texas, or merely hoping Sherman's Southern expedition would turn into a Union debacle.

Defeated on 30 November by troops under General John Schofield at Franklin, he continued to maneuver in a desultory way towards Nashville. Unfortunately, his force was now so small that his options for prosecuting the war effort were marginal.

And, upon reaching Nashville, he found himself opposed by famed Union commander George H. Thomas. Thomas had earned enduring glory as the "Rock of Chickamauga" and granite was indeed the major component of his being. Thus, when Hood accepted battle on 15-16 December 1864, Thomas drove him off easily. Though Union losses were considerably higher due to their constant posture of assault, no less than three Southern generals were captured with their units. The remnant of the once mighty Army of Tennessee straggled east to join General Joseph Johnston for his last stand in the Carolinas. It was the last battle of import west of the Blue Ridge Mountains.

Nashville National Cemetery, located in nearby Madison, was established in 1867. The location was chosen for its proximity to the Nashville battlefield and others. Franklin and Gallatin, Tennessee and Cave City and Bowling Green, Kentucky had been the site of sharp collisions between the two sides during the conflict.

The sixty-five-acre plot reached this size in 1879. Several thousand Union war dead were reinterred here in addition to three well-known Union leaders buried much later. These were Colonel Edward S. Jones, Third Pennsylvania Cavalry and later area founder of the Grand Army of the Republic; Colonel James W. Lawless, Fifth Kentucky Cavalry, an Irish immigrant who spent most of his life in the U.S. Army; and Chaplain Erastus Cravath, 101st Ohio Infantry, one of the founders of Fisk University in Nashville and its president for twenty-five years.

Two Medal of Honor winners also rest here. Pvt. Charles Cantrell received his award for valor in action in Cuba during the Spanish War. Cpl. William Lyell was posthumously decorated for heroism during the Korean War in 1951.

Nashville National Cemetery is laid out basically in two large loops on either side of the Nashville & Louisville Railroad. It has interment for over 24,000 American servicemen. This includes 4,141 unknowns, mostly Union casualties reinterred here shortly after the Civil War. Because of the cemetery's comparatively large size, gravesites will probably be available into the next century.

SHILOH NATIONAL MILITARY PARK

Shiloh, Tennessee

Ten miles south of Adamsville, Tennessee and twenty-three miles north of Corinth, Mississippi, lies Shiloh National Military Park and Cemetery. Administered by the Department of the Interior, it is the site of one of the most significant--and sanguinary--struggles of the Civil War.

Union forces under Ulysses S. Grant had shattered the Confederate cordon defenses along the Cumberland and Tennessee Rivers and moved south in a two-pronged effort aimed at Nashville and Memphis. The western force was composed of the forty-thousand-man Army of the Tennessee under Grant himself. In early April 1862, he paused at Pittsburgh Landing on the Tennessee River prior to driving on the main Confederate depot at Corinth. He was awaiting the arrival of the Army of the Ohio under General Don Carlos Buell which was to join him there.

Ulysses S. Grant

Confederate commander A.S. Johnston, having been forced to

abandon Kentucky and much of Tennessee because of Grant's offensive, resolved to be pushed back no farther without a trial of arms. He concentrated forty-four thousand men of the Army of the Mississippi at Corinth and moved north to attack Grant before Buell could arrive.

The Confederate army struck Grant's encampment on the morning of 6 April 1862, and one of the most doggedly contested and gallantly waged struggles of the Civil War was on. Though initially routed, many Union units rallied along the sunken road in front of the river and exacted such a fearful toll on the attackers that the name "Hornet's Nest" was applied to the position. In order to capture the road, the Confederates eventually massed sixty-two cannon, which until that time was the heaviest concentration seen on this continent. The Union units there were all but exterminated, but their sacrifice had bought Grant time to establish an impregnable defense line in front of Pittsburgh Landing.

Johnston's plan had been to launch a massive flank attack with his right wing that would tear the Union troops away from the river and allow them to be rolled up. It soon became obvious that just the reverse was happening. Frantic in his efforts to retrieve the plan, Johnston was killed leading attacks against the Union left. General P.G.T. Beauregard assumed command.

By late afternoon, Grant's forces were safe in their defense lines. Confederate attacks were repulsed time and again. Union gunboats on the river hurled enfilading fire into the Confederate lines to help stem the tide.

That night the vanguard of Buell's forces crossed the river. At dawn on 7 April, Grant launched a counterattack with fifty-five thousand men. The Confederates attempted to stand but were eventually driven from the field. They withdrew south of Shiloh Church and then began the dispirited march back to Corinth.

Shiloh has come to symbolize the cruel and divisive American civil struggle. When it was over, twenty-three thousand Americans had fallen in the bitter woods along the Tennessee River. But more importantly, for the first time a Confederate army had been beaten in open battle. And Abraham Lincoln had found a general who knew how to fight--and win.

Shiloh National Cemetery, part of the national park, was opened in 1866, as were most Civil War sites. Though technically still open, it no longer receives interments. Most of the nearly ten thousand dead buried there are unknown Union and Confederate soldiers reinterred from temporary burial trenches after the war. The eleven-acre site is easily accessible to tourists from many different directions.

STONES RIVER NATIONAL BATTLEFIELD

Murfreesboro, Tennessee

The national park at Stones River is located twenty-seven miles south of Nashville and it lies in what is today the northwest corner of Murfreesboro. Here, in late 1862, occurred one of the most costly and least-known struggles of the American Civil War.

By the latter part of 1862, following Union occupation of Nashville, it became obvious that central Tennessee would be a major battleground in the Civil War. With Grant's campaign pressing down on Vicksburg, it was mandatory that the Confederacy prevent a further splitting of the South by Union forces poised to strike at Chattanooga and Atlanta.

On 26 December 1862, Union General William S. Rosecrans moved out of Nashville with forty-five thousand men, intending to sweep aside the Confederate Army of Tennessee under General Braxton Bragg and capture Chattanooga. Four days later, along the banks of this small backwater of the Cumberland River, the two sides collided.

At dawn on 31 December the Confederates attacked, attempting to turn the Union right flank. The night before, both sides had steadied their resolve with popular songs. But there was no singing now, just the horrid roar of battle. At one point, the din became so great that Confederate soldiers are said to have paused in their onslaught to stuff their ears with cotton.

By mid-morning the Union lines had been driven back almost to the Nashville Pike. But there the Northerners held, following "Old Rosy's" directive to "contest every inch of ground." Troops under Generals Philip Sheridan and George Thomas beat off the last Southern thrusts in hand-to-hand combat.

There were no concerts that night, and it was a dreary New Year's Day for the two armies as they faced each other the next morning. Bragg, perplexed to find the tenacious Rosecrans had not retreated, launched another assault on 2 January. It scored initial success but was eventually repulsed. In the end, it was the Confederates who withdrew.

Both sides claimed victory, but without much conviction. Over twenty-three thousand Americans had fallen in the battle, staggering losses for both sides. The loss of the farming belt of middle Tennessee was a body blow to the Confederates.

Rosecrans turned Murfreesboro into a bastion. He constructed

Fortress Rosecrans nearby, the largest earthwork fortification of the Civil War. From this bastion, Union troops succeeded in capturing Chattanooga and Atlanta. The Confederate failure at Stones River was the beginning of the end. For the Army of Tennessee, one of the South's most successful and resilient forces, the end was nigh.

Stones River National Cemetery was established in 1865. All Union dead from the battlefield were relocated here. Of the 6,100 total, 2,572 were unidentifiable. No Southern soldiers lie here. They were taken to the nearest Southern community or simply covered in unmarked mass graves. Thousands of these slain are buried in the park ground, but exact locales are long since lost.

Just to the south of the cemetery is McFadden's Lane. The fighting here marked what might best be termed the Confederate high tide. Breastworks thrown up by Bragg's men may still be viewed by tourists today. Also nearby is the monument erected by the survivors of Colonel William Hazen's brigade to their fallen Union comrades. The short, truncated monument rests above the graves of fifty-six Northern enlisted men who died on that bloody field. It is also the nation's oldest monument of Civil War vintage.

Since that time, Stones River National Cemetery has served as final resting place for American veterans through the Vietnam war. The only monument in the cemetery itself is the Cumberland Monument, erected by the survivors of Colonel O.L. Shepherd's brigade to their comrades. As of 1980, 6,931 burials had been made here. However, with the expansion of the National Cemetery System under the Veterans Administration, the site was closed to future interments even though space remained available.

FORT BLISS NATIONAL CEMETERY

Fort Bliss, Texas

Fort Bliss National Cemetery was established in 1939 and it is the only location of its type providing service to veterans in western Texas as well as large areas of Arizona and New Mexico. Prior to the opening of Houston National Cemetery in 1965, it was one of only two available sites in the state.

In June 1936 Congress directed that the cemetery be established on the most suitable land on the reservation. Its first superintendent was Mr. Elmer Swanton. The first interment occurred on 7 March 1940 when the remains of Sgt. James Featherstone, U.S.A., were committed. Music for the occasion war provided by the band of the famed Seventh Cavalry.

Since 1848 this strategic post has been in existence in the vicinity of El Paso, Texas. However, the name "Fort Bliss" was not bestowed until 1854 in honor of Colonel William V.S. Bliss who had died the previous year.

Bliss was born in New York in 1815 and graduated from the Military Academy in 1833. He saw service in various Indian wars and later returned to teach mathematics at West Point. He saw additional service as chief of staff to General Zachary Taylor, with whom he served throughout the Mexican War, and in which he was decorated for meritorious service at the Battles of Palo Alto and Resaca de la Palma. In 1848 he married Elizabeth Taylor, daughter of "Old Rough and Ready," and later served as private secretary to that worthy during his brief presidency. Following the demise of his father-in-law, he was reassigned as adjutant general to the army's Western Command. He died of yellow fever in Pascagoula, Mississippi on 5 August 1853. His remains were originally interred in a private cemetery in New Orleans, his gravesite marked by a $10,000 white marble column.

By 1950, removal of the Bliss monument and remains had become critical. The old cemetery wherein he lay had become disused and virtually abandoned. In 1955 the land was condemned by New Orleans. Therefore, in 1955, U.S. Army personnel removed the colonel to a triangular piece of ground in Fort Bliss National Cemetery along the main entrance driveway. His costly monument was renovated and now stands in a different part of the cemetery, designed to serve as a monument to the reservation and cemetery itself.

Among the others buried here is General William Glasgow, who at the time of his death at the age of 101 in 1967, was the longest-living graduate of West Point. General T.V. Stayton, who served with distinction in World War II and Korea, and later as commanding general of Fort Bliss, also rests here. Sgt. Ambrosio Guillen, USMC, killed in action in Korea on 25 July 1953, is the one Medal of Honor recipient known to be interred here.

Both allies and enemies have found their final home in the old post section of the cemetery. During World War II, the air cadets of the government of China received their training at this reservation and the remains of fifty-five of them will stay forever. In addition, one will find the burial places of forty-four Axis prisoners of World War II. Each year the government of West Germany conducts memorial services for its fallen soldiers.

As of 31 December 1968 the cemetery comprised sixty acres. However, it appeared that thirty additional acres would be assigned by the army to make certain that interment space was available through the year 2030, though this has been held in abeyance because the site gets limited usage due to geography. At present 8,222 committals have been carried out, including numerous unknowns.

FORT SAM HOUSTON NATIONAL CEMETERY

San Antonio, Texas

San Antonio was one of the earliest American settlements in Texas. Set in the south-central part of the state in what Sam Houston described as a "howling solitude," it gradually became one of the premier cattle-and-oil-producing areas of the nation.

Texas Ranger

Located 150 miles west of Houston, Fort Sam Houston is a relative newcomer to the area, only rising to major status with the advent of World War II. It is the heir of innumerable U.S. posts and forts in Texas established almost 150 years earlier. Today it serves as the major training facility for army medical and support personnel.

Directly to the south of "San Antone" lies the town of Brownsville, one of the chief trading ports of the Confederacy from 1861 to 1865. It was an easy task to ship cotton and other commodities across the Rio Grande to the Mexican town of Matamoros, thereby side-stepping the crippling Union blockade. And it was near here at Palmito Ranch that the last conflict of the Civil War took place nearly a month after Lee's surrender at Appomattox. One hundred miles southwest of San Antonio lies the border town of Eagle Pass. It too was a major smuggling area, and through it passed thousands of expatriate Confederates and their families fleeing their homes to Mexico after the Southern collapse.

The original post cemetery at Fort Sam Houston was set aside in 1926. On 1 July 1930 it was expanded into a national location. It currently consists of 107 acres. However, at present, only 75 of these have been developed, with the remainder held in reserve.

The current number of interments is over fifteen thousand. Six Medal of Honor winners rest here. They are Col. C.H. Bolton, U.S.A.; Sgt. W. E. Harrell, USMC; Lt. L.H. Hughes, USAF; Col. S. L. Weld, U.S.A.; Pfc. M.A. Lee, U.S.A.; and Lt. J.P. Robinson, U.S.A. Most of these men were decorated for valor in World War II.

Also interred here is one Raymond Gardner. Long known as "Arizona Bill," Gardner served for years as an Indian scout in the American Southwest. He was one of those whose dogged persistence led to the final defeat of the last heroic (if futile) resistance of the Apaches under Geronimo and others. Reputedly, Gardner was an associate of Tom Horn, Indian scout cum lawman and hired assassin, during the controversial and tragic Horn's more admirable days.

Because of the myriad of Axis prisoner of war camps in Texas during World War II, many such prisoners also lie in the Fort Sam Houston National Cemetery. No less than 104 of them, including a Japanese, can be identified here.

The cemetery will remain open for the foreseeable future. Supervision of nearby San Antonio National Cemetery is also entrusted to the staff of this location.

HOUSTON NATIONAL CEMETERY

Houston, Texas

Houston National Cemetery is another of those locales which reflects the shifting demographics of the modern United States. It was primarily developed to serve the needs of the huge veteran population to be found in southern and eastern Texas. The largest concentration in the United States is found here--not, oddly, California or Florida, as might be thought.

On 2 May 1963 the Veterans Administration purchased a 420-acre tract of land in Harris County about fifteen miles north of downtown Houston. The two-million-dollar project was completed and the cemetery opened on 7 December 1965. However, only 50 acres are presently open for interments, with four miles of circular roadways offering easy access to all gravesites. The remaining land will be developed as needed.

The most noteworthy feature of the location is a large hemicycle. Including a chapel with a seventy-five-foot bell tower, the structure comprises two sweeping arcs which enclose an amphitheater. Some three thousand participants can gather here for memorial services. The chapel contains one of the largest carillons in existence, containing 330 bells of Flemish, Italian and English manufacture. The chapel's power is such that the bells could be heard for several miles, but amplification is adjusted to confine the sound to the cemetery area. The carillon cost $55,000 and was presented to the national cemetery by members of various local veterans groups on Memorial Day, 1970.

A portion of the site has been designated a Medal of Honor Section. Two men rest here at present. They are S. Sgt. Marcario Garcia and Captain James H. Fields, both of whom were decorated for valor during World War II. Their graves are marked by granite monuments inscribed with replicas of the medal.

The first interment in Houston National Cemetery was that of J.F. Evans, a decorated veteran of World War II campaigns in New Guinea and the Philippines. His committal occurred on 9 November 1965. Perhaps the best-known veteran here is Albert Thomas, a U.S. Army veteran of World War I, who was a Texas congressman for thirty years. He deserves much credit for the eventual establishment of this national cemetery. He was buried here just a year after its opening.

At this time, fourteen thousand veterans and their dependents have been interred here. Increasing numbers are expected as large numbers of American veterans discover the proximity and availability of the location. A former cemetery director, Mr. William Spivey, was a Pacific veteran of World War II who spent thirty years in government service.

KERRVILLE NATIONAL CEMETERY

Kerrville, Texas

The community of Kerrville lies in south-central Texas about fifty miles north of San Antonio, between the Llano and Guadalupe Rivers. Nearby tourist attractions include Century Caverns to the east and Frio Canyon to the west. Medina Lake to the south is a water-sports area.

Numerous old army posts from the days of the Texas frontier are located in the general vicinity. One of these, and the closest, is Fort Martin Scott, named to commemorate a fallen American of the Mexican War of 1846 to 1848. It served as a forage depot for the U.S. Army for many years, but was abandoned with the outbreak of Civil War and never reoccupied.

Kerrville National Cemetery is an adjunct of the V.A. Medical Center located on Road Spur 100 about three miles from the town. The cemetery was opened in 1923, apparently while the medical facility was administered by the state of Texas or other organization. After the Veterans Administration was established in 1930, it supervised the cemetery.

The cemetery comprises 1.7 acres of land in which 460 American veterans have found their final resting place. No interments have been made since its closing in 1957. The cemetery is maintained by the engineering branch of the adjacent hospital.

SAN ANTONIO NATIONAL CEMETERY

San Antonio, Texas

It was called San Antonio de Bejar and it is one of the cities most associated with the advancement of the American frontier. Still surrounded by palm trees and banana plants, the town appears in many ways not to have changed since its founding in the early eighteenth century by Mexican settlers. It has been referred to as "an amalgam of ox-cart and intercontinental missile" in tourist brochures and commercial publications such as *National Geographic*, and the appellation is indeed appropriate.

In addition, few areas are richer in colorful American history. Any survey of the region's past must begin with the Alamo. Here, for thirteen immortal days during the struggle for Texas independence in the winter of 1836, William Travis, Davey Crockett, Jim Bowie and 187 other gallant (if reckless) plainsmen reduced one of the finest armies Mexico ever fielded to a veritable shambles. But the Mexican army's overwhelming numbers brought the extermination of the Americans to the last man. At the time, Alamo Mission was a mile out of town. Today it is virtually in the midst of the downtown area. This has rendered the sense of perspective at the site suspect, but not the sense of history.

Leading away from the Alamo vicinity is the Paseo del Rio. Here in the middle of Texas is a lengthy promenade lined with old-time shops and lush, tropical greenery. Directly behind today's city hall lies Old Military Plaza, containing the residence of the Spanish governors. A brooding statue of Moses Austin, the man whose efforts led to American colonization of the area, towers nearby. In the governor's palace one will find things just as they were in bygone days when Spanish bureaucrats staged fantastically colorful parties and balls in an almost frenetic attempt to stave off the surrounding wilderness.

Virtually next door is La Villeta where one can step across the threshold of time into nineteenth-century Spanish Texas as Travis and his men knew it. Here in the shadow of oilmen's skyscrapers, a one-block area of the old city has been religiously maintained in situ. Many of those early skills such as pottery-making and glassblowing are still on display.

On the southeast outskirts of the city one will find another manifestation of Spanish Empire. Old San Jose Mission is one of the first built in the continental United States and is today designated a national historic site.

But San Antonio is as much a part of modern society as it is of the past. It is surrounded by major American military bases and has become a retirement haven for vast numbers of veterans. The small San Antonio National Cemetery at 517 Paso Hondo Street is a reflection of the area's contribution to national defense. However, due to lack of space, it has been closed for many years and has been supplanted by the larger burial facility at Fort Sam Houston a few miles away. The staff of the latter site now administers the San Antonio locale as well. However, a walk through the grounds of this site, containing some of the oldest markers in the National Cemetery System, is an experience the visitor with a sense of tradition may find as valuable as a tour through the better-known and more flamboyant locations.

ALEXANDRIA NATIONAL CEMETERY

Alexandria, Virginia

Alexandria National Cemetery, Battleground National Cemetery in Washington, D.C., and Arlington National Cemetery were established with the same stroke of Edwin M. Stanton's pen in 1864. For much of the Civil War, the vicinity was a major staging area for the Army of the Potomac. Supply centers, tent encampments and training fields extended for miles in all directions. Naturally, many of the soldiers stationed here came to grief through disease or other unrelated causes.

As a capacity house watched a performance of *Our American Cousin* in Ford's Theater in Washington on the evening of 14 April 1865, shortly after ten o'clock the rear door to President Lincoln's box was silently opened. A twenty-seven-year-old actor named John Wilkes Booth stole in.

The son of English tragedian Junius Brutus Booth, this volatile, young Southern sympathizer had long chafed under the opinion that he was inferior to his father and his brother as a thespian. Having joined the Virginia militia regiment that helped end the John Brown incident at Harpers Ferry in 1859, he was no stranger to intrigue. With the war going badly for the South, he had spent the last six months of it plotting various means of kidnapping or killing Abraham Lincoln.

Now he had his opportunity to avenge the lost cause. After firing the bullet that killed the president, he leaped from the stage in a properly dramatic gesture and broke his leg. Maintaining his stage presence long enough to bellow "Sic semper tyrannus," he fled backstage and vanished with a fellow conspirator. He was finally hunted down in a barn near Bowling Green, Virginia on 26 April and shot to death. But he had kept his vow of becoming the most immortal actor in the history of the American stage!

Thousands of Union troops had joined the manhunt for the fugitive assassin. At the time, northern Virginia was filled with Confederate diehards, deserters and just plain renegades. It was inevitable that clashes would occur. Before Booth died, no less than four Union troops died in various actions. All of these men found their final resting place at Alexandria National Cemetery.

In addition, some 125 unknown Union soldiers from locations throughout Virginia were reinterred here after the war. Most of those buried in this four-acre site were either Union war dead or veterans of

Mr. Lincoln's army who died in the ensuing years. Though evidence is scant, the cemetery may have provided space for the committal of veterans of subsequent American conflicts as well.

As of 1980, Alexandria National Cemetery is closed to future activity and no expansion is projected. It is administered by the cemetery director of the facility at Winchester, Virginia.

BALLS BLUFF NATIONAL CEMETERY

Leesburg, Virginia

In addition to being one of the earliest and greatest of Union fiascoes, the Battle of Balls Bluff irreparably damaged the career of a man now regarded as a fine American soldier. On 21 October 1861, Colonel Edward D. Baker, a former congressman and personal friend of President Lincoln, was authorized to make a reconnaissance in force across the Potomac River fords near Leesburg. In a magnificent display of ineptitude, Baker managed to get his command ambushed by Confederate forces under garrulous leader Nathan "Shanks" Evans. Before it was over, 921 Union soldiers had been killed, wounded or captured while Southern losses were but 150 men. Baker himself fell in the battle, but he was not the most famous casualty of the struggle.

That honor goes to Charles P. Stone, the Union general who was tactically responsible for the operation. An 1845 graduate of the U.S. Military Academy, Stone had enjoyed an illustrious career in the Corps of Engineers that included teaching at the academy and service in the Mexican War. But it was the debacle along the Potomac which brought him fame.

Arrested three months after the battle, he was confined without trial or charges for 189 days. Rumors of treason were rife but no evidence was ever advanced and no reason for his detention was ever offered. Finally released in August 1862, he went on to give excellent service during the conflict. Despite the recommendations of such leaders as Hooker and Grant that he be assigned responsible duties, he was kept under constant surveillance by Union agents and remained in menial tasks throughout the war.

He eventually gave up all hope of achieving any significant status and resigned from the army in September 1864. He later entered the service of the Khedive of Egypt in the 1870s and returned home in 1883 in time to put his engineering background to work as project chief on the foundation for the Statue of Liberty. He died in 1887, still the center of one of the most mysterious affairs in Civil War history.

Baker's blunder was not the final military action in the vicinity of Leesburg. The Army of Northern Virginia crossed the Potomac at White's Ford just a few miles north during Lee's first northern invasion. To the strains of "Maryland, My Maryland" they marched on through Frederick and other towns towards their rendezvous with destiny at Antietam.

Balls Bluff National Cemetery was officially established in 1865. Only a fraction of an acre in size, it is the smallest facility of its type on the North American continent. It was basically used to provide burial space for unknown Union soldiers whose bodies were discovered in the area around Leesburg after the cessation of hostilities. There are only fifty-four Union remains in the cemetery; sadly, all but one are unknown. In later years, a former Union army captain often visited the site to ponder the fates which had spared him, though grievously wounded, and claimed so many of his comrades. However, at his own death in 1935, Oliver Wendell Holmes did find his final resting place in a national cemetery--Arlington.

Balls Bluff National Cemetery is closed to future interments. In fact, none were made after the initial efforts in 1865. The cemetery is under the administration of the cemetery director of the national cemetery at Winchester, Virginia.

CITY POINT NATIONAL CEMETERY

Hopewell, Virginia

The existence of a military burial grounds at this location reflects the stalemate incurred by General Grant in his attempts to conquer the Southern capital from 1864 to 1865. Once halted in his efforts to turn Lee's flank and fall on Richmond, he crossed the James River, secured supply lines from the Yorktown Peninsula, and entrenched before Petersburg. Petersburg was a major logistical point and key railroad terminus on the Petersburg and Lynchburg Railroad running to the north. Constant probes, raids and trench assaults produced a steady supply of casualties on both sides.

More importantly, City Point became the major support depot for the receipt of men and material for Grant's proposed advance on Richmond in the spring of 1865. For many months that winter, City Point and its small neighbor, Harrison's Landing, were among the busiest locales in the United States. Few areas of their size on earth have ever seen such a passage of thousands of men and hundreds of thousands of tons of supplies in such a short time. Period photographs show endless trains of mule-drawn wagons queuing to receive the mountains of equipment and material awaiting them. Finally, the army literally built its own railroad to the front lines.

But from June 1864 to April 1865, desperate and determined resistance by Lee's troops held Grant at bay and came to symbolize the brutal civil struggle. And it was not always trench warfare. Numerous Union cavalry raids to destroy sections of track near Richmond were repulsed. A Confederate attack near the Union base at Bermuda Hundred in September 1864 became known as the Hampton-Rosser Cattle Raid. Routing Pennsylvania and District of Columbia cavalry units, the rebels managed to abscond with twenty-five hundred head of beef for Lee's starving soldiers. Behind them they left over four hundred Union casualties after a brief battle. Union attempts under Butler and others to capture Richmond from north of the James River led to a series of Union defeats such as that at Drewry's Bluff.

A huge Union hospital was constructed at City Point. The death toll from wounds and their concomitant infections was high. Disease also exacted a considerable toll. Most of these casualties were immediately buried at the cemetery located there. After cessation of hostilities, the hospital burial grounds became part of the expanded City Point National Cemetery authorized in 1866 on the banks of the

Appomattox River. Today it lies within the city limits of Hopewell.

The seven-acre cemetery contains 5,561 graves. Among these are many recovered from Chesterfield County, Charles City and around Bermuda Hundred as well as other areas of conflict. Though authorized in 1866, the land was not actually purchased by the government until 1872.

City Point National Cemetery differs from most of the others in the Richmond Complex in two distinct ways. The number of identified dead vastly exceeds those unknown. Only fifteen hundred unknowns rest there. Also, City Point contains a large number of Confederate dead, at least 118 of which are known for certain.

The fighting was of such scope that interments have continued to the present time. In 1955 some seventeen remains were excavated from a vacant lot in Hopewell, apparently the site of an abandoned cemetery. In 1959 two Union bodies were discovered during construction of I-95 north of the city. These were the last interments in City Point.

In the cemetery stands a marble spire twenty feet high. It was erected in 1865 by direction of General B.F. Butler, former commander of the Army of the James, as a monument to all those who fell under his command from April 1864 to January 1865.

This cemetery now is administered by the Richmond National Cemetery Complex, and is closed to future interments.

COLD HARBOR NATIONAL CEMETERY

Mechanicsville, Virginia

Located on Virginia State Highway 156 about nine miles east of Richmond, Cold Harbor is primarily a battlefield site. The small size of the cemetery gives little indication of the ferocity of the struggles waged here on two separate occasions. A large part of two Union campaigns in the Civil War was waged here, both designed to capture Richmond.

The first of these, McClellan's Peninsula Campaign of 1862, collapsed as a result of the Seven Days Battles that summer. The fighting at Gaines Hill, just outside Cold Harbor, on 26 and 27 June was one of the sharpest and costliest struggles. Both sides inflicted heavy losses on the other, but it was McClellan who retreated. Peace descended on the area for two years.

In early spring 1864, a huge Union army under Grant plunged into the Virginia wilderness, seeking to destroy Lee's forces and capture Richmond. Constantly striving to outflank the Confederate right wing, Grant was repulsed again and again. On 3 June he was brought up short in front of Lee's heavily entrenched positions at Cold Harbor. Fearful Lee might escape his clutches if he delayed, Grant ordered a sanguinary and ill-advised assault. He was defeated as both sides again suffered greatly. In valiant but pointless charges against the Confederate center, Union forces under General Meade lost seven thousand men in one short hour.

Lee was able to establish his defenses around Richmond, and trench warfare ensued. It was another ten months before the Southern cause was extinguished. However, as Douglas Southall Freeman, Lee's greatest biographer, observed, "Lee had won his last great battle in the field."

Today, within the two-acre national cemetery, row after row of headstones provide poignant reminder to the struggle here. But nothing can truly memorialize the intrepidity displayed by both sides. Nearly 2,000 interments were made here, 1,313 of which were unknowns. Most identifiable dead were removed from the battlefield and several thousand rest at Arlington.

With the establishment of Cold Harbor National Cemetery in 1866, an intensive search over twenty-two square miles of terrain located the initial graves of many who fell in action but could not be evacuated for various reasons. But hasty and inadequate burials made the later work of registering these graves all but impossible. It was beyond the capability of the registration parties to identify most of these men. Because of this, an inordinately high percentage of those brought to Cold Harbor are known but to God.

In 1877 a large marble sarcophagus was erected at the cemetery by the U.S. government in memory of those unknowns who perished in the Peninsula Campaign at Mechanicsville, Gaines Mill and Savage Station. However, the later collision at Cold Harbor provides most of the commemorative artifacts. A tall granite statue bearing a soldier at parade rest was erected by the state of Pennsylvania in 1909 to immortalize all those who fell in operations in the Cold Harbor vicinity between 12 May and 15 June 1864. Another monument, supplied in 1909 by the New York Monuments Commission, commemorates the 219 men of the Eighth New York Artillery who died in the Battle of Cold Harbor.

Cold Harbor National Cemetery is a part of and administered by the Richmond National Cemetery Complex.

CULPEPER NATIONAL CEMETERY

Culpeper, Virginia

Culpeper National Cemetery lies in north-central Virginia in an area where much of the Civil War raged for several years.

Just to the north lies Manassas, Virginia, site of the first major confrontation of that long struggle--Bull Run. And, following the reversals of Union fortunes in the Peninsula Campaign of 1862, Union forces under General Pope were driven from this area a second time by Robert E. Lee. In August 1862 there were a number of sharp clashes in the area at Cedar Mountain, Chantilly and Second Manassas, as Lee broke through Union opposition and launched his first invasion of the North, a campaign which was to end on the reddened banks of Antietam Creek only three weeks later. In June 1863, one of the few purely cavalry battles of the war occurred as J.E.B. Stuart's horsemen screened Lee's final and most portentous invasion of Union soil, an invasion that ended three weeks later at a Pennsylvania farming community called Gettysburg. Later, the Army of the Potomac encamped at the site of Brandy Station during the winter of 1863 to 1864. Numerous skirmishes developed along the Rappahannock and Rapidan Rivers.

Union casualties from all these battles rest in Culpeper National Cemetery, officially established in 1867. Reinterments began at once, but as usual in Civil War graves registration, identification was doubtful. As of 1869 1,327 Union decedents had been reinterred here but 880 were unknown. Among those who are known are Lt. Col. Virgil Broderick, First New Jersey Cavalry, and Lt. Isaac M. Ward, Sixth U.S. Cavalry, both of whom fell 9 June 1863 at the Battle of Brandy Station.

Culpeper National Cemetery has since provided burial space for American veterans of all later wars. However, its initial size of only 5.7 acres limited interment space, and it was closed in November 1972. Fortunately, local veterans groups came to the rescue and donated an additional 11.2 acres of land adjacent to the original locale. As of January 1978 Culpeper was once again able to provide for the care of American veterans in need of a final resting place.

There are no less than five monuments within the confines of the original location--all raised by Union veterans groups in memory of their fallen comrades. These include edifices donated by the Second Massachusetts Infantry, Twenty-eighth New York Regimental Association, State of Pennsylvania, Tenth Maine Infantry and Ohio Regimental Association.

At its present size of seventeen acres, Culpeper National Cemetery should remain open until about the year 2000, at which time its thirteen thousand gravesites should be claimed.

DANVILLE NATIONAL CEMETERY

Danville, Virginia

Located in south-central Virginia, just north of the North Carolina border, Danville, Virginia is one of those cities which remains as much a citadel of Southern hospitality and culture as in pre-Civil War days. It was and is a central terminus on the Richmond and Danville Railroad and lies but fifty miles south of the site of Lee's final surrender at Appomattox.

But Danville is equally close to the location of the South's final capitulation of the war. This occurred south of Danville and, contrary to common belief, it was not the surrender of Robert E. Lee. Confederate General Joseph S. Johnston, the man Lee had replaced prior to the Peninsula Campaign of 1862, had been charged with the defense of the Carolinas against the Union forces under Sherman advancing from the south. But the Union army opposing him was too strong for serious resistance. Riding the crest of his victorious march through Georgia, Sherman brushed aside Johnston's forces at every turn.

Not until the remnant of the old Army of Tennessee joined him at Smithfield on the Carolina Railroad in February 1865 did Johnston feel he had the material and manpower for a final stand. This occurred at Bentonville from 19-21 March, but it too ended in another defeat for the failing Confederate cause.

Learning of Lee's surrender, Johnston asked for and received an armistice from Sherman, who then accepted the formal surrender of the last active Confederate field army on 26 April 1865 at Bennett's House near Hillsboro, North Carolina. Thus, Danville lies almost equidistant between the sites of the final two capitulations which forever ended hopes of Southern independence.

Because of its railroad location, Danville had served throughout the struggle as a marshaling area for supplies and troops on their way to the Army of Northern Virginia. It also made a perfect site for a Confederate prison camp.

Danville National Cemetery contains the remains of 1,171 known Union prisoners and 143 unknown. All perished in captivity while being held in the ramshackle tobacco warehouses of the area. Most died in late 1864 or early 1865 when the Confederate food and medical situation became desperate. Only four other Union war dead lie here. All were members of the VI Corps killed in skirmishes shortly before Johnston's surrender.

The 3.5-acre cemetery was closed to future interments as of 23 October 1970 due to lack of space. At that time, 2,215 American veterans had been buried there, including a number from the Vietnam conflict. Two memorial plaques are in the facility, one an upright bronze cannon near the entrance and the other containing the words of Lincoln's Gettysburg Address.

FORT HARRISON NATIONAL CEMETERY

Richmond, Virginia

Situated on the Varina Road about eight miles southeast of Richmond is another of the small cemeteries which came into being due to the protracted struggle around the Confederate capital. In this cemetery lie numerous Union soldiers who perished in 1864 and 1865 in Grant's relentless drive for final victory.

The siege operations around Petersburg demanded the bulk of attention from Grant and the Union army. However, the campaigns in and around Fort Harrison were a manifestation of Union efforts to reach Richmond through the side door north of the James River. Forts Harrison and Gilmer were fortified positions on the outer defense cordon of the capital, south of Darbytown and the nearly impassable White Oak Swamp. A heavy Union assault captured Fort Harrison on the morning of 29 September 1864, but attacks against Fort Gilmer to the north were repulsed with considerable bloodshed. Stiff counterattacks by Lee failed to retake Fort Harrison, but did halt any Union plans to exploit their limited advantage. It was many weeks before Fort Gilmer had to be abandoned by the Confederates.

In April 1865 the position was temporarily renamed Fort Burnham, in honor of Union General Hiram Burnham, killed at Chapin's Farm in operations around the area.

Among those Union casualties who rest here are many who fell in other areas of battle. On 13 August 1864, acting on erroneous information that Lee's defenses at Deep Bottom Run (a boggy backwater of the James) had been degraded to provide reinforcements elsewhere, Grant launched a sledgehammer blow to sever Confederate supply lines along the Weldon and Petersburg Railroad toward Richmond. The main attack was delivered by the II and X Corps supported by a cavalry division. After several days of hammer-and-tongs battle, the Union forces managed to seize most of their objectives around Fussell's Farm, and captured several hundred prisoners. However, Lee's heavy counterattacks restored the line and prevented any breakthrough.

In later years, Grant often lamented his many assaults during the Petersburg siege and the losses incurred. However, he apparently felt they were necessary to destroy the resiliency of his opposition. Perhaps he was correct. At least history rarely queries successful generals. And Grant is one man whose image actually seems enhanced by the passage of time.

With the end of the war, a site was appropriated for a national cemetery in the area. Portions of land were purchased in increments, the last in 1873. The 1.55-acre site contains Union remains reinterred from areas around Forts Harrison and Gilmer and from forty other locations within a five-mile radius. Here again, the number of identifiable remains was quite small. As of 31 March 1961 some 846 interments had been made but almost 600 were of unknowns. All graves here are of Union war dead and the cemetery is unavailable for future burials. Fort Harrison National Cemetery is administered by the Richmond Complex.

FREDERICKSBURG AND SPOTSYLVANIA NATIONAL MILITARY PARK

Fredericksburg, Virginia

On 7 November 1862 General Ambrose E. Burnside, hero of the Battle of Antietam during the Civil War, replaced the less-than-mercurial George McClellan as commander of the Union Army of the Potomac. He cautiously advanced south, seeking Lee's forces, attempting to follow up the victory at Antietam.

However, Burnside's advance was so dilatory that Lee chose to make his stand without awaiting reinforcements along the excellent defensive terrain offered by the Rappahannock River. On 13 December 1862 Burnside finally tried to force a crossing of that river at the small town of Fredericksburg, Virginia. When enemy sharpshooters inflicted some losses on his troops as they laid pontoon bridges across the water, he ordered a senseless bombardment of the town; this destroyed most of the town but did little to dislodge Lee's defenders.

Eventually the Union forces launched heavy attacks against the northern flank of the Confederate lines at Mayre's Heights. The suicidal charges lasted all afternoon, until 12,700 Union casualties were piled in windrows at the base of the position's stone wall and sunken road. Even so, Burnside remained astride the river for two days before withdrawing on the night of 15 December.

Lee has often been criticized for not following up his victory and seeking to destroy Burnside's army completely. However, he suffered fifty-three hundred casualties, and Union artillery dominated the area from Stafford Heights across the river. The slaughter of Antietam was too fresh a memory for Lee to seriously consider a continuance of the struggle under such negative conditions. At any rate, he had successfully ended the career of yet another opponent. Burnside was soon relieved of command. He was not the first nor the last to meet such a fate while confronting Marse Robert.

Fredericksburg National Cemetery was established on 15 July 1865. Twelve acres in extent, it lies atop Willis' Hill, part of the famous Confederate defense position along Mayre's Heights. Early accounts indicate Union interments from this battle as well as the later struggles at Chancellorsville, the Wilderness and Spotsylvania, totaled 15,243. Illness, of course, added its share to the grim scroll.

The cemetery was closed due to lack of space in the 1940s.

However, by then it had supplied burial space for American veterans of later wars through World War II. As of 1960 total interments were 15,333, including 12,746 unknown Union soldiers. Even today, remains dating to the Civil War are still unearthed during work on the national park and environs. These periodically add to the total of unknowns who rest in the site.

Several monuments have been raised here. One is to General Daniel Butterfield and the V Corps he commanded at the Battle of Fredericksburg. Others commemorate General Andrew Humphreys, who commanded a division of that corps, and the 127th Pennsylvania Regiment which suffered heavy losses there. Also noteworthy is the gravesite of Lt. Col. Edward Hill of the Sixteenth Michigan who perished during the battle while winning the Medal of Honor.

Fredericksburg National Cemetery and its concomitant national park is administered by the Department of the Interior.

GLENDALE NATIONAL CEMETERY

Glendale, Virginia

The Battle of Glendale, sometimes known as Frayser's Farm, marked the final retreat of General George McClellan and the abandonment of his Peninsula Campaign of 1862, only weeks after he was within sight of victory. It was a bitter and vigorously contested rearguard action like Savage Station, White Oak Swamp and the culminating debacle at Malvern Hill on 1 July 1862.

McClellan's defeat was a tribute to the aggressive defense of Richmond by Robert E. Lee. Attempting to split the Union army, he had launched a series of clashes known historically as the Seven Days Battles. Though his tactical victories were few, Lee triumphed completely in the strategic campaign. It was Lee who was usually repulsed in his attacks on Union forces entrenched against him; it was McClellan who invariably retreated.

Lincoln in General McClellan's Tent

And indeed, Lee's campaign here was an incredible gamble on his part. Only McClellan's vacillation allowed it to succeed. In vain did Union generals such as Joseph Hooker tell McClellan that Lee's covering force between the Union army and Richmond was but a thin crust easily penetrated; little did McClellan realize how easily the enemy capital could be seized. However, McClellan was too preoccupied with his lines of supply and the main depot near Harrison's Landing. The famous raid by Confederate cavalry under J.E.B. Stuart just prior to the commencement of Lee's offensive indicated areas of vulnerability which tormented McClellan constantly. Therefore, he allowed himself to be steadily driven back by an enemy which lacked the manpower and material to vanquish him in open battle.

Nowhere is McClellan's faulty estimate of his own power better displayed than in the Battle of Glendale. Superior Union artillery emplacements and tenacious infantry units threw back Lee's strong assaults again and again. Yet by 2 July the highly-touted Peninsula Campaign was an abject failure. Richmond was saved, though only at frightful cost to the belligerents.

McClellan would later achieve some success at Antietam in repulsing Lee's first invasion of the North--but his days were numbered. Never again would he retrieve his reputation in the eyes of "Father Abraham," and Lincoln would soon find it necessary to replace him. Lee's career, meanwhile, was on a meteoric rise that would gain him acceptance as one of the Great Captains of History.

All this was true despite twenty thousand Confederate casualties in the Seven Days Battles to the Union's seventeen thousand. But regardless, the disgruntled, disgusted Union army soon huddled in the protection of Union gunboats on the James, drinking the dregs of a dismal, disheartening defeat.

The land comprising Glendale National Cemetery was appropriated in 1866 and the two-acre plot was purchased finally in 1873. It is located on Virginia State Highway 156 approximately fifteen miles southeast of Seven Pines National Cemetery. It is also within sight of the battlefield at Malvern Hill.

As with other cemeteries in the area, all those interred here are Union casualties of the Civil War. Most are monuments to the exigencies of hasty, battlefield burials and the ravages of time after initial committal. As of 31 March 1961, 1,209 interments had been made. Of these, a staggering 961 bore markers with the simple inscription "Unknown." The cemetery is closed to future use and is administered by the Richmond National Cemetery Complex.

HAMPTON NATIONAL CEMETERY

and

HAMPTON V.A. NATIONAL CEMETERY

Hampton, Virginia

Hampton is located on the tip of the Yorktown Peninsula south of the historic battlefield and is a few miles from such colonial sites as Jamestown and Williamsburg. Also nearby was the site of the powerful Union army bastion in the Civil War, Fortress Monroe, not far from Old Point Comfort. With the area used as a staging base for numerous Union operations during the Civil War, a cemetery became mandatory.

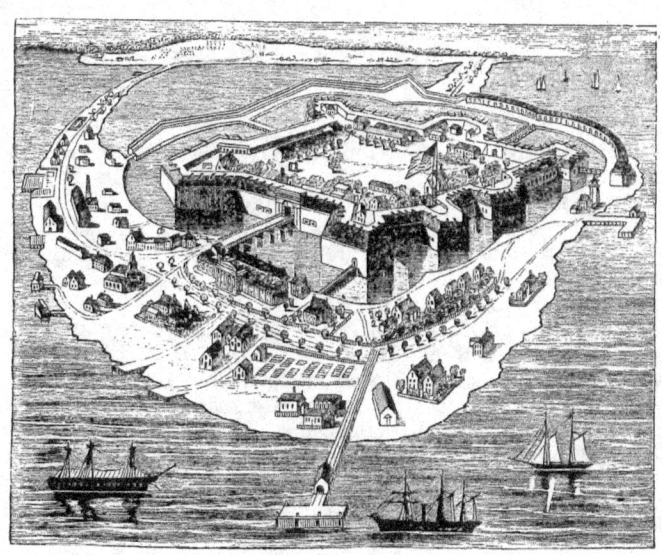

Fortress Monroe

Between Hampton and Norfolk lies the placid body of water called

Hampton Roads. Today it is home for the U.S. Atlantic Fleet. And during the Civil War it was a major area of operations for the Union navy endeavoring to strangle the Southern war effort through blockade. Thus, it was here in the early days of March 1862, that naval warfare and seafaring ventures in general were subjected to the greatest change they had known in four thousand years of recorded history.

When the Union navy evacuated Norfolk in 1861, it had burned the fine screw frigate *Merrimack*. Confederate forces raised it and improvised an ironclad ram renamed *Virginia*. Some 263 feet long, its sides sloped at thirty-five degrees and were constructed of wrought iron four inches thick, and then greased with tallow. From a distance it resembled a floating barn roof.

On 8 March 1862 the ram debouched into Hampton Roads and promptly sank or destroyed three Union vessels of the blockading force. Then, with night coming on and its commander, Commodore Franklin Buchanan, wounded, the vessel steamed back up the James with every intention of returning the following day to finish off the Union blockaders.

However, at dawn the following morning, the ram encountered an even stranger ship than itself. Awaiting the *Virginia* was U.S.S. *Monitor*, at the time known as Erickson's Folly after its Swedish inventor. One hundred and seventy-two feet long and displacing twelve hundred tons, the vessel was surmounted by a 140-ton turret housing two eleven-inch smoothbores. Indeed, its most apt description was "a cheesebox on a raft."

The ensuing battle was indecisive. But it became apparent that the U.S.S. *Monitor* had met the challenge of Southern ironclads and the wooden-walled Union navy would never be driven from Confederate coasts. A few weeks later the *Virginia* had to be blown-up by its crew when threatened by the advance of McClellan's forces in the Peninsula Campaign. The *Monitor* was lost in a storm the following winter. But in their passing, they had forevermore changed human endeavors on the sea.

On 3 February 1865 a meeting was held on a ship anchored just off Old Point Comfort in an attempt to achieve peace. President Lincoln and Secretary of State Seward represented the U.S. government while Robert Hunter and J.A. Campbell were the Confederate agents. The meeting resulted from the efforts of one F.P. Blair, an intimate of Confederate President Jefferson Davis, after an unofficial discussion with that worthy a few weeks previously.

However, the conference failed completely. Despite the tenuous and desperate situation of the Southern cause, Southern negotiators continued their strident demands for independence. Lincoln and Seward could make no headway against such adamant refusal to face reality. Besides, neither Lincoln nor Seward was prepared to condone any agreement that provided for a continuation of slavery or a separation of the Union. Consequently, the meeting was adjourned in deadlock and never re-opened. The last hope for the South to obtain any terms other than abject, unconditional surrender had been squandered.

The two national cemeteries lying in the area, though neither large by the standards of the system, both represent their own individual chapters of American history. The original Hampton National Cemetery, now lying at the corner of Cemetery Road and Marshall Avenue, is the resting place of most of those Union veterans who fell during the actual conflict. Casualties from clashes in the vicinity of Fortress Monroe ran into the hundreds. These included Federal forces slain in the battle of Hampton Roads, mainly naval personnel from the frigates *Congress*, *Cumberland* and *Minnesota* lost to the *Virginia* on 8 March 1862. Pennsylvania and New York units firing from shore also sustained some losses.

The national cemetery attached to the Hampton V. A. Medical Center is one of the newer facilities in the system. Dating from the National Cemetery Act of 1973, the installation was initially used only for the interment of veterans who succumbed while in V.A. hospitals. All such restrictions have now been lifted. Most of those American servicemen at rest here were veterans of the Spanish conflict.

Due to a lack of available gravesites, both locations have been closed for some years. Both are administered by the staff at the original Hampton National Cemetery. This facility, 26.5 acres in extent, contained 21,390 burials as of 31 May 1980. The smaller half-acre V.A. location held 22 committals, apparently all Spanish War era fatalities.

Poplar Grove National Cemetery
Marker of a Union Dead from the Civil War
--*National Archives photo*

POPLAR GROVE NATIONAL CEMETERY

Petersburg, Virginia

Poplar Grove is yet another cemetery established during the Civil War period in response to the general crisis in burial arrangements in the Union army. Here the fighting concerned capture of Petersburg; located just south of Richmond, Petersburg was often considered the key to the Confederate capital. And here too, the disposal problems of the dead of both armies were the same as elsewhere. Most were buried where they fell, ofttimes in unmarked mass graves.

The Petersburg Campaign began in June 1864. With his efforts to outflank Lee repeatedly blocked, Grant resolved to capture this crucial communications center. Foiled by the incompetence of subordinates in the North, the Union commander in chief finally realized he must undertake a siege. Ten long months of brutal trench warfare ensued, marked alternately by brilliance and lack of resolution by both sides. Before it was over, forty-two thousand Union and twenty-eight thousand Confederate soldiers would become casualties.

The most memorable incident was the Petersburg Mine Assault of 30 July 1864, commonly referred to as "The Battle of the Crater." The idea originated with Colonel Pleasants of the Forty-eighth Pennsylvania. The former coal miners of his unit managed to run a shaft 511 feet below the Southern emplacements, a mine large enough for the stacking of eight thousand pounds of black powder. Though Grant was less than enthusiastic, he allowed the attack to be launched at dawn on 30 July.

The explosion annihilated the Nineteenth and Twenty-second South Carolina regiments of Lee's army, but the massed Union troops did not satisfactorily exploit the breach. Of the fifteen thousand engaged, over four thousand became casualties when Lee managed to restore his line with savage counterattacks. Grant summed it up as "a stupendous failure."

And there were other battles in the area. The fact that the Army of the Potomac did not always retain the field added to the burden of recovering these dead after the war. Identification was all but impossible. For instance, of the 646 men reclaimed from "The Crater," not a single individual could be identified.

A year after the cessation of hostilities, it became obvious that a national cemetery would be mandatory in or around Petersburg. The area chosen was six miles southwest of the town on land where the

Battle of Peebles Farm had raged in late 1864. It was chosen for its central location, and because of the existence of the Poplar Grove Church. This edifice had been constructed as a combination house of worship and hospital by the Fiftieth New York Engineers during February 1865. The building survived until 1868 when the army tore it down due to zooming maintenance costs.

By 1869, graves registration details had reinterred victims of the Petersburg Campaign from no less than nine separate Virginia counties. When completed, the operations had committed the remains of 6,142 Union and 36 Confederate soldiers--all but a few, unknowns. In addition, the cemetery provided burial space to veterans through the Korean War. However, its approximately ten acres were filled in 1957 and it was closed with approximately seven thousand gravesites filled. Poplar Grove National Cemetery is a part of the Petersburg National Battlefield administered by the Department of the Interior.

RICHMOND NATIONAL CEMETERY

Richmond, Virginia

Little more than one hundred miles separated Richmond and Washington during the Civil War. Yet the amount of hardship, toil and blood necessary to bridge that short span was incalculable. Only after four years of the most bitter and savage conflict ever seen on the North American continent was the issue resolved. With the fall of Richmond and the surrender of the Army of Northern Virginia on 9 April 1865 at Wilmer McLean's house near Appomattox, the American Civil War ended and passed into history, subsequently engendering an inordinate amount of myth and legend.

Here at Richmond, both materially and psychologically, the course of history was determined. Exactly how many men fell from the start of Grant's campaign in the spring of 1864 until its end a year later is unknown. Some estimates range as high as one hundred thousand Union and seventy thousand Confederate casualties from all causes. And this may not include numerous incapacitations among troops in rear areas before reaching the area of conflict. Suffice it to say that if the highest price a man can place on something is to purchase it with his blood, then the real estate of south-central Virginia is the most expensive soil in the United States.

For Richmond, the war, but not the destruction, ended at 8:15 on the morning of 3 April 1865. Then Union General Weitzel of the XVIII Corps accepted the surrender of the capital in a formal surrender ceremony on the steps of city hall. Into the bag went six thousand Confederate prisoners, mainly those in hospitals.

However, even then the city was fighting for survival. No sooner did Lee abandon the city the night before than it began to burn due to flaming and exploding war material. As Union troops marched in, they stacked their arms and joined the citizenry in battling the conflagration. Probably in no other civil war in history has there been such a strange sight. Perhaps in no other nation on earth could it happen.

Lee's flight to the southwest merely served to prolong the issue. Even he could no longer seriously believe the issue was in doubt. The fall of the Richmond Arsenal and the Tredegar Iron Works doomed the Confederates from receiving even the most rudimentary armaments again.

Richmond National Cemetery lies just inside the defense fortifications Lee had maintained during the siege. It is almost ten acres in extent, the largest of the cemeteries in the Richmond National Cemetery Complex. However, it contains only an infinitesimal fraction of those who fell in and around the Confederate capital. Not that it matters really. No amount of white markers marching across acres of greensward could truly convey to us the bitterness, obscenity, savagery and magnificence of the fratricidal struggle which rent this nation from 1861 to 1865. Richmond National Cemetery is merely a symbol of it. Perhaps that should be enough.

The site of the cemetery was appropriated in 1866 along with the other five local national cemeteries administered by its director. Actual purchase of the land through various additions continued through 1906 when the cemetery reached its current size. Reinterments were made from Confederate cemeteries at Hollywood and Oakwood cemeteries as well as from the Union prison at Belle Island where numerous captives perished during incarceration. Reinterments were also made as need arose from sites near Seven Pines, Cold Harbor and various locales in Chesterfield and Hanover counties. Seventy different areas within a twenty-five-mile radius of Richmond eventually supplied war dead to the cemetery, mainly unknown Union soldiers.

By 1868, only two years after it was established, over 6,000 interments had been made. Of this number, only 800 were identified. Unlike most other cemeteries in the Richmond Complex, this cemetery has provided burial space for American servicemen who served a united nation in subsequent conflicts through World War II. As of 31 March 1961, 8,348 interments had been made in its hallowed ground, most of whom were casualties of war.

However, in 1980, Richmond National Cemetery was closed to future interments due to committal of all available space. All information or correspondence concerning any national cemetery in the Richmond Complex should go through the administrator of this facility.

SEVEN PINES NATIONAL CEMETERY

Sandston, Virginia

In the spring of 1862, General George McClellan, recently promoted to command of the Army of the Potomac, resolved on a daring gambit to seize Richmond and end the war. Transporting most of the Union forces from Washington via water to Fortress Monroe at the tip of the Yorktown Peninsula, he began to move laterally west between the James and York rivers towards the Confederate capital.

The plan was a boldly conceived stroke and, for a man of more resolution, it might have proven decisive. Unfortunately, McClellan's tactical deficiencies prevented this brainstorm from becoming a triumph of strategic genius.

He managed to capture Yorktown and Williamsburg before Confederate leaders truly understood the threat he posed. But then his own dilatory tactics rescued them. By the end of May 1862 he advanced until balloon observers could see the spires of the enemy capital. At this point, McClellan, still not believing it could be this easy, unwisely divided his forces to protect his lines of communications. The Union army found itself separated by the Chickihominy River, a low, marshy stream bordered by swamps and often impassable due to spring rains that would turn it into a morass of bogs and tangled undergrowth. But McClellan surrendered the initiative and established a defense line along the Williamsburg Road.

It was here that Confederate commander, Gen. Joseph E. Johnston, struck him on 31 May at the Battle of Seven Pines (Fair Oaks.) For

Hospital at Fair Oaks

two days they slugged it out as Johnston sought to defeat the scattered Union army in detail. Despite their difficulties, the Union troops fought him off time and time again. Johnston himself was grievously wounded before the attacks ended.

But McClellan had suffered heavy losses and this further magnified a naturally timid personality. For nearly a month he sat in his positions, making no further advance on Richmond. His only activity was occasional probes to the northeast and south of the enemy capital.

He was found here in late June by Robert E. Lee, recently appointed by President Jefferson Davis to succeed the wounded Johnston. McClellan was soon driven from the area despite a series of clashes of which only the last could be called a Confederate triumph tactically.

After the war, Colonel James Moore, Quartermaster Corps, was assigned the task of selecting a site for a national cemetery. He chose Seven Pines, primarily as a tribute to the Union victory there. It now lies at the junction of Virginia State Highway 156 and U.S. Route 60 outside Sandston, Virginia.

The original purchase of land in 1866 was small, only 1.6 acres. An additional strip was added in 1875. Remains of fallen Union troops were removed from Seven Pines and innumerable farm yards, stream beds and ditches within a four-mile radius of the cemetery.

As of 31 March 1961 some 1,427 bodies had been reinterred to the cemetery. Because so many of them rested for years in unmarked battlefield graves, only 190 of them could be identified. Those buried in the Seven Pines National Cemetery are strictly Union casualties of the Civil War. It is closed to future interments. Like others in the area, it is administered by the Richmond National Cemetery Complex.

STAUNTON NATIONAL CEMETERY

Staunton, Virginia

Nestled in one of the most scenic areas of the United States, the southern Shenandoah Valley, Staunton, Virginia is also the possessor of a national cemetery. Located only a few miles southwest of the southern tip of spacious Shenandoah National Park, Staunton is one of the most historical cities in all Virginia.

The city was a central point on the Valley Pike, known as the Great Wagon Road, during the early days of expansion prior to the Civil War. It was also a major terminus on the old Valley Railroad which wends its way from the southern valley, east through Rockfish Gap in the Blue Ridge Mountains and joins the Orange and Alexandria Railroad to terminate near the nation's capital.

It was from near here in the spring of 1862 that Confederate general T.J. "Stonewall" Jackson launched his fabled Valley Campaign; his role in the campaign is regarded as one of the greatest examples of leadership, daring and resolution in human history. Ensconced at Swift Run Gap, he was ordered by the Confederate leadership then facing the threat of McClellan's Peninsula Campaign, to march up the valley, threaten Washington, and thereby relieve some of the pressure. Feinting departure from the valley to join the Confederate forces at Richmond, he quickly loaded his troops onto a train at Staunton and struck west to surprise and rout the Union forces of Fremont at the Battle of McDowell on 8 May 1862. Wheeling north, he used the central ridge of Massanutten Mountain as a screen and inflicted a series of defeats on befuddled Union generals in the next month. He won victories at Front Royal, Middletown, Winchester, Harrisonburg, Cross Keys and Port Republic, and found time to raid the Union arsenal at Harpers Ferry. By the time he returned in safety to Staunton, he had acquired a vast wagon train of war booty for the hard-pressed defenders of Richmond. He had also eliminated an estimated forty-thousand Union soldiers as casualties, prisoners or deserters.

Of course the Shenandoah would see much more travail in the bitter struggle. In the fall of 1864, General Philip Sheridan would virtually lay it waste from Harpers Ferry to Lexington in the south. Not even Staunton would be spared. The final Union triumph would occur only twenty miles east at Waynesboro on 2 March 1865. Here Brevet General George A. Custer led one of the most stirring and successful cavalry charges of the Civil War in overwhelming and destroying the

Confederate forces under General Jubal Early.

But Staunton is known for more than its Civil War history. To the northwest at Mount Solon lie the natural limestone formations called the Natural Chimneys. An annual jousting tournament is held here, one of the oldest continuously held events on the continent.

At Steele's Tavern in Rockford County to the southeast, a young man named Cyrus McCormick first demonstrated his grain reaper in 1831.

Only thirty-five miles to the south along the North James River lies Lexington, Virginia, containing famous Virginia Military Institute. Here "Stonewall" Jackson first taught school. And from here sallied forth the corps of cadets on 15 June 1864 to help defeat the Union forces at New Market, temporarily stemming their advance into the valley. Ironically, upon returning home they found that raiding Union cavalry had trampled their school books into the mud while looting the institution.

Stonewall Jackson

Staunton can also lay claim to being the birthplace of one of America's greatest diplomats. In 1856 a son was born in the parsonage of the Presbyterian church to Pastor Joseph R. Wilson. That son, Woodrow Wilson, would later become the twenty-eighth president of the United States.

Staunton National Cemetery is one of the smallest either on foreign or domestic soil. It is two acres in size and has only 1.15 acres devoted to burials. Originally opened in 1864, it is known locally as "The Yankee Cemetery." This is due to the fact that 529 of the 965 men interred there were Union soldiers whose bodies were not discovered until long after the fighting, and were interred in unknown graves. The cemetery lies on Richmond Avenue (U.S. Route 250) and is easily accessible via all the major traffic arteries through the Shenandoah Valley.

WINCHESTER NATIONAL CEMETERY

Winchester, Virginia

On Fame's eternal camping ground
Their silent tents are spread,
And glory guards with solemn round
The Bivouac of the Dead

Thus goes one of the more memorable verses of Lt. Col. O'Hara's immortal Civil War paean. Ten plaques containing the stanzas of the poem line the central pathway in Winchester National Cemetery. And few cities on this continent have ever played a more strategic role in our history.

But a century before the bloodbath which followed South Carolina's secession from the Union, the strategic site of Winchester had already been noticed by a young Virginia surveyor named George Washington. Departing the area in the summer of 1755, Washington served as aide to Major Edward Braddock during the fabled and ill-fated British expedition to seize Fort Duquesne (Pittsburgh), Pennsylvania. Following Braddock's great defeat, Washington covered the British retreat with his American militia, and brought them safely back to Winchester. Later, the Lord of Mount Vernon made contingency plans to use Winchester as a base for guerrilla war along the eastern coast in case of defeat by the British during the Revolutionary War. That he never had to employ this strategy detracts not in the slightest from its foresight.

The guns had barely ceased belching flame at Fort Sumter in 1861 before both Union and Confederate commanders espied the importance of Winchester at the head of the Shenandoah Valley. The valley was one of the most fertile on the continent, and indeed worthy of its name "Granary of the Confederacy." It also provided a major recruiting area for Lee's army. It is little wonder therefore, that the city reportedly changed hands seventy-one times during the ebb and flow of conflict. There were at least three major engagements here, and interment files at the national cemetery list 4,448 Union soldiers buried here as a result. Some 2,338 are unknowns. However, numerous Confederate war dead from the last battles in September 1864 also found a final resting place here. It is an interesting footnote that no less than two future American presidents fought at Winchester during the last Valley Campaign--James A. Garfield and Rutherford B. Hayes.

Winchester National Cemetery was dedicated on 8 April 1866.

Even before that, reinterments were underway to reclaim Union dead from such distant points as the southern Shenandoah battlefields and even Harper's Ferry and Romney, West Virginia. Since then the remains of American veterans of every war through Vietnam have been committed also. But the cemetery has been closed in recent years due to a lack of burial space.

In 1868, the state of New Hampshire began to erect here marble headstones over its dead, and the federal government soon emulated this policy. This alleviated the problem of identification due to perishable wooden markers, which had plagued burial details throughout the war. In addition, no less than six different Union states have raised some thirteen separate monuments in the cemetery, both to units and individuals.

The current cemetery director is also charged with the administration of nearby Balls Bluff National Cemetery, Leesburg, Virginia.

YORKTOWN NATIONAL CEMETERY

Yorktown, Virginia

Out they marched that day, 19 October 1781, a bedraggled and downcast line of soldiery. The scarlet coats were dusty and torn, the gold buttons either missing or tarnished. Their drummers pounded a slow, mournful beat. The band played a popular song, "The World Turned Upside Down," but that day it sounded like a funeral dirge. And indeed, for the seemingly omnipotent British Empire, the world would never be the same. Lord Charles Cornwallis had surrendered at Yorktown. American independence was a reality!

The campaign which led to the penultimate British debacle in the New World had begun two years previously with the shift of emphasis of British operations to the southern colonies. However, success continued to elude them. Finally, overextended British forces in Virginia under Cornwallis were ordered to establish communications

Surrender at Yorktown

with British headquarters in New York under General Clinton. It was impossible to march north through hordes of congregating American forces. Therefore, on 4 August 1781 Cornwallis moved into the tip of the Yorktown Peninsula hoping to keep a link open by sea. Within a month, George Washington had besieged him with seventeen thousand American and French troops.

The British strategy might have prevailed had the normally dominant British navy been able to hold command of the sea. But it was not to be. The French navy held hegemony over the waters off the eastern coast just long enough to assure the demise of the last major field army the British maintained on the North American continent.

The siege dragged on for weeks, highlighted by artillery duels and the storming of an occasional redoubt as Washington tightened his stranglehold. Cornwallis hung on grimly, even attempting to break out on 16 October. Failing, and facing starvation as well as a constant artillery pounding, he asked for terms on 17 October. Two days later the British world had turned upside down. In London Lord North provided the best epitaph for British rule south of Canada. "My God," he moaned, "it is all over!"

Not only during the American Revolution was Yorktown a battleground. It was the site of a Confederate post under General John Magruder at the time of McClellan's Peninsula Campaign in 1862. He evacuated the town with little difficulty and even made a brief stand near Williamsburg to buy time for the Confederate forces assembling near Richmond. Otherwise, the area escaped the worst ravages of civil strife.

Today Yorktown is part of the huge complex of colonial Americana. Williamsburg, and sites such as White House Landing and King and Queen Courthouse, present incisive and comprehensive views of a way of life two centuries gone.

Yorktown National Cemetery was selected as a location in 1866 primarily due to the Peninsula Campaign. Approximately three acres in extent, the cemetery contains 2,183 gravesites. Of these, about 1,400 are unknown, the majority being Union soldiers. The cemetery also contains ten Confederate soldiers buried there before the Union army appropriated it officially as a national cemetery. Reinterments were made to Yorktown from twenty-seven locations within a fifty-mile radius. It cannot be precisely determined, but it is believed that a number of colonial veterans, including five Negro soldiers, are interred here. Because of the lack of earlier records, the cemetery is considered a Civil War site. It has been officially closed to further burials.

GRAFTON NATIONAL CEMETERY

Grafton, West Virginia

Set in the north-central part of the state, not far west of legendary Harper's Ferry, Grafton is known as the "Memorial City" because it contains the only national cemetery in all of West Virginia. And the site was chosen almost by accident.

In 1865, Samuel Burdett, commander in chief of the former members of the Grand Army of the Republic and an Iowa Congressman, was touring the battlefields of the area while vacationing with relatives in nearby Pruntytown. Envisioning having the Union war dead concentrated in one location, he introduced a bill to that effect in the House and soon saw his dream realized.

Under orders from the War Department to find a suitable site, Major R.C. Bates selected Grafton. A contract was signed between the government and a local family named Yates for approximately four acres of land lying between the Baltimore and Ohio right of way and Walnut Street in the western end of the city. Cemetery development and reinterment work commenced in 1867. However, the handicaps of inclement winter weather and the large number of bodies to be reclaimed prevented the site from being dedicated as planned on Memorial Day, 1868. Finally on 14 June Company B, Seventeenth West Virginia Regiment formed up amidst martial music and led the procession to officially open the cemetery. Today Grafton sees one of the more poignant ceremonies in the nation. Every Memorial Day some two thousand local school children march through the streets to the cemetery to decorate the graves, a tradition observed since 1869.

Grafton provides one of the more unique sites in the National Cemetery System, perched as it is on three separate terraces. Interred here are some 1,250 Civil War dead, both Union and Confederate. Of these, 644 lie in unknown graves, although some do show the home state of the decedent. In the years since its opening, the cemetery has provided burial space for American veterans of all subsequent wars and the current number of committals stands at 2,095. These veterans represent twenty-four states and thirty-two counties of West Virginia. Among them are a dozen members of the famous American Volunteer Regiment, which adopted the baggy, red pants and fez of the French Zouaves during their Civil War service.

On the night of 22 May 1861, Confederate pickets over a bridge on the B & O Railroad near the town of Feuterman espied the approach of two Union soldiers apparently on a scout from Grafton. Refusing to halt when challenged by the Southerners, these Union men continued to advance until the inevitable gun battle erupted. One Confederate had his ear shot off and Private Bailey Brown, Union army, fell dead with a bullet through the heart. He was later interred at Grafton National Cemetery and a ten-foot monument stands at the foot of his grave. Thus, Grafton claims the distinction of being the final resting place of the first Union soldier to fall in battle during the Civil War.

The cemetery remains open to interments at present. However, limited acreage indicates it will shortly be closed. An enlargement is planned, but has not yet occurred due to limited availability of suitable land.

WOOD NATIONAL CEMETERY

Wood, Wisconsin

In the heavily wooded farm country to the north of the Madison-Milwaukee axis lies Wood National Cemetery. The surrounding terrain is some of the most lush and productive in the American Midwest. Minnesota may be the land of ten thousand lakes, but Wisconsin takes a back seat to nowhere in the attractiveness of its landscape.

Long the center of America's dairy industry, the farming feats of the area are legion. Two-hundred-pound cheeses are occasionally turned out just to prove the possibility of such a stunt.

Central Wisconsin abounds in fish and wildlife. Lake Mendota maintains the most liberal quotas of game fish in the Midwest. In the winter, the area becomes a snowy wonderland of winter sports. Among the most fascinating and dangerous is iceboat racing on various lakes. These sleek craft can scream across the ice at speeds upwards of eighty miles per hour.

Nor is Wisconsin a stranger to historic events. Just northeast of Madison lies the Menominee Reservation. This tribe was one of a score of groups which joined in the epic Pontiac Revolt of 1769 against British penetration south of the Great Lakes. Menominees helped overrun several British forts and fought in the abortive siege of Fort Detroit. Some served in Pontiac's unsuccessful attempt to block British relief columns at the Battle of Bushy Run. However, like most tribes, the Menominees entered an irreversible decline following Pontiac's defeat. Today they are among the least-known tribal entities in the Midwest.

And it was in this area that the Indians of the Midwest made their final stand against white encroachments in 1832 under Chief Black Hawk of the Sauk and Fox tribe. At the time, the Indian leader knew it was a forlorn gamble against impossible odds. But when he found white settlers ensconced on his own doorstep, it was definitely time for action!

At first he enjoyed a modicum of success. His May 1832 rout of the forces under Major Isaiah Stillman on ground which today is a Chicago suburb, inspired confidence in his followers. However, the local settlers were not so much astonished as they were vengeful. Within months he had been driven into southwestern Wisconsin along the Mississippi River. There General Zachary Taylor, who had campaigned so successfully against the Seminoles, led a militia force through Bad Ax Swamp to administer the defeat that broke the back of the revolt. One of his subordinates was a young captain of militia named Abraham Lincoln.

Somehow Black Hawk survived the revolt and even became a local celebrity. He died in 1838. By that time the remnant of his tribe had either ceased to exist or fled west to join the Sioux nation.

In natural disasters alone, Wisconsin can claim fame. A hundred or so miles northeast of Madison lies the lumber-milling town of Peshtigo. In 1871 a fire began here that consumed the town and soon swept across northern Wisconsin, moved by the whims of gale force winds, until it had become the worst forest fire in American history. At least twelve hundred people perished. To this day nobody knows how much acreage was destroyed and how many structures razed.

Wisconsin supplied vast reservoirs of manpower to the Union in the Civil War. Among its regiments, the Second, Seventh, Twenty-sixth, Thirty-sixth and Thirty-seventh were the most noteworthy. The Seventh served in every battle fought by the Army of the Potomac. The Thirty-sixth was heavily involved in the Siege of Petersburg and has been intimately identified with it. At the "Battle of the Crater" the regiment lost 145 of 250 men in action.

Because of these contributions to the war effort, citizens of Wisconsin wondered aloud why they were not granted a national cemetery as were Illinois and other states. Therefore, they took the initiative themselves. On 1 May 1867 a National Asylum for Disabled Volunteer Soldiers was opened in Wood, Wisconsin. The name was changed to National Home in 1873 and its jurisdiction was transferred to the Veterans Administration in 1930.

The first interment in its cemetery was Union veteran John K. Afton on 22 May 1871. The forty-acre cemetery remains open today. Its most notable feature is an obelisk with a statue of a soldier dedicated to all who have served in the armed forces.

Perhaps the best-known individual buried there is General K.T. Knox. Originally from Pennsylvania, his father later entered law practice with Edwin M. Stanton in the 1850s. Knox served with distinction in the Union army from 1861 to 1865 and later was assigned as military advisor to President Andrew Johnson. In 1889 he became governor of the Wood National Home. He was still in that capacity at the time of his death in 1891.

The V.A. Hospital cemetery at Wood, Wisconsin officially became part of the National Cemetery System in 1975. As mentioned, it remains available for interments, and according to current estimates, should remain open into the next century.

THE FUTURE

It is not the function of this book to discuss Arlington, but rather to provide a general survey of the nation's history as it correlates with the remainder of the National Cemetery System. Arlington, the national shrine, has been the subject of numerous literary endeavors. For those interested in pursuing that aspect, two of the better tomes available in the average municipal library are *In Honored Glory*, (Peter Andrews, 1966, G.P. Putnam and Sons), and *Arlington: Monument to Heroes*, (John V. Hinkel, 1970, Prentice-Hall, Inc.). It was estimated that by 1981 its projected 270,000 gravesites would be filled or committed. However, in 1980 an additional two hundred acres of adjacent army land was acquired and this has sustained burial space until the present time. For a brief listing of those distinguished Americans, military and civilian, who rest at Arlington, Appendix B is available at the end of this book.

Nor has this book devoted attention to those overseas locales administered by the American Battle Monuments Commission. Adequate information on these is available to the reader from other sources.

Rather, this effort has concentrated on the remainder of our national system, cemeteries which many Americans do not even realize exist, though they may literally live within a stone's throw of them. Aside from Arlington, there are nearly one hundred and twenty such locations in the continental United States, as well as the National Memorial Cemetery of the Pacific in Hawaii. In the survey which has preceded, each of these has been studied in, at best, a superficial manner. The emphasis has been not on the cemetery itself. Indeed, there is merit to the view that if you have seen one, you have seen them all. I can only hope that the main thrust of my work has not escaped the reader's notice--and that is the history of the United States which is represented in each site, and the pageant of American life, both past and present.

No American should fear to take such a journey into the past. I believe that if every American did, we would be a much stronger and more viable nation. Knowledge of what has gone before can add resiliency to any society, and a grasp of enduring trends can provide much consolation to those terrified by current events that seem without control or direction. A nation's history can give perspective to many of those fears which darken our lives as a community, and which make us feel that we are in a game where the rules don't fit.

The United States National Cemetery System is unique. Some Latin American nations (Argentina, Paraguay, et al.) do maintain small plots near their national capitals for certain deceased leaders; however, no attempt is made to render them coherent or logical. In medieval Byzantium, most of the ruling Comneni Dynasty were entombed beneath the various cathedrals of Constantinople, but few of those tombs survive today.

The notorious sacking and pillaging of the city in 1204 during what is euphemistically referred to as the Fourth Crusade did most of the damage. The little reconstruction that was attempted was destroyed in 1453 when the empire expired at the point of Turkish swords.

The nations of Europe do not follow a policy of maintaining a visible national symbol and "last post" for those who have served their nations. Only London's Westminster Abbey conveys some of the sweep and scope of British history. France and Germany do maintain assorted memorials to their war dead but nothing even remotely resembling an Arlington is extant. Because of their colonial history, these nations opted for burying their war dead in foreign locales or in mass graves on the battlefield. Apparently this was a manifestation of the principle Out of sight, Out of Mind. Throughout Africa, Asia and elsewhere, one can find European names on headstones in the most unlikely cemeteries.

The Union of South Africa does maintain a national burying ground at Maitland. Along with Westminster Abbey, it is one of the few concerted efforts to consciously promulgate a sense of national history. Specific information, however, remains scarce.

Only in distant China does another example of a national burying ground exist. The old Forbidden City of Peking served for many centuries as a resting place for the rulers of numerous Chinese dynasties. However, how much of this once sacred, historical locale has survived the ravages of communism and China's internal upheavals is problematical.

So, only in this country has it been long recognized that a national network of monuments, shrines, encampments, homes and cemeteries is one of the most effective and articulate means of preserving heritage and tradition.

However, as late as 1961, what many considered to be a pernicious threat to that concept was posed by congressional legislation. A moratorium was declared on the expansion and establishment of future national cemeteries, both those administered by the Department of the Army and those under the auspices of the Department of the Interior, National Parks Service. In that year, a study was published by Congress stating that the existing system was both "inadequate and discriminatory." Since many Americans did not live in immediate proximity to a national cemetery, it was felt that such cemeteries offered them little service. Also, in view of the fact that some forty million Americans conceivably could qualify according to long-range actuarial tables, the existing facilities, many of them already filled, could not provide adequate gravesites for even a portion of those eligible.

Some authorities, many politicians and most veterans' groups loudly denounced the survey. Whether rightly or wrongly, it was argued that Congress had kowtowed to civilian funeral directors, private memorial park owners and other interests. It was true that certain death benefits to veterans under the Veterans Administration and Social Security systems did exist and could be applied to defraying costs at private funeral establishments. It was also true that only the private sector would thereby benefit. Many veterans, as well as consumer and preservationist groups, believed there had been more than a little subterranean lobbying prior to the congressional action of 1961, lobbying that would lead to the government eventually abandoning many cemeteries and their historical adjuncts.

Despite the brief, if loud, fire-storm of controversy over the decision, the National Cemetery System was allowed to lapse for over a decade. And indeed, those opponents of an expansion of the system certainly had some merit to their arguments.

The primary consideration was, of course, financial. A cemetery is not something one can fill, close and forget. Friends and relatives invariably survive. In addition, policy allows for the interment of spouses or other next of kin in the same gravesite as the eligible veteran. Consequently, a steady continuance of burials obtains even after a national cemetery is officially closed. This necessitates a staff of a dozen administrators, clerks, mechanics, landscapers and laborers at even a modest-sized facility.

It is also true that many cemeteries, mostly those at historical sites, are often far removed from major metropolitan areas. Undeniably, history and demographics do not always coincide.

However, critics of the moratorium complained that, while death benefits from various governmental agencies could be used to pay the costs of interment at a private facility, they were equally efficacious in transporting the deceased to a national cemetery where he might prefer to reside and where a plot was without charge.

Particularly was this so in the decedent affairs of retired military personnel. Their numbers remain constant at approximately three and one-half million. Many of these individuals regard burial among other "brothers of the cloth" as much a benefit of their career service as commissary prices, health benefits and retirement checks.

It is a further fact, claimed critics, that the march of technology has noticeably cut the maintenance cost of a national cemetery. Mass production of markers at two sites in Georgia and Vermont have kept this expense nominal. New strains of grass, requiring less mowing and other upkeep, have helped pare landscaping costs. Backhoes are now used for grave excavation, so that large staffs of laborers with their unavoidable salaries have also been eliminated. In addition, since the land is usually wholly owned by the federal government to begin with, little expense is incurred in acquisition and development. Added pressures from inflationary spirals, now dominating every American's lifestyle, are also beginning to affect the style of their earthly departure. Inflation has constantly eroded the purchasing power of many retired veterans, especially those who left the service before the great advances in pay commencing in 1970. Their retirement checks have not kept pace with those of their colleagues recently leaving the military. Interment in a national cemetery is once again becoming a most attractive prospect for those who may find it impossible to afford similar services in the civilian sector.

It is difficult to ascertain just how much influence on subsequent events was exercised by this vocal and political remonstration. What is known is that in 1973, after considerable debate, Congress reversed course. The National Cemetery Act of 1973 signed into law in June 1974 by President Nixon, amalgamated the cemeteries of the national monuments and those of the Veterans Administration into a National Cemetery Service to be administered by the latter organization. Only Arlington and the Soldiers' and Airmen's Home in Washington, D.C., as national shrines, were excluded and continued to operate under the auspices of the U.S. Army. Another dozen or so sites of extreme national historical importance were left to the charge of the Department of the Interior, National Parks Service. However, the Veterans Administration was left with the bulk of the cemetery administration.

Under the Veterans Administration's driving leadership, the feasibility of expansion came under serious study again in 1975. Between then and early 1978, six more sites were designated as regional locations to make certain that proper space would always be available to those demanding it. These included Riverside, California; Bourne, Massachusetts; Fort Custer, Michigan; Calverton, New York (Long Island); Indiantown Gap, Pennsylvania; and Quantico, Virginia. From 1987 to 1989 three new ones were added at Ft. Mitchell, Alabama; Phoenix, Arizona; and Bushnell, Florida. Larger than the original cemeteries, they were designed to cut costs as much as possible. A simple accounting study shows that one large cemetery, employing modern advances, can be administered and maintained for only half the cost of six or eight smaller ones comprising the same acreage.

This regional concept was a compromise between cost-conscious Washington and a large body of veterans' groups which insisted on available burial grounds for their members. While many of those seeking interment in these locations might find it necessary to arrange for transport over hundreds of miles, it is still the most appropriate and fair method for solving the complex issues involved. Those individuals adamant upon interment in a national cemetery surely will arrange transport, setting aside the necessary funds prior to the time of need.

These assorted new locales, all opened in the last decade or so, now provide several thousand additional acres of land capable of receiving over two million gravesites. This has virtually doubled the size of the initial National Cemetery System.

However, one thing neither Congress nor the Department of Veterans Affairs has been able to settle on, is a replacement for Arlington; despite the small expansion previously mentioned, Arlington will no longer have available space by 1990, except for active-duty casualties. As a chronicle of the nation's past, the old Lee estate is unparalleled. A walk through its verdant, shady greensward is a communion with America vastly superior to that offered in any classroom or textbook. By osmosis, if no other way, such a walk can produce a sense of perspective that the average American sorely needs in his hard-pressed and often unrewarding daily life.

But today there seems no assurance that the next century and a half of American history will be similarly preserved, at least not in the area of our nation's capital.

This would be quite tragic. People and monuments are what a nation's history, and its aspirations for the future, are all about, even if on occasion these aspirations are inflated and grandiose.

A perusal of any map of the Washington vicinity will show even a casual observer that ground is available. To the north of the city lie Greenbelt and Anacostia River parks, small parts of which encompass more area than Arlington. In and around Washington, D.C. much ground is dormant. From St. Elizabeth's Farm to the south, through the little-used Washington Naval Air Station and Bolling A.F.B., on up through East and West Potomac Park to Rock Creek Park in the northwest is much usable space. Yet, despite pressure from the Department of Veterans Affairs, no decision has been announced.

This book has been an attempt to delineate aspects of American history, both good and bad, through our country's National Cemetery System. It would be a national tragedy if our leaders in Washington allowed their interest in America's past and future to wane. Such cavalier disregard for our history would greatly trouble all students of history and concerned Americans. We live at a time when self-centeredness is a cherished virtue, and the most grievous sin is not to get mine first. Such an attitude inspires the view that if it has not happened to me, then it cannot be important.

The fate of our historical sites and our knowledge of them is inextricably bound up with our future as well as our past. The National Cemetery System is not a refuse pile of forgotten ancestors and old soldiers who forgot to duck in time. Each cemetery is a repository of history. Each is a part of our heritage, tradition, culture and shared national experience which are the glue of our society. When that glue begins to dissolve through neglect, we find ourselves in our current predicament--a nation which has forgotten its past, forgotten where it has been; and a nation, therefore, which cannot know where it is going.

APPENDIX A

The following is a listing of those national cemeteries maintained by the United States government overseas. They are administered by the American Battle Monuments Commission, Washington, D.C. 20314. All, of course, are closed to future interments, since they contain only those American servicemen who died during wars on foreign soil. The numbers in parentheses indicate the number of interred and the number of missing commemorated respectively.

World War I Cemeteries

Belleau, France (2,288 - 1,060)
Brookwood, England (468 - 563)
Flanders Field, Belgium (368 - 43)
Meuse-Argonne, France (14,246 - 954)
Oise, France (6,012 - 241)
St. Mihiel, France (4,153 - 284)
Somme, France (1,844 - 284)
Suresnes, France (1,541 - 974)

World War I Memorials

Audenarde, Belgium
Bellicourt, France
Brest, France
Cantigny, France
Chateau Thierry, France
Gibraltar
Kemmel, Belgium
Montfaucon, France
Montsec, France
Sommepy, France
Tours, France

World War II Cemeteries

Ardennes, Belgium (5,313 - 462)

Brittany, France (4,410 - 498)
Cambridge, England (3,811 - 5,125)
Epinal, France (5,255 - 424)
Florence, Italy (4,402 - 1,409)
Henri-Chapelle, Belgium (7,989 - 450)
Lorraine, France (10,489 - 444)
Luxembourg, Luxembourg (5,076 - 370)
Manila, P.I. (17,208 - 36,279)
Margraten, Holland (8,301 - 1,722)
Normandy, France (9,386 - 1,557)
North Africa (2,840 - 3,724)
Rhone, France (861 - 293)
Sicily-Rome, Italy (7,862 - 3,094)

Mexican War

Mexico City (750) victims of the war with Mexico 1846-1848

Because of local complaints and treacherous politics in various parts of the world, there has been talk of bringing home those buried in certain locales. Locales most commonly mentioned are Mexico City, North Africa and Manila. Nothing official has been determined, however. If the project commences, the reinterments would probably occur at centrally located sites with plenty of room, such as Jefferson Barracks, Missouri, or Fort Snelling, Minnesota.

APPENDIX B

The following listing is of some of the more prominent Americans interred at Arlington National Cemetery. It is by no means exhaustive but will give an excellent idea of the scope of the American heritage entailed in that national shrine.

Gen. H.H. "Hap" Arnold, U.S.A.F.
Lt. Floyd Bennett, USNR, aviator.
Pvt. William B. Blatt, Union Army, first battle casualty.
Gen. Tasker H. Bliss, U.S.A.
William Jennings Bryan
Adm. Richard E. Byrd, explorer.
Gen. Claire L. Chenault, U.S.A.F.
Gen. John L. Clem, U.S.A.; at twelve, "Drummer Boy of Chickamauga."
Gen. George Crook, U.S.A.
Jane Delano, Superintendent, Army Nurse Corps.
Gen. William J. Donovan, U.S.A.
Gen. Abner Doubleday, U.S.A., inventor of baseball.
John Foster Dulles
Gen. Robert A. Eichelberger, U.S.A.
James V. Forrestal, first Secretary of Defense.
Gen. Roy S. Geiger, U.S.M.C.
Gen. William Gorgas, U.S.A., built Panama Canal.
Adm. William F. "Bull" Halsey, U.S.N.
Cpl. Ira Hayes, U.S.M.C., famed for flag-raising at Iwo Jima.
Oliver Wendell Holmes
Frank Knox, Secretary of Navy and former Rough Rider.
Adm. William L. Leahy, U.S.N.
Major Pierre L'Enfant, planned Washington, D.C.
Maj. Johnathan Letterman, U.S.A. Surgeon.
Adm. Jonas Ingram, U.S.N.
Gen. Philip Kearny, U.S.A.
John F. Kennedy, President of U.S.
Gen. Walter Kreuger, U.S.A.
Gen. John A. Lejeune, U.S.M.C.
Robert Todd Lincoln, Secretary of War and president's son.
Gen. Arthur MacArthur, U.S.A.
Lt. Comdr. John McCloy, U.S.N., twice awarded Medal of

Honor.
Gen. George C. Marshall, U.S.A.
Gen. Nelson A. Miles, U.S.A.
Adm. Marc A. Mitscher, U.S.N.
Gen. Floyd L. Parks, U.S.A.
Gen. John J. "Black Jack" Pershing, U.S.A.
Adm. David D. Porter, U.S.N.
James Wesley Powell, western explorer.
Maj. Walter Reed, U.S.A. Surgeon, conquered yellow fever.
Gen. William S. Rosecrans, U.S.A.
Gen. John M. Schofield, U.S.A.
Adm. Forrest P. Sherman, U.S.N.
Gen. Philip H. Sheridan, U.S.A.
Adm. William S. Sims, U.S.N.
Gen. Walter Bedell Smith, U.S.A., Chief of Staff to Eisenhower.
William Howard Taft, President of U.S.
Adm. Joseph K. Taussig, U.S.N.
Gen. Lucien Truscott, U.S.A.
Gen. Hoyt Vandenberg, U.S.A.F.
Gen. Jonathan M. Wainright, U.S.A., defender of Bataan.
Gen. Walter H. Walker, U.S.A.
Gen. Oscar Westover, U.S.A.F.
Gen. Leonard Wood, U.S.A.

APPENDIX C

The U.S. government has stringent restrictions on its decorative and upkeep policies for national cemeteries and these are strictly adhered to. Those below are generally applicable to all such facilities.

1) Entrance gates are open to public from 8:00 A.M. to 5:00 P.M. every day and from 8:00 A.M. to 7:00 P.M. on Memorial Day.

2) No picnics are allowed.

3) Visitors who litter or deface the landscaping will generally be prosecuted. (Note: often with tenacity.)

4) All graves are donated at government expense and are decorated with small national flags the day before Memorial Day. Flags are not allowed at other times.

5) Cut flowers may be placed on graves anytime. Temporary containers may be left but they and floral tributes are removed from graves when they become faded and unsightly.

6) Artificial flowers are permitted only from October through April. Plants, statues, vigil lights and other unnatural commemorative objects are not allowed and will be removed.

7) All inquiries should be directed to the cemetery director for specific answers to other requests. Appendix D provides the mailing addresses of all national cemeteries in the system.

APPENDIX D

The following list is of the cemeteries currently extant in the National Cemetery System. For those wishing to acquire specific information on any site, inquiry should be directed to the cemetery director. Those cemeteries still open to receive interments are indicated by an asterisk (*). All national cemeteries administered by the Department of the Interior are located at various national historical sites, monuments, military parks, and battlefields.

Ft. Mitchell Nat. Cem.*
Phoenix City, Ala. 36868
(Opened 1987)

Mobile Nat. Cem.
Mobile, Ala. 36604

Sitka Nat. Cem.*
Sitka, Alaska 99835

National Memorial Cemetery of
  Arizona*
Phoenix, Ariz. 85024
(Opened 1989)

Prescott Nat. Cem.
Prescott, Ariz. 86313

Fayetteville Nat. Cem.*
Fayetteville, Ark. 72701

Ft. Smith Nat. Cem.*
Ft. Smith, Ark. 72901

Little Rock Nat. Cem.*
Little Rock, Ark. 72206

Ft. Rosecrans Nat. Cem.
San Diego, Calif. 92106

Golden Gate Nat. Cem.
San Bruno, Calif. 94066

Los Angeles Nat. Cem.
Los Angeles, Calif. 90049

Riverside Nat. Cem.*
Riverside, Calif. 92508
(Opened 1978)

San Francisco Nat. Cem.
The Presidio
San Francisco, Calif. 94129

Ft. Logan Nat. Cem.*
Denver, Colo. 80235

Ft. Lyon Nat. Cem.*
Ft. Lyon, Colo. 81038

Barrancas Nat. Cem.*
Pensacola, Fla. 32508

Bay Pines Nat. Cem.
Bay Pines, Fla. 33504

Florida Nat. Cem.*
Bushnell, Fla. 33513
(Opened 1988)

St. Augustine Nat. Cem.
St. Augustine, Fla. 32084

Marietta Nat. Cem.
Marietta, Ga. 30060

National Memorial Cemetery of
the Pacific*
Honolulu, Hawaii 96813

Alton Nat. Cem.
Alton, Ill.
(Contact Jefferson Barracks, Mo.)

Camp Butler Nat. Cem.*
Springfield, Ill. 62707

Danville Nat. Cem.*
Danville, Ill. 61832

Mound City Nat. Cem.*
Mound City, Ill. 62963

Quincy Nat. Cem.
Quincy, Ill.
(Contact Keokuk, Iowa)

Rock Island Nat. Cem.*
Rock Island, Ill. 61299

Crown Hill Nat. Cem.
Indianapolis, Ind. 46208

Marion Nat. Cem.*
Marion, Ind. 46952

New Albany Nat. Cem.
New Albany, Ind. 47150

Keokuk Nat. Cem.*
Keokuk, Iowa 52632

Ft. Leavenworth Nat. Cem.*
Ft. Leavenworth, Kans. 66027

Ft. Scott Nat. Cem.*
Ft. Scott, Kans. 66701

Leavenworth Nat. Cem.*
Leavenworth, Kans.
(Contact Ft. Leavenworth, Kans.)

Camp Nelson Nat. Cem.*
Nicholasville, Ky. 40356

Cave Hill Nat. Cem.
Louisville, Ky.
(Contact Z. Taylor, Ky.)

Danville Nat. Cem.
Danville, Ky.
(Contact Camp Nelson, Ky.)

Lebanon Nat. Cem.
Lebanon, Ky. 40033

Lexington Nat. Cem.
Lexington, Ky.
(Contact Camp Nelson, Ky.)

Mill Springs Nat. Cem.*
Nancy, Ky. 42544

Perryville Nat. Cem.
Perryville, Ky.
(Contact Camp Nelson, Ky.)

Zachary Taylor Nat. Cem.*
Louisville, Ky. 40207

Alexandria Nat. Cem.*
Pineville, La. 71360

Baton Rouge Nat. Cem.
Baton Rouge, La. 70806

Port Hudson Nat. Cem.*
Zachary, La. 70791

Togus Nat. Cem.
Togus, Maine 04330

Annapolis Nat. Cem.
Annapolis, Md. 21401

Baltimore Nat. Cem.
Baltimore, Md. 21228

Loudon Park Nat. Cem.
Baltimore, Md.
(Contact Baltimore, Md.)

Massachusetts Nat. Cem.*
Bourne, Mass. 02532
(Opened 1980)

Ft. Custer Nat. Cem.*
Ft. Custer, Mich.
(Opened 1982)

Ft. Snelling Nat. Cem.*
St. Paul, Minn. 55111

Biloxi Nat. Cem.*
Biloxi, Miss. 39531

Corinth Nat. Cem.*
Corinth, Miss. 38834

Natchez Nat. Cem.*
Natchez, Miss. 39120

Jefferson Barracks Nat. Cem.*
St. Louis, Mo. 63125

Jefferson City Nat. Cem.
Jefferson City, Mo. 65101

Springfield Nat. Cem.*
Springfield, Mo. 65804

Ft. McPherson Nat. Cem.*
Maxwell, Nebr. 69151

Beverly Nat. Cem.
Beverly, N.J. 08010

Finn's Point Nat. Cem.
Salem, N.J. 08079

Ft. Bayard Nat. Cem.*
Ft. Bayard, N.Mex. 88036

Santa Fe Nat. Cem.*
Santa Fe, N.Mex. 87501

Bath Nat. Cem.*
Bath, N.Y.
(Contact Woodlawn, N.Y.)

Calverton, Nat. Cem.*
Calverton, N.Y. 11933
(Opened 1978)

Cypress Hills Nat. Cem.
Brooklyn, N.Y. 11208

Long Island Nat. Cem.
Farmingdale L.I., N.Y. 11735

Woodlawn Nat. Cem.
Elmira, N.Y. 14901

New Bern Nat. Cem.*
New Bern, N.C. 28560

Raleigh Nat. Cem.*
Raleigh, N.C. 27610

Salisbury Nat. Cem.*
Salisbury, N.C. 28144

Wilmington Nat. Cem.*
Wilmington, N.C. 28401

Dayton Nat. Cem.*
Dayton, Ohio 45428

Ft. Gibson Nat. Cem.*
Ft. Gibson, Okla. 74434

Roseburg Nat. Cem.
Roseburg, Oreg. 97470

White City Nat. Cem.*
White City, Oreg. 97501

Willamette Nat. Cem.*
Portland, Oreg. 97266

Philadelphia Nat. Cem.
Philadelphia, Pa. 19138

Indiantown Gap Nat. Cem.*
Annville, Pa. 17003
(Opened 1982)

Puerto Rico Nat. Cem.*
Bayamon, P.R. 00619

Beaufort Nat. Cem.*
Beaufort, S.C. 29902

Florence Nat. Cem.*
Florence, S.C. 79501

Black Hills Nat. Cem.*
Sturgis, S.Dak. 57785

Ft. Meade Nat. Cem.
Ft. Meade, S.Dak.
(Contact Black Hills, S.Dak.)

Hot Springs Nat. Cem.
Hot Springs, S.Dak. 57747

Chattanooga Nat. Cem.*
Chattanooga, Tenn. 37404

Knoxville Nat. Cem.
Knoxville, Tenn. 37917

Memphis Nat. Cem.*
Memphis, Tenn. 38122

Mountain Home Nat. Cem.*
Mountain Home, Tenn. 37684

Nashville Nat. Cem.*
Madison, Tenn. 37115

Ft. Bliss Nat. Cem.*
Ft. Bliss, Tex. 79906

Ft. Houston Nat. Cem.*
San Antonio, Tex. 78209

Houston Nat. Cem.*
Houston, Tex. 77038

Kerrville Nat. Cem.
Kerrville, Tex. 78028

San Antonio Nat. Cem.
San Antonio, Tex.
(Contact Ft. Houston, Tex.)

Alexandria Nat. Cem.
Alexandria, Va. 22314

Balls Bluff Nat. Cem.
Leesburg, Va.
(Contact Winchester, Va.)

City Point Nat. Cem.
Hopewell, Va.
(Contact Richmond, Va.)

Cold Harbor Nat. Cem.
Mechanicsville, Va.
(Contact Richmond Va.)

Culpeper Nat. Cem.*
Culpeper, Va. 22701

Danville Nat. Cem.
Danville, Va. 24541

Ft. Harrison Nat. Cem.
Richmond, Va.
(Contact Richmond, Va.)

Glendale Nat. Cem.
Glendale, Va.
(Contact Richmond, Va.)

Hampton Nat. Cem.
Hampton, Va. 23669

Hampton V.A. Nat. Cem.
Hampton, Va.
(Contact Hampton Nat. Cem., Va.)

Quantico Nat. Cem.*
Quantico, Va. 22134
(Opened 1983)

Richmond Nat. Cem.
Richmond, Va. 23231

Seven Pines Nat. Cem.
Sandston, Va.
(Contact Richmond, Va.)

Staunton Nat. Cem.
Staunton, Va. 24401

Winchester Nat. Cem.
Winchester, Va. 22601

Grafton Nat. Cem.
Grafton, W.Va. 26354

Wood Nat. Cem.*
Wood, Wis. 53193

ADMINISTERED BY DEPT.
OF THE ARMY:

U.S. Soldiers' and Airmen's
  Home Nat. Cem.
Washington, D.C. 20011

Arlington Nat. Cem.*
Arlington, Va. 22211

ADMINISTERED BY DEPT.
OF THE INTERIOR:

Battleground Nat. Cem.
Washington, D.C.

Andersonville Nat. Cem.
Andersonville, Ga. 31711

Chalmette Nat. Cem.
Arabi, La. 70032

Antietam Nat. Cem.
Sharpsburg, Md. 21782

Vicksburg Nat. Cem.
Vicksburg, Miss. 39180

ADMINISTERED BY DEPT.
OF THE INTERIOR (continued)

Custer Battlefield Nat. Cem.
Crow Agency, Mont. 59022

Gettysburg Nat. Cem.
Gettysburg, Pa. 17325

Andrew Johnson Nat. Cem.*
Greenville, Tenn. 37743

Ft. Donelson Nat. Cem.*
Dover, Tenn. 37058

Shiloh Nat. Cem.*
Shiloh, Tenn. 38376

Stones River Nat. Cem.
Murfreesboro, Tenn. 37130

Fredericksburg & Spotsylvania
  Nat. Cem.
Fredericksburg, Va. 22401

Poplar Grove Nat. Cem.
Petersburg, Va. 23803

Yorktown Battlefield Nat. Cem.
Yorktown, Va. 23690

Most of the smaller facilities in the system are now nearing exhaustion of space. Almost all have applied to acquire more land adjacent to existing sites, and thus remain in service until past the year 2000. However, it cannot be currently predicted which ones will be authorized to do so.

APPENDIX E

No two national cemeteries are alike. Their physical layout must take into account the available land and any inherent historical features. Such planning creates some remarkable vistas. Only one factor is constant. Each is developed with a "loop drive," which encompasses all major areas of the location and from which smaller roads lead to secondary interment fields. This way, no gravesite is more than a few hundred paces from some type of paved easement. Below are a few examples of typical national-cemetery-site layouts.

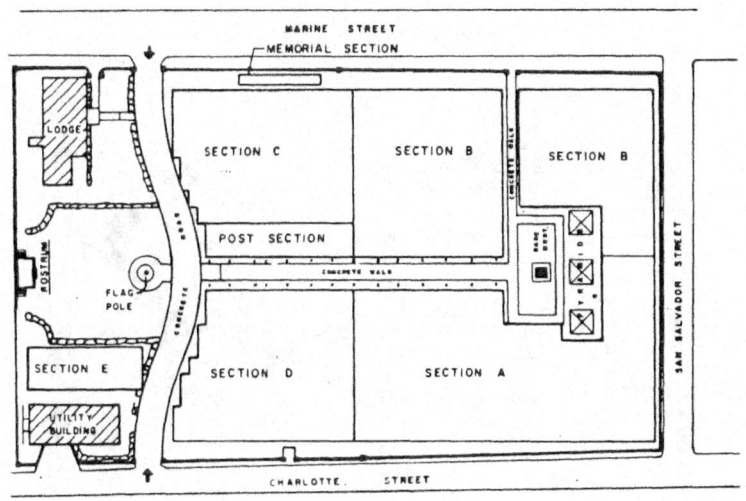

ST. AUGUSTINE NATIONAL CEMETERY

ST. AUGUSTINE, FLORIDA

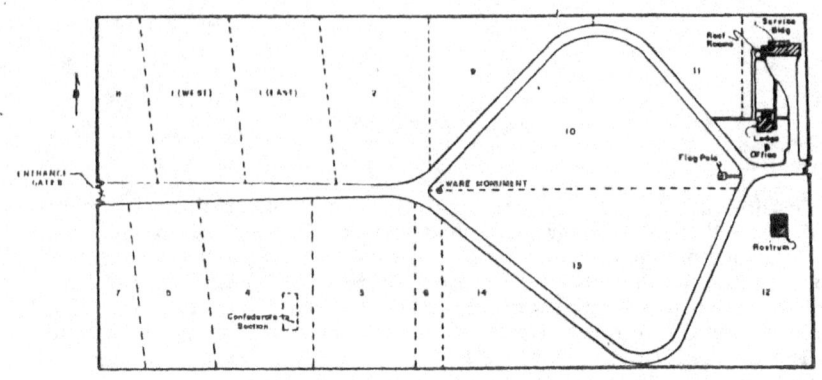

FORT SCOTT NATIONAL CEMETERY

FORT SCOTT, KANSAS

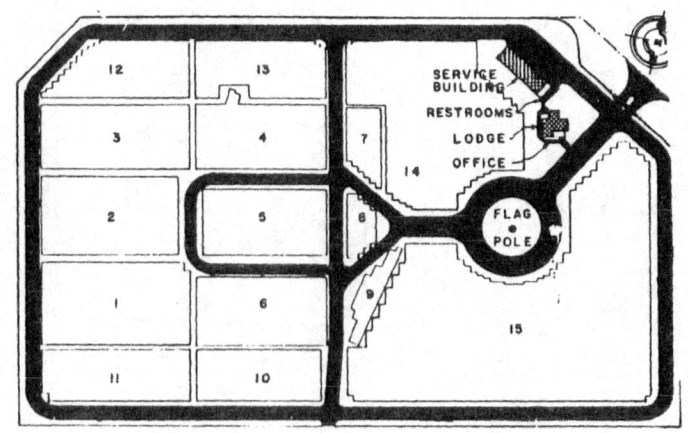

FORT SMITH NATIONAL CEMETERY

FORT SMITH, ARKANSAS

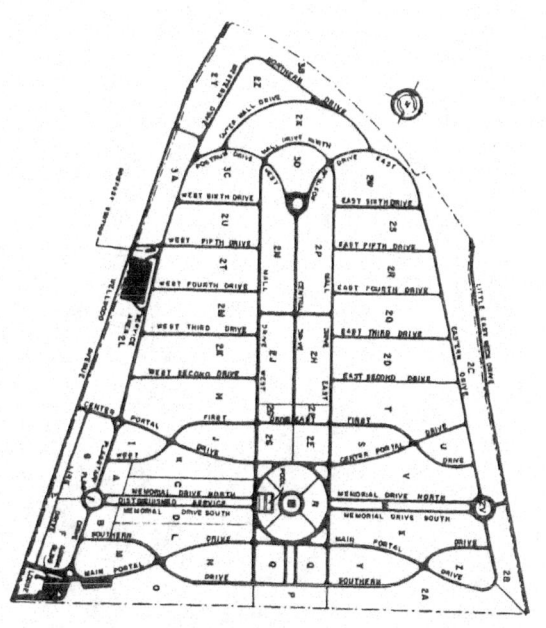

LONG ISLAND NATIONAL CEMETERY

FARMINGDALE, NEW YORK

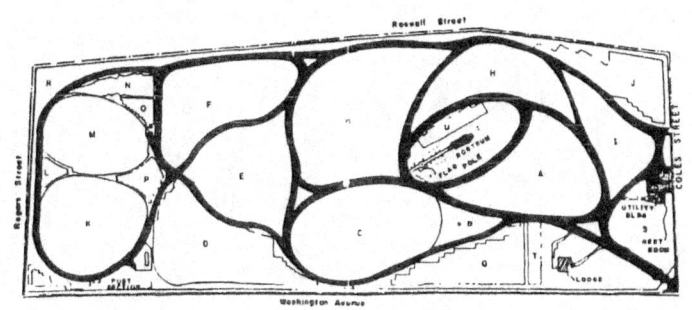

MARIETTA NATIONAL CEMETERY

MARIETTA, GEORGIA

APPENDIX F

Eligibility Requirements for Interment in a National Cemetery

The following extracts are from government pamphlet VA-DMA-IS-1 dated 1 May 1979 and supply the basic eligibility rules for assignment of gravesite space in any national cemetery.

Persons Entitled to Interment

Veterans discharged under other than dishonorable conditions and all active personnel who die while in service.

Members of reserve components whose deaths are service-connected.

Officers of the National Oceanic and Atmospheric Administration.

Commissioned officers of the public health service who have been detailed for duty with any of the regular armed forces.

The spouse and/or minor children of an eligible (usually interred in the same plot in accordance with the one-family, one-grave policy to maximize the yield per acre of usable gravesites).

Persons Not Entitled to Interment

Father, mother, brother, sister or in-laws of an eligible regardless of the circumstances of his or her death.

Those called for the draft but never actually inducted.

Remarried spouses (unless second marriage is terminated by conditions other than death of second spouse).

Those convicted of subversive activities after 1 September 1959. Eligibility can only be reinstated by specific presidential pardon.

Any man or woman whose separation from the armed forces was under dishonorable conditions. Eligibility can only be reinstated by a subsequent service tour in which discharge is honorable.

ADAMS, Samuel 135
AFTON, John K 258
AGUINALDO, Emilio 28
ALLEN, James 73
ANDERSON, 126 Bloody Bill 125
    Major 35 Robert 35 81
ANDREWS, James 192
ARIZONA BILL, 214
ARMISTEAD, 170
ARNOLD H H "Hap", 267
AUDUBON, John J 174
AUGUR, C C 164
AUSTIN, Moses 219
BAKER, Benjamin 134 Edward D
    28 223
BALTIMORE, Lord 105
BANKS, 96 N P 95 101 Nathaniel
    69
BATES, R C 255
BAYARD, George D 139
BEASLEY, John 9
BEAUREGARD, 116 P G T 182
    208
BELL, Harry 73
BENNETT, 231 Floyd 267
BENT, Charles 141
BENTEEN, Frederick 183
BILLY BOWLEGS, (Indian) 161
BLACK HAWK, (Indian) 71 257
    258
BLACK KETTLE ,(Indian) 31 32
BLAIR, F P 240
BLATT, William B 4 267
BLISS, Elizabeth 211 Tasker H
    267 William V S 211
BLUNT, James F 162
BOGUS CHARLEY, (Indian) 165
BOLTON, C H 214
BOOTH, John Wilkes 56 221
    Junius Brutus 221
BORGLUM, Gutzon 190

BORLAND, Col 17 Senator 17
BOWIE, Jim 219
BRADDOCK, 251 Edward 251
BRADFORD, William 17
BRADY, Matthew 171
BRAGG, 192 210 Braxton 37 85
    91 191 197 209
BRANTLEY, C B 120
BRAVE BEAR, (Indian) 133
BRECKENRIDGE, John C 88
    John C 97 101
BRODERICK, Virgil 229
BROWN, Bailey 256 John 221
    Wilson 118
BROWNLOW, Walter P 203
BRYAN, William Jennings 267
BRYANT, William M 154
BRYSON, Mizell 40
BUCHANAN, Franklin 240 James
    97 President 193
BUDWIN, Florena 182
BUELL, 92 208 Don Carlos 81 91
    207
BUFORD, Gen 170
BURDETT, Samuel 255
BURGOYNE, 181
BURNHAM, Hiram 233
BURNSIDE, Ambrose B 108
    Ambrose E 151 197 235
BURR, Aaron 117
BUSH, George 103
BUTLER, B F 226 Benjamin F
    157
BUTTERFIELD, Daniel 236
BYRD, Richard E 267
CABRILLO, Juan R 21
CALAMITY JANE, 189
CALIFORNIA JOE, 133
CAMPBELL, J A 240
CANBY, E R S 10 141 166
CANTRELL, Charles 206

CAPTAIN JACK, (Indian) 165 166
CARLETON, James 139 James R 13
CARLTON, C H 185
CASE, Francis 183
CHAPIN, 233
CHARLES V, 39
CHENAULT, Claire L 267
CHIVINGTON, Col 32 John M 31
CHRISTMAN, William 4
CLAIBORNE, William 105
CLARK, George Rogers 55 65 John 48
CLAY, Henry 87
CLEM, John L 267
CLEMENTS, Isaac 57
CLEVELAND, Grover 66
CLINTON, Gen 155 254
COCKBURN, George 109
COFFIN, Levi 67
COLE, Henry G 48
COLORADAS, Mangas 139
CORDOBA, 39
CORNWALLIS, 105 124 174 254 Charles 155 253
COSGROVE, Silas 69
COX, Jacob 66
CRAVATH, Erastus 205
CREEKMORE, Randolph 18
CRITTENDEN, George 89 John 131
CROCKETT, Davey 219
CRONAN, William S 22
CROOK, Gen 133 George 267
CURLEY, (Indian) 131
CURTIS, Samuel 15
CUSHMAN, Pauline 28
CUSTER, 130 131 133 159 185 George A 183 249 George Armstrong 129
CUSTIS, George Parke 1
DADE, 42 Francis L 41
DALTON, 18
DAVIS, Jefferson 123 240 248 Jefferson C 2 79 N H 139
DEEL-IN-WATER, (Indian) 75
DELAHARPE, Bernard 19
DELANO, Jane 267
DELANZOS, Dona Ana 177
DESOTO, Ferdinand 39
DEWERT, Richard 150

DILLINGER, John H 66
DONOVAN, William J 267
DOOLIN, 18
DOUBLEDAY, Abner
DOUGLAS, 56 61
DRAKE, Francis 178
DUKE, Ray E 192
DULLES, John Foster 267
DUPONT, Samuel 179
EARLY, 34 Jubal 35 128 250 Jubal A 33
EARNSHAW, William 201
EARP, Nicholas 26
EISENHOWER, 268
ELIZABETH I, (queen of England) 153
ELLSWORTH, Richard C 184
ERICKSON, 240
EVERETT, Edward 169
EWELL, Gen 170
FAIR, George Washington 159
FAIRBANKS, Charles Warren 66
FARRAGUT, Admiral 101 201 David 95 97 105 David G 9 118
FIELDS, James H 215
FILLMORE, Millard 93
FIREY, L P 108
FLOYD, John B 193
FOOTE, Andrew H 193
FORREST, Nathan B 10
FORRESTAL, James V 267
FOX, Cyrus 134
FREDERICK The Great, (of Prussia) 136
FREMONT, 249 John C 23
FRY, S S 90
FRYER, Pauline 28
FUNSTON, Frederick 28
FUSSELL, 233
GA-AH, (Indian) 37
GARCIA, Marcario 215
GARDNER, Raymond 214
GARFIELD, James A 251
GARNIER, Baptiste 133
GATES, Horatio 181
GATLING, Richard J 66
GEIGER, George 159 Roy S 267
GENTRY, Richard 124
GEORGE III, (king of England) 174
GERONIMO, (Indian) 13 37 214

GERONIMO (continued)
  Chappo (Indian) 10
GIBSON, Gen 162
GLASGOW, William 211
GOES AHEAD, (Indian) 131
GORGAS, Josiah 120 William 267
GRANGER, Gordon 88
GRANT, 29 33 90 95 96 116 120 133 180 192 197 208 209 223 227 233 243 Gen 225 Ulysses 3 Ulysses S 6 59 115 119 123 157 159 167 193 207
GRATTEN, Lt 133
GREENE, Nathaniel 155
GUILLEN, Ambrosio 212
HALLECK, Henry W 115
HALSEY, William F "Bull" 267
HANKS, Nancy 69
HANSON, C S 85 Roger 88
HARRELL, W E 214
HARRISON, Benjamin 65-67 Caroline S 66
HARVEY, William "Coin" 15
HATCH, Edward 74 J P 179
HAYES, Ira 267 Rutherford B 251
HAZEN, William 210
HENDRICKS, Thomas A 66
HERKIMER, Nicholas 144
HICKOK, Wild Bill 189
HILL, Edward 236
HOLMES, Oliver Wendell 224 267
HOOD, John B 47 205
HOOKER, 223 Joseph 238
HOOKER JIM, (Indian) 165
HOOVER, Herbert 185 President 142
HORN, Tom 214
HOUSTON, Diana 162 Sam 162 213
HOWE, Gen 135 174
HUGHES, L H 214
HUMPHREYS, Andrew 236
HUNTER, Robert 240
HURLEY, Patrick J 142
INGRAM, Jonas 267
JACKSON, 69 100 139 Andrew 9 17 40 48 153 161 Andrew "Old Hickory" 99 Stonewall 192 250 T J "Stonewall" 249

JEFFERSON, 190 Thomas 173
JOHNSON, 126 196 A E V 125 Andrew 153 195 258 Jeremiah 26 "Liver-eating" 26
JOHNSTON, 208 248 A S 115 207 Joseph 151 205 Joseph E 2 247 Joseph S 231
JONES, Edward S 205 Herbert C 22 John Paul 103
JULIAN, J R 148
KEARNY, Philip 267 S W 141 Stephen W 22
KEENE, Gen 100
KELLEY, H Jackson 165
KEMPER, James L 137
KENNEDY, 108 John F 267
KEOKUK, (Indian) 71
KEY, Francis Scott 109
KINTPUASH, (Indian) 165
KNAAK, Albert 186
KNOX, Frank 267 K T 258
KREUGER, Walter 267
L'ENFANT, Pierre 267
LAFARGE, Oliver 142
LAMY, John B 142
LANE, Jim 125
LAWLESS, James W 205
LEADBETTER, Daniel 197
LEAHY, William L 267
LEAVENWORTH, Henry 73
LEE, 2 3 34 80 96 107 108 149 157 170 171 225 227 231 233 235 238 243 245 251 Harry 1 M A 214 Mary 4 Robert E 6 123 169 229 231 237 248 Robert Edward 1
LEJEUNE, John A 267
LETTERMAN, Johnathan 267
LILLY, Eli 66
LINCOLN, 34 61 108 180 190 238 Abraham 31 36 56 69 79 85 119 145 169 195 208 221 258 Mr 222 Nancy 69 President 3 96 180 221 223 240 Robert Todd 267
LITTLE BAT, 133
LOCKWOOD, Charles A 23
LOGAN, John A 6 29
LONG, Stephen 17
LONGSTREET, James 170 197
LUCY, (Indian) 186

LURCH, Thomas 72
LYELL, William 206
LYMAN, Theodore 47
LYON, Gen 128 Nathaniel 15 31 127
MACARTHUR, Arthur 267
MAGNER, Edmund 160
MAGRUDER, John 254
MAKSOUTOFF, Polina 11
MALEDON, George C 204
MALLET, 141
MALLON, George H 112
MARGOLIS, Louis 160
MARION, Francis 182
MARS, Kayo 160
MARSHALL, George C 268
MASTERS, Edgar Lee 61
MCCALL, Jack 189
MCCLELLAN, 2 107 108 227 238 240 248 249 254 George 235 237 247
MCCLOY, John 267 268
MCCORMICK, Cyrus 250
MCDOWELL, 249 Irwin 28
MCELROY, John 43
MCINTOSH, James 18
MCKEE, Hugh 88
MCLEAN, Wilmer 245
MCPHERSON, James Birdseye 133
MEADE, 171 Gen 227 George B 170 George C 185
MEIGS, 4 5 M C 18 Montgomery C 4 116 117 123 Montgomery Cunningham 3
MILES, Nelson A 37 268
MILLER, Silas 62
MILNER, Moses 133
MITSCHER, Marc A 268
MOORE, James 248
MORGAN, John 85 87 John H 88 203
MORRISON, James 88
MORROW, Alexander 75
MORSE, Samuel F B 110
MOSBY, John S 128
NAPOLEON, 99
NELSON, William "Bull" 79
NIMITZ, Chester 23 105
NIXON, President 262
NORTH, Lord 254

O'HARA, Lt Col 251
O'ROURKE, Patrick 134
OLD JOHN, (Indian) 164
PAKENHAM, Edward 99 100
PALMER, Ernest 147
PARKER, Isaac 204 Isaac C 18
PARKS, Floyd L 268
PATRICK, M R 160
PEARY, Robert E 103
PEMBERTON, 120 John C 119
PENDYGRAFT, Ray 86
PERSHING, John J "Black Jack" 268
PETTIGREW, 170
PHILLIPS, L H 48 William A 162
PHIPS, William 178
PICKERSGILL, Mary 110
PICKETT, 149 170 George W 165
PITCAIRN, 173
PIZARRO, 39
PLEASANTS, Col 243
PLESS, S W 38
POE, Edgar Allan 110
POLK, James K 153 155
PONTIAC, (Indian) 257
POPE, 107 Gen 229
PORTER, David D 119 268
POTTER, L P (Mrs) 180
POWELL, James Wesley 268
PRATHER, Abner 25
PRESTON, William 118
PRICE, Sterling 15 116 127 128
PYLE, Ernest T 51
QUANTRILL, 77 William 125
RALEIGH, Walter 153
RAMSEY, Alexander 111
RAY, Bernard 147
REED, Walter 268
REEVES, J W 37
REN, Marcus 131
RENNIE, Col 100
RENO, Marcus 159
RIGGS, George W 35
RILEY, James Whitcomb 66
ROBINSON, J P 214
RODMAN, Thomas C 63
ROGERS, Diana 162
ROOSEVELT, President 167 Theodore 66 190
ROSECRANS, 116 197

ROSECRANS (continued)
  William S 91 192 209 268
  William Starke 21
ROSS, Edmund 196
SAINT LEGER, 144
SCHOEPF, 89
SCHOFIELD, 158 John 205 John M 268
SCOTT, Martin 217 Winfield 35 75 Winfield S 1 111
SEDGWICK, John 31
SET-THEM-UP, (Indian) 75 76
SEWARD, Secretary of State 11 240
SEXTON, James 80
SEYMOUR, Governor 145
SHAFTER, William 28
SHAGNASTY JIM, (Indian) 165
SHANKS, Nathan "Shanks" 223
SHELBY, J O 125
SHEPHERD, O L 210
SHERIDAN, Philip 29 209 249 Philip H 34 91 268
SHERMAN, 29 69 74 96 120 133 151 158 179-181 192 197 205 Forrest P 268 William T 62 73 81 123
SIBLEY, Gen 141
SIMON, 108
SIMS, C C 38 William S 268
SLEMMER, A J 37
SMITH, 92 164 Andrew J 163 E Kirby 83 91 95 96 G W 179 Kirby 19 20 87 96 Preacher 189 Thomas A 17 Walter Bedell 268
SNELLING, Josiah 111
SOLLY, Cornelius 159
SPIVEY, William 216
SPOTTED HORSE, (Indian) 134
SPRUANCE, Raymond A 23
STAINT LEGER, Col 143
STANTON, 4 Edwin M 196 221 258 Edwin McMasters 3
STAYTON, T V 212
STEELE, 20 Frederick 19
STEEN, Alexander 18
STICK-OUT-BELLY, (Indian) 76
STILLMAN, Isaiah 257
STONE, Charles P 223
STONEMAN, Gen 156

STUART, J E B 170 229 238
STURGIS, 185
SULLIVAN, Timothy 26
SWAMP FOX, 182
SWANTON, Elmer 211
TAFT, William Howard 268
TALIHINI, (Indian) 162
TARKINGTON, Booth 66
TARLETON, 182
TAUSSIG, Joseph K 268
TAYLOR, Elizabeth 211 Richard 10 96 Zachary 39 40 93 211 257
TECUMSEH, (Indian) 67
TERRY, A H 157
THOMAS, Albert 215 George H 89 192 205 Lorenzo 63
THOMPSON, Wiley 39
THORSON, John 72
TOWNSEND, E D 137
TRAVIS, William 219
TRIMBLE, 170
TRUSCOTT, Lucien 268
TRYON, William 151 155
TURNER, Richmond K 23
TYNDAL, Robert H 66
VANAUSDELN, B C 168
VANDENBERG, Hoyt 268
VANDORN, Earl 15 116
VANHORN, Robert 28
VONROMMEL, Erwin 24
WADSWORTH, C W 78
WAINWRIGHT, Jonathan M 268
WALKER, Walter H 268
WALLACE, Lew 33
WALTERS, Henry 128
WARD, Isaac M 229
WARE, Eugene F 75
WASHINGTON, 1 105 107 136 174 190 George 110 135 251 254
WEATHERFORD, William 9
WEG, Frank 186
WEITZEL, Gen 245
WELD, S L 214
WELLINGTON, 99
WESTOVER, Oscar 268
WEYMAN, 136
WHIPPLE, A W 13
WHITE, Reuben 120
WHITSON, Calvin 18

WHITTIER, John Greenleaf 107
WILLIS, Edward 13
WILSON, Joseph R 250 William 28 Woodrow 7 250
WINDOLPH, Charles 183
WIRZ, Henry 44
WOOD, Leonard 268
WOOL, John E 164
WOOLWORTH, Robert 177
WRIGHT, Gen 33 Orville 67 Wilbur 67
YOES, Jacob 18
YOUNG, Brigham 61
YOUNG CHICKEN, (Indian) 75
ZOLLICOFFER, 90 Felix 89 91

www.ingramcontent.com/pod-product-compliance
Lightning Source LLC
Chambersburg PA
CBHW051630230426
43669CB00013B/2246